The Fifteenth Crusade

A Novel in the
Future Church

John Wright

**For Colleen and Linda
with gratitude for your
love and support**

Anyone who renders
loving service to a child of
God magnifies the glory
of the Lord and builds the
Kingdom of God on earth.
Carmen Ortiz Freeman
(1973-2046)

Prologue

Since the time of Christ, theologians, philosophers, Popes and even some scoundrels have restated Christ's exhortation to love God and one another. In 1963, the loving and lovable Saint John XXIII commissioned leaders of the Catholic Church to fashion a compassionate and wide-ranging re-statement of Christ's message to outdistance post-Modernism's secular message. He called for a message that would "throw open the windows" of the Church and aid the flock to embrace personal salvation. More than one commentator observed that the effort "opened Pandora's box". At least one noted that it allowed the "devil's stink" into the Church.

In the sense that politics is people engaging in the art of the possible, popes are politicians. Popes are also personalities, some extroverted, some introverted, some affable and some rigid. Popes effect policy by alternating the emphasis of the papacy as Christ did in his ministry, one day demonstrating tolerance and kindness for the adulteress and other days emphasizing adherence to a new law of love with its own disciplines to his disciples.

Pope Paul VI followed St. John XXIII facing a flock and a world that was beginning to wobble with wars, secularisms, assassinations and uprisings. He was challenged by an age eager to throw off the constraints of an entrenched Church leadership. He was required to utilize both his energy and theological capital to respond to the challenge of a generation eager to assert individual rights of every sort. He resisted and severely disappointed those who implored him to find a new theology that included approval of artificial birth control. In refusing to do so, he lost a legion of the baptized. While open to all religions, nations and opinions, he proved himself resolute in affirming the natural law as the predicate for judging moral behavior.

His successor the last Italian Pope and the only pope to have lived his entire life in the twentieth century expired after just thirty three days in the Chair of Peter. He was followed by St. John Paul II a man of gentle smile, vigor, great warmth and strength of personality. He helped to break the grip of Communism on Eastern Europe and enthusiastically spread the gospel of life and love. A principal of the St John XXIII's Council, he engaged in a personal and global mission to share the gospel of Jesus with the poor and powerless. But during his reign, the Church was subjected to the evil imposed by pedophile priests and muddled through a thoroughly non-Christian response. The damage was so great that the Church would never fully recover and would carry the scars far into the twenty first century.

There continued alternating papal styles from Benedict XVI to Francis with emphasis on compassion or authority in its attempt to form a more open but at the same time orderly Church with a common interpretation of the gospel and to engage in the joining of man in communion. The effort to successfully reflect the message of Jesus continued until 2058 when Francisco Augustine, a man of unusual background and experience was lifted from obscurity to lead a struggling Church.

Chapter 1

Francisco Augustine

Remembering

The roar of the fire trucks, the deafening pitch of the police sirens and the wail of the hundreds of ambulances that respond to the emergencies of the thirty million souls who inhabit the city of Lagos begin to subside at about three each morning. With the exception of the homeless and those who labor at irrational hours, people return to their homes. A peaceful quiet finally settles on the city. In the tiny chapel attached to the emergency room of St Monica's Hospital, the quiet is welcomed this day by a large man sitting in the front pew wearing a surgical gown, mask, head covering and gloves. The thin steady flame of the lone sanctuary lamp is witness to both the presence of the Eucharist and the absence of any air movement in the makeshift preserve. The cobalt blue of the sanctuary lamp's glass lends an azure tint to the limited light in the chapel.

At fifty six and having been a part of the Catholic Church for all those years, he can't remember ever having seen a blue glass in a sanctuary lamp. In his weariness, he wonders if there is some Church rule or regulation requiring red glass. That was the only color he had ever seen in any sanctuary lamp. His mother had always placed her candles in red glasses before the statue of The Lady of Guadalupe that graced the living room in their home. Then, he remembers the first time he had seen blue glass candle holders. His daddy was gunned down and people from the neighborhood had set up an instant memorial with flowers, candles and small teddy bears in front of the Allsave Foods where he had fallen. There were some blue candle holders there.

As he sits alone in the very warm chapel, he realizes just how exhausted and hungry he is. But hunger and exhaustion have been his frequent companions over the last few years. There have been many times when that was the case. He's in enviable physical condition for a man of his years, but some days exhaustion sets in. His normal routine has been to sleep five hours and rise at four A.M. each day. As his feet touch the floor in the early morning, he invokes God with his common prayer "God you are the one in whom all things begin, exist and will continue. You made the world of love. You made each of us in your image to know and to love you and your children. When we reject your love and act selfishly, not loving and acting contrary to your will, we break the loving bond you share with us. To heal the bond and free us from our sins, you came as man. You lived, you loved, you laughed, you taught, you healed, you felt impatience, anger, doubt and fear. You knew rejection and pain. You died in agony on the cross to show us pure love and to teach us how to love.

You come to us in the Spirit to enlighten, inspire and energize us. You come in your glorified body in the Eucharist to heal and nurture us. By your presence in us, God, please help us to believe, to hope and to love so that we may see clearly what you desire of me during this day. Make me willing to love and help me to see you in each of your children".

At this hour he would normally be pressing himself to fifty push- ups, a hundred sit ups and a run at near his top speed for fifteen minutes on the treadmill in his small austere office while listening to the news of the world. At six four, he has trimmed from the two hundred thirty five pounds of his playing days to two hundred five. He is still a physical specimen and has retained a very low BMI. He enjoys excellent health and unusual energy. On a normal day after exercise, he showers, meditates for half an hour and then prays in his attempt to put himself in the presence of God, a condition which he hopes will last the entire day. He wants diligently to see the child of God in everyone whom he encounters during a day, but some days he finds it more difficult than others. He fights the stress of the coming day with prayer and exercise.

This is not a normal day. He's not entirely certain why he sits alone in the simple chapel on the third floor of St Monica's Hospital in Lagos. He was told by the doctors that he needed to be attired in a hospital gown, surgical mask and surgical gloves for his and other's protection. He knows why he is in Lagos, but that's a very different matter.

Near midnight, he had been summoned to the emergency room next to the chapel from his own small private chapel attached to his bedroom and located in the abandoned psychiatric wing of the hospital. The doctors had said that they needed to determine if he was contagious. He felt fine, but he was horrified when he learned that two of his three dinner companions had earlier been brought to the emergency room with severe illnesses. One had died almost immediately upon entering the emergency room and the other was struggling on a respirator. The Nigerian emergency room doctor assumed it was some gastronomic illness because they had eaten together. But, he was doubtful that someone would expire so quickly from just food poisoning. To be certain however, the doctor pumped the stomachs of both men and took blood samples sending the specimens to the hospital lab which was operating at skeleton strength. The emergency room doctor called in a German contagious disease specialist who was in Lagos as a representative of the United Nations. He also called in the Pope's personal physician, Dr. Bender, who was also an attending physician.

When he arrived in the hospital and before he came to the chapel, the doctors had asked him what he had eaten the day before. He shared that he had eaten his normal oatmeal breakfast, for lunch, ante-pasta, a small roll and a glass of red table wine and at dinner time, he had had a few of bites of the fruit salad, a roll and then retired to his chapel. He left the table prior to the dinner being served. Menudo, one of his favorite meals, was to be served. Sister Sophia, the Nigerian nun who headed the kitchen, had obtained his mother's recipe for menudo and had perfected it. She served it twice a month usually on Wednesday and he normally ate ample portions.

However, last night, he had skipped the dinner and retired to his private chapel to pray and to think. While at the dinner table, he and his three companions had discussed the American church situation over a glass of red table wine prior to dinner and he felt a need to fast and pray for the Americans. The number of Catholics practicing the faith had diminished all over the world. It had happened so rapidly and radically in the United States that he sensed he needed the guidance of the Holy Spirit in order to sort out what he must do. His practice in those cases was to fast and pray.

While he sat quietly in the hospital chapel, he occasionally drifted off. He hadn't slept in nearly twenty four hours and though he was disciplined, he was also human and required sleep. He desperately needed a cup of powerful Columbian coffee, a drink to which he had become mildly addicted. While playing football at Northwestern University he had roomed with the place kicker, a young soccer player from Columbia who had "hooked" him on strong Columbian coffee. The caffeine had sustained him though many a weary moment in his career. His addiction had strengthened while in Brazil. The moment he had finished celebrating his mass each day he would head for the coffee pot. He kept a coffee maker in his small apartment and made his own very strong coffee while writing or thinking. On the road, he looked for a McDonalds and was now eligible for their less expensive "senior coffee". He had tried "Starbucks" a few times but felt guilty about indulging himself at the cost. He felt the money could be saved and spent on more worthy causes than his addiction.

The late July 2060 date turned his mind to the thought that on August 2nd, it would be fifty years from the date of his father's death. How could it be that long? The day and the events surrounding it were still very fresh in his mind. Lately, when he thought of his dad and his mother, he wondered what their lives with God were like. He frequently pondered what eternity will be like. He was six when his father died and he was livid with God for a very long time. Now he enjoyed a better relationship with him. He was sometimes overwhelmed just with the thought of his mom and dad being with God. He looked forward to that day when he would join them, his Jordan and his child.

The last fifty years of his life had passed so swiftly and were so surprising in their outcome that when he would meditate, he would frequently want to stay in that concentrated mode focused on matters of the soul. It provided him respite from the speed, the profound challenges and complexity of his life. From time to time, he wondered where the next years would take him and the struggling, but growing Church of which he was such an important part.

As he sat upright in a light sleep, his mind shifted as it often did to some of the bumps along the improbable path that had led him to the circumstance in
which he found himself, being attended by the Pope's personal

physician, located more than half way around the world from his birthplace and in good health, but dressed in a hospital gown. Where was this matter taking him?

Chapter 2

Bad Start to a New Year

Face Down on the Ground, Hands Behind Your Head!!!

August 23, 2019 dawned with a downpour but the weather cleared at mid-day and the humidity blanketed the city's south side. August in Chicago frequently produced a dew point that dampened the spirit as well as the body. It could smother initiative as well. But not today. Late in afternoon, the St. Rita Mustangs would hold their first football practice of the season. St. Rita's had had a string of bad years on the gridiron. But this was going to be St. Rita's year. It was also going to be Oscar and Diego's year to break into the starting lineup, at least in their thinking and planning. They were sophomores and they were ready, in top condition and eager. Both had been able to play enough in their freshman year to earn coveted St. Rita football letters.

Practice had begun with endless wind sprints and calisthenics. After two and a half hours of constant drills with just two water breaks, both Diego and Oscar were exhausted and thirsty. They showered quickly, left the muggy gym and headed for refreshment. They dragged themselves to the "White Hen", the local convenience store. They were both serious about heading straight home to sleep, but first they needed to hydrate. Then they would head straight to bed.

The first shots screamed over their heads. At least one smashed the first floor window of the darkened three flat located next to where they were standing sipping their 32 oz.

drinks. The shots came from an older slow moving four door Buick. Oscar dropped to the ground immediately. He hadn't been hit, but his mom had told him to "always make the smallest target possible if someone is shooting at you". Diego simply froze but dropped his drink. The second set of at least four shots hit the concrete stairs of the three flat and they could see the sparks fly. Oscar lit out in the opposite direction of the Buick with Diego right behind him. They passed two three flats and then there was a gangway about fifteen foot wide that led into the backyard of a single family home. The width of the opening allowed them to make a more difficult target by zig zagging their way to the back of the house hoping to find protection.

When they got to the backyard they found the house had no garage. They needed cover. There was a single car garage behind the house next door. They didn't have time to go any farther. They headed straight for the door to the garage, but it was locked. Oscar leapt onto a big plastic garbage can that was next to the door and mounted it with his feet spread in order to put his weight on the top of the sides where it was solid enough to hold him. He lifted himself onto the roof. Diego was right behind. They decided to lie on the other side of the roof where there was a tree overhanging the garage and they could see a portion of the street and part of the alley.

They were well hidden, but the leaves on the roof were wet and slippery from the rain earlier in the day. After four or five minutes, a car with its lights off crept slowly down the alley. It was the same Buick. It stopped at the garage just to north. Both Oscar and Diego froze. They were lying motionless and quiet, barely breathing. Two heavyset Hispanics exited the back of the car, both with pistols drawn. "I'm going to get that f...... money no matter if I have to kill that whole damn family". Oscar recognized "Hoghead" Fernandez. "Hoghead" jiggled the handle on the garage door next to where Diego and Oscar were lying. It was locked. So he kicked it, broke it open and found nothing. The two men walked to the garage where Oscar and Diego were hidden but didn't kick in the door. "S..., I'll get those ass..... tomorrow or the next day or the next. But I will have my money". They got back in the car, the lights came on and the Buick drove away. Oscar and Diego resumed breathing, remained on the roof for another ten minutes and finally got down from their perch.

They were three blocks from Oscar's house. They took a minute to discuss whether it would be better to go to Diego's rather than Oscar's. Oscar decided that he had to go home in case his younger sister was there by herself. It was Friday night and she was probably out with her friends, but if she was home, he needed to be there. His mom, Lt. Evelyn Chavez, was on the three to eleven P.M. shift, running Cell Block Three at the Cook County Jail and wouldn't be home for at least three hours. Oscar was aware that "Hoghead" knew where the family lived because "Hoghead" knew Oscar's older brother Jorge all too well. "Hoghead" had been the one to get Jorge "strung out". Jorge had tried to work off his debt in the employ of "Hoghead" but the drugs he was supposed to peddle proved to be too tempting to Jorge's voracious habit. He was in debt to "Hoghead" to the tune of more than three grand. The sum was equivalent to Jorge's drug use over a period of some three weeks.

Jorge was residing in the Lake County Indiana Jail having been placed there by the Cook County Sheriff to insure he wasn't in any danger from residing in the location of his mother's employment. "Hoghead" and a lot of "Hoghead's" friends were frequent residents of the jail. Jorge was awaiting trial on eight or ten counts of burglary and half dozen drug charges. He wouldn't be available to pay his debt for some time. His lawyer was a Public Defender with a ton of other cases. As a victim of burglary himself, the Public Defender was not all that eager to see Jorge back on the street any time soon.

Oscar's little sister, Sarah, was at home with a couple of her girlfriends. Though they were two years younger than the boys, they adored Diego and were excited to see him even though both he and Oscar were covered from head to toe with moss and dirt from lying in the leaves. Oscar went immediately upstairs to shower. The girls surrounded Diego as he sat on the couch and each bid more eagerly for his attention. He had to get up from the couch for fear that they would pounce on him. He went to the kitchen, got a drink of water and sat at the kitchen table. Two of the girls sat down with him. Sarah went to the refrigerator and brought Diego a Pepsi, but nothing for the other girls. Then she put a large bag of popcorn into the microwave.

Sarah had had a crush on Diego from the first time she saw him when she was in fourth grade. She dreamed about him and had a dozen or so pictures of him in her phone, pictures that he didn't know she had taken. One of them was taken when he was bare-chested asleep only in his boxers. She had snuck into Jorge and Oscar's room one night when Diego was staying over in Jorge's vacant bed. She had snapped a picture while he was sleeping.

When Oscar came downstairs, he called Diego into the back bedroom. He went to the closet and opened it. There was a collection of sports equipment including a basketball and a couple of sixteen inch softballs, the spheroid popular in Chicago for smaller fields and played slow-pitch with no gloves. He took the basketball out of the closet, pulled apart the seams and opened it. He reached in and pulled out a Glock 9mm and a snub- nosed Smith and Wesson .38 caliber. He checked both safeties. Both guns were loaded. He looked at Diego and asked if he had ever fired either type of gun. Diego said that he had never had anything to do with guns because of his father.

Oscar indicated that both guns belonged to Jorge. He wouldn't need them for a long while. Oscar hated guns as well, but now they had no choice but to have protection. They were already targeted. He told Diego that the police might go to "Hoghead" and tell him to "knock it off" but they wouldn't arrest him. Oscar observed "if the cops arrested everyone who shot at somebody in Chicago, they'd have to build five more jails". Chicago had had the strictest gun laws of anywhere in the United States for forty years, but the murder rate had been the highest in the country for more than the last twenty years.

There were just too many gangs and guns. The police, despite heroic attempts, couldn't get a hold on the violence. Guns were relatively cheap and easy to come by. In 2018, the New York Times quoted a suppressed Justice Department report showing that nearly half the boys over fifteen in Chicago carried guns and more than a quarter of the girls did so. The mayor was so tied up in labor negotiations and budget matters that he had little time or energy to devote to the problem. The president was so busy boosting the "Green" lobby and protecting the teachers' unions from the deadly advance of charters and vouchers for children who were wasting in and dropping out of failing schools that he failed to notice the weekly carnage in the major cities of his country. When kids killed people with guns, baseball bats, flashlights and knives, he talked about the evils insurance companies. His wife was so caught up in promoting broccoli and carrots in every school lunch that she had little time to devote to the killing. She was persuaded that all those people, who at eighty and ninety, were straining the health care system had been short changed by their mothers who sent them to school with a peanut butter sandwich, apple and cookie. She wouldn't be satisfied until all schools were in the healthy food and condom business. The ACLU continued to block a "stop and frisk". In 2019 when Mayor Perez's nephew was killed by a bullet not intended for him when he was coming home from his junior prom, there was another attempt to pass one, but with no success. Kids had lots of guns.

Oscar told Diego that they had to protect themselves and that he should take the .38 caliber and carry it all the time, at least until they could get "Hoghead" off their backs. He impressed on Diego that the biggest issue was to make certain that the safety was on at all times, except when he needed to shoot, which he hoped never would happen. He told him that he should keep the weapon in his backpack. They had never had a metal detector or a backpack search at St. Rita's since they had been going to school there.

Diego fretted for a minute, but then decided that he didn't want to face another situation like tonight without some self-protection. He took the gun. Oscar showed him how to take the safety off and put it on. Then he went back to the closet with the basketball and came out with the softball and pulled the seams apart. It contained the ammunition. He handed Diego a box with just twelve .38 caliber bullets. He said that if they needed more than that, they were" screwed". That was all Jorge had left. He had no idea of where the other dozen bullets had gone but he doubted they were used for target practice. The Glock had a clip of just ten and no extras.

They went back to the kitchen and the popcorn, but on the way Oscar turned off all the lights in the front of the house and closed the door
to the kitchen. When it came time for the girls to leave, Oscar and Diego got their backpacks. They all left through the back door. Oscar, Diego and Sarah walked the girls to their front doors just two blocks away. The girls and Sarah couldn't figure out why they were being walked home but they were happy because it was one more chance to impress Diego. Later, when

Diego started for home three blocks away, he put the gun in his right front pocket, but didn't take the safety off. He had practiced removing the weapon from his pocket and releasing the safety a couple of times and was satisfied he was quick enough to make it work for him. He took a round- about way home and kept a close eye.

A Short Lived Respite

Three weeks went by with no sign of "Hoghead". So the boys relaxed a bit and life went back to normal, but they both kept the guns in their backpacks. St. Rita's had easily won their first game of the season with a blowout of St. Leo's. While neither one of them had broken into the starting lineup, both boys got a lot of playing time, Diego more on offense and Oscar more on defense. On Wednesday night after football practice, they both stayed behind to lift weights until it was dark. They left the gym tired but buoyed by the progress of the team and their own hopes for eventual stardom. They were the last ones out of the gym. The gym door had closed behind them and the panic bar had locked when they saw the dark Buick parked at the corner. It started moving slowly toward them. They had a choice of running or hitting the deck.

Both remembered Oscar's mother's admonition regarding the small target. Both hit the deck at the same time. This time they heard the shrill whiz of the shots as they came overhead and hit the steel of the gym door and ricocheted. Both pulled the backpacks to their sides and removed the guns, flipped off the safeties and fired almost simultaneously. Oscar got off all ten of the shots he had available and Diego got off four quick rounds. They got lucky. At least one of the shots caught the right rear tire and one or more must have hit the gas tank in the right place. The car didn't explode but by the time the car reached the end of the block, it was in flames.

Diego couldn't explain it later, but somehow, he had the presence of mind and presumably the forgiveness in his heart to use his cell. He called 911 to report the fire. He didn't mention the gunfire but some other caller must have. It turned out that his good deed did not go unpunished. Cell phone calls to dispatch were easily traceable and the police immediately began looking for him. As the boys turned and ran from the scene, they entered the gangway between two large houses near the school. When they got to the alley behind the houses, they heard the sirens of what must have been half dozen emergency vehicles. They continued on the way to Diego's house moving in a zigzag pattern only in alleys.

A block before they got home, a car with its lights on entered the alley and started toward them. Oscar thought perhaps it was "Hoghead" or one of his friends in a different car. He pulled his weapon and aimed. He forgot that he had emptied the weapon shooting at the Buick. Immediately the red, white and blue strobe lights on the car came on and Oscar and Diego froze. Both dropped their guns. A single female officer exited the patrol car weapon in hand pointed at the boys. There was no need to do a "stop and frisk". She screamed "Down on your face, hands behind your head". A very large male officer exited the other side of the car and came toward them with his weapon drawn.

The second officer patted both boys down and picked up both guns. He could smell the powder residue indicating they had been fired recently and he checked them to see if they had any remaining rounds. He put them in an evidence bag he had pulled from his pocket. He put the evidence bag on the hood of the car and returned, put his knee and the two hundred fifty pounds of his girth square in the middle of Diego's back while he cuffed him, pulling the plastic ties as tight as he could without completely cutting off the circulation. For a moment, Diego lost his breath, but didn't say anything.

He was scared. It looked as though the dream of breaking into the starting lineup this year or maybe any year was fading quickly. When the officer cuffed Oscar in the same manner, Oscar grimaced and cursed under his breath, but didn't utter a word. The officer ripped the wallets of both boys from their backpacks. Other than the female officer's "face down" order, not a word had been said. The male officer went to the evidence bag and put the wallets in a similar bag and then placed them in the trunk of the car. He opened the right side door and walked Diego back to the vehicle with his left hand on Diego's belt and right squeezing his neck at the pressure point. He did the same with Oscar and placed him on the left side. The officers assumed from Diego's and Oscar's size that they had arrested adults. Both boys weighed more than two hundred pounds and stood over six foot two. But after they had put them in the station lock up, they looked at the wallets. Their school ID cards said both were only fifteen and neither had a driver's license. Because they were juveniles, the uniform officers didn't interrogate them. Juveniles were always turned over to the Youth Division Officers for interrogation. They didn't even ask them whether they had been involved in the earlier shooting where the fire occurred. They knew that both weapons had been fired. They turned the weapons over to the evidence office.

They then took a bathroom break, had a snack and coffee and took a long time to write the arrest report. Both officers thought it was a good idea to have the boys cool their heels and think about their circumstance. After nearly an hour and half, they went to the Youth Officer and explained the arrest. The police hadn't called their parents or allowed them a call. That would be the job of the Youth Officer.

The Youth Officer thanked them for their thoughtfulness

in bringing him a couple of oversized shooters. The Youth Division in the Chicago Lawn Station was undermanned to begin with and he was operating by himself tonight. His normal partner had testified in court earlier in the day on a murder case and had taken compensatory time that evening with no replacement. It was Wednesday and no one really liked working the day after payday. The Youth Officer had already had a shooter that evening who the transportation team had taken to the Audy Home, the euphemism for the county juvenile jail. The Youth Officer was not authorized to release any juveniles involved with guns. All gun cases were held until the next day when the prosecutor could review the facts. There was no question about this being a gun case. The weapons were in evidence.

The Youth Officer would have to wait until one of the transportation officers came back to the station. There always had to be a second officer present in the room during the interrogation. Two officers at the interrogation of juveniles was a relatively new requirement. The ACLU had won a case from Mississippi at the Supreme Court where a Youth Officer slugged a kid for spitting in his face twice. The precedent was set for the nation at a considerable cost. But the Youth Officer was comfortable with the requirement. He knew that the protection of constitutional rights and that law and order were never cheap.

When he finally got to the questioning, he was pleasantly surprised. Both boys were respectful. When he learned that Diego was the son of Sergeant Frankie Freeman, he felt a need to exercise some special care in managing the boys' cases. He had known Frankie from working in the same station for five years and admired him. The boys' story was a little hard to swallow, but they were totally consistent when they were questioned separately. They both said that they knew that they should have come to the police with the first shooting at the "White Hen".

But the Youth Officer gave them credit for being good shots and for taking the initiative because he knew that nothing would have happened if they had reported the first shooting. He didn't say anything to the boys

about it but he thought that considering the times, they had used their heads, armed themselves and had taken care of business. It was the prosecutor's business to sort it out. He was tired and he had two more cases waiting for him. He sent the boys to The Audy Home. The Youth Officer knew that because they would be coming into Audy after mid-night, they would not be fed a meal. He took two large "Baby Ruths" from his desk drawer and gave them to them.

The Audy Home

The overhead speaker crackled and a loud gravelly male voice with some edge yelled. "I will push the buzzer that opens the door. When the door slides open, you will enter the interlock, the space ahead of you and turn to your right. If you don't understand what I have said, raise your hand." Diego didn't raise his hand. He thought "If I don't understand what he said, how in the hell am I going to know if I should raise my hand". The door slid to the right and Diego entered. Gravelly said "On the bench to your left there is a set of underwear, a jumpsuit and sandals. Pick those items up and hold them in your arms. If you have any false teeth or partials, remove them and place them in the bowl on the steel counter. They will be returned to you. If the cops did not already relieve you of the contents of your pockets, leave the contents on the counter. When I open the door behind you, walk into the room, remove your shoes and all your clothing and leave them on the floor. Put on the underwear, the jumpsuit and the sandals. Don't worry about someone seeing you or whether the items fit. No one can see you except me and I don't like to look at dumb kids undress. It's not my thing. Wait until someone opens the door. Nice to have you aboard Mr. er, er Freeman. Enjoy your cruise with us."

Diego heard the massive thick steel door open and then clang behind him. When he entered the ten by ten foot room where he was to be interviewed, he almost gagged. The room smelled of something with which he was not familiar, but he didn't like it. There was a very large Black woman in a uniform sitting behind a desk in the small well lit room with some pictures obviously done by little kids taped to the wall. A steel chair was welded to the desk. A name plate declared that she was the Reception Officer. She motioned to Diego to sit in the chair and introduced herself as Gladys Bright. In a wholly unexpected warm friendly voice she said "Well Diego Freeman you have come to visit us on this fine Wednesday night. We prefer to have our guests check in earlier in the evening, but you and your friend Oscar are our latecomers tonight. We apologize for the smell from the sewer backup. But we have had a rash of young men stuffing their jumpsuits down the toilets piece by piece and it always stops up the sewer. The sewer has the "muffin eaters" but they just can't keep up. Do you expect to stay with us for very long and may I ask what occasions your visit? Tell Gladys what you did to get here."

Diego was disarmed by her friendliness and said "My friend and I shot at some people who were trying to kill us. We had to".

Miss Bright said "Now let's see here. Your mother has been called to come tomorrow to see us. You will have to go before a Referee tomorrow who will decide if you are to become a guest of ours. It says here that you will also have to see the prosecutor who will determine if and how he is going to charge you. We will just have to see. I need to check to make sure the information on the sheet the Youth Officer prepared is complete.

Let's see. You are fifteen, there are seven children in the family and your father is deceased. You are a sophomore at St. Rita's. You are six foot two inches tall and weigh 206 pounds. Good grief boy, what is your mama feeding you? Your mother is Hispanic and your father is Black, was Black. Your father was a police officer, a sergeant killed in the line of duty? Child what's wrong with you, don't you get it; you are supposed to be one of the good guys, not a shooter. What in the world were you doing with a gun anyway? Leave the guns to the dummies". Diego sighed "It's a long story".

Miss Bright said "Let's get you processed and give you a house. You can tell the referee and the prosecutor the whole story tomorrow. We're going to put you in one of our special guest holding rooms for the night until your mother comes. Then you will be put in the visiting room with her until you are called to go to a Referee. You will probably have a lawyer from the defender's office with you and your mother. When you go to the Referee, you'll do yourself a big favor by keeping your mouth shut unless he or she asks you to speak. Don't blame anyone other than yourself. Say a prayer and keep your fingers crossed that the Referee will allow you to go home with your mother. You really do not want to be our guest. The food is lousy and the accommodations and entertainment are just not that attractive. The Referee may be able to settle the case right there and if so, consider yourself fortunate. Then for heaven's sake keep your nose clean and stay out of places like this. Do you hear me?"

"Yes, Miss Bright" Diego responded. She rang a buzzer and short young Hispanic man came and greeted him with "Well, my goodness me, Miss Bright, you certainly have tall guests tonight. And who is this"

"This handsome young man would be Juan Diego Ortiz Freeman. He is going to a holding cell until his mother Carmen arrives. Please be gentle with him. Your wallet is safe. He is a shooter. But he doesn't have a gun and from now on he is going straight, very straight." Diego was led to Holding Cell 8. Again the door clanged behind him. He sat on the bunk for a moment and assessed his situation. He murmured "Nuts, nuts". There was a steel toilet attached to the wall and no windows.

He lay on the steel bunk and thought how stupid he and Oscar were. He was tired and began to nod off. As he lay half asleep his thoughts went back to the date and time where they always went when he was sad. He was six and Angel, the last born Freeman was on her way. He thought of his mother and how disappointed in him she would be. She would say that she couldn't believe a child of hers was in detention, that none of his brothers had ever gotten into trouble and that his father would be terribly sad to think a Freeman was in jail. She would be the deeply loving mother she always was, but she would be scared and wonder about his future. The others were doing well. Would Diego be her cross, would he be the one to break her heart? And Diego thought to himself that maybe he had already done so by being there.

There was a very dim light covered by a wire mesh high above the door of the cell. Diego was exhausted and drifted off almost immediately. He was startled awake. There was movement outside the steel door. The clanging of the huge steel and reinforced glass door on the interlock at the front of the unit was so loud that it roused him from a deep sleep. It awakened him to his circumstance. He was in trouble, serious trouble. He didn't mean harm to anyone. It seemed unfair that all they were doing was trying to stay alive and they are now in jail.

When he was being processed by the intake officer, he had been given a pair of jockey shorts that were once white, but were now a dull gray. He was outfitted with the freshly laundered yellow jumpsuit but it was at least three sizes too small for his frame. His feet were barely covered by the pair of blue cloth sandals. He was assigned to his five by nine foot "house" with a yellow tile base for the bed and a thin gray plastic mattress covered by a gray sheet. He prayed that this was not his future.

The Audy smell was a very strong pine disinfectant and it reminded him of the night at the visitation for his father's funeral in the basement of the church. The basement at St Rita's always smelled like pine disinfectant. The visitation for his father was the first time Diego had smelled the disinfectant and he associated it with death. Later when he attended St. Rita's school, he learned the <u>why </u>of the strong disinfectant. At one point, the basement served as the gym for the school although the ceiling was only fourteen foot high. There was a small stage at one end and two baskets had been set up for basketball but the shots couldn't be higher than the low ceiling. There was a cold air register with an exhaust grate at one end of the room and two inlet grates where the heat was piped in.

There were no bathrooms in the basement and when there was no supervision, some of boys would use the grates to relieve themselves. During the summer the smell was gross but when the heat came on in the winter it was unbearable. It took the janitor a long time to learn the cause but once he did, he began throwing buckets of the pine disinfectant into the grates to fight the smell. He always lost the battle.

Diego was shocked that he found himself in Audy at age fifteen. Both he and Oscar had been arrested once before when they were thirteen, but that was minor and they hadn't been shipped off to Audy. That arrest was more of an embarrassment than big trouble. When Oscar and he had planned that day, they had nothing in mind but a swim. It was Oscar's thirteenth birthday. It was the middle of July and very hot and humid. The back door to the Mapes Hardware store had been left open.

There wasn't anyone in sight and there were a bunch of new electric hand tools that apparently had just been delivered. He and Oscar had grabbed as many "dremmels" and small drills as they could carry and tried their new formed sales partnership on Western Ave. Mr. Mapes, the owner, happened by in his truck and saw them. He went back to the store, checked on the delivery, part of which was missing and called the police. He went with them to where Diego and Oscar had set up shop. When they saw the tan unmarked car approach, Oscar started toward it thinking that maybe they had customers.

Mr. Mapes was agreeable to having them taken to the station and processed by the Youth Officer. They would be on the record in case they decided to make a career out of theft. They were held at the station until their mothers could pick them up. But when the Youth Officer called Diego's mom, she was at St. Rita's working and could not come until after lunch had been served to the priests in the monastery and the cleanup was finished. So he sat in a room at the station for three hours. Both Oscar and Diego had avoided arrest until now.

Diego thought it odd that they would call a place like "Audy", a home. It was a mess. But it was a place to put kids for a while until the prosecutors could get it together and judges could decide what to do with the "dummies". Audy had been established back in the 1890's to protect kids from adult convicts in the jails. Some women from Hull House founded and led by the renowned social worker, Jane Addams, pressed the county to put kids in their own jail.

There was a pamphlet that was in the cell that told kids about how they would be processed. It included a section on how the place came to be. It was named for a guy named Audy who ran the place and died of a heart attack as a young man. Diego thought that there should be a place named for his dad. Maybe someday he'd be able to do something that could make that happen. He'd rather have it be a stadium, a place where people wanted to be, not a jail.

It occurred to him that whoever was running the place now was stealing his paycheck. Even though every wall and door had been painted with at least a dozen coats of light green paint, the place was dark and dingy. He thought maybe that the county building couldn't afford to pay their electric bill. He knew he couldn't complain. He was the one who put himself there. It was, after all, a little bit like the Freeman home with respect to the lighting. Since his daddy was killed, the Freeman family had gone short on electricity. The house was always dark. There were now seven kids. His baby sister Angel was born two months after his daddy died. There wasn't much left to what his mom made working in the kitchen at the school after she paid the mortgage and bought food. She received a part of his daddy's pension pay and some social security but eight people living in the house was tough on any budget.

His mom, Carmen, had insisted that Renaldo, Jose and Rosa attend community college. And Tony would follow. None of them was able to work full time with their class schedules. All of the older kids had part time jobs, but with tuition, they couldn't contribute that much to the household. But Carmen was happy with the fact that she had three in college. All three would eventually go on to the university and secure degrees. The city and the union made a one-time payment after Frankie died, but that money didn't last that long. The fact that he was in the employ of a private company at the time of his death technically ruled out being killed on the job. The Mayor had his staff do a slight of hand and managed to get a partial pension to Carmen. Mr. Goldman, owner of Allsave, the grocery where Frankie was killed stepped up and created small trust funds for the seven children's college tuitions. The Chicago Tribune wrote a story with a picture of Mr. Goldman and the seven kids. Mr. Goldman didn't know it at the time and neither did Diego, but Diego wasn't going to need the scholarship. He certainly could not see that possibility from where he was now sitting.

Carmen and Frankie had been saving small amounts to eventually buy a house. Five years after Frankie died, Mrs. Diaz, the bookkeeper at the parish had shown Carmen how she could buy a house if she could find one that was big enough for the family but not too expensive. Providence cared for her when an old friend, a partner of Frankie's on the job, had gone into real estate. He found her the perfect house for the family right in the neighborhood. She and Mrs. Diaz inspected it and worked out the numbers for the mortgage and the taxes. She had to watch her pennies, but it turned out to be the right step. Carmen kept telling the kids "Daddy is looking after us from heaven". She believed it firmly and she was making believers of the kids.

The church helped some, by raising her pay a bit and not requiring as many hours. But the church always looked like it was poor too, so she didn't push Father Kevin for raises. After Frankie died, she didn't want to spend too much time away from the kids. Father Kevin had no problem with Carmen bringing the two youngest to the kitchen while she cooked. Carmen could see clearly how Frankie's death had begun to affect both Diego and Isabel. She had a sense of how angry, despondent and confused Diego was and she seemed not to be able to do anything about it. He was just six, but he brooded. He had gone into a shell and tried to stay away from the family as much as he could.

He would go to the room he shared with Isabel. Six months after Frankie was killed, she decided to move Diego in with Renaldo. Jose and Tony could live together. Rosa would have her own room. Isabel and Angel could live in her room until they grew too old for that arrangement. At fifteen, Renaldo was trying to take as much of his father's role as he could manage.

When Carmen asked him to have Diego in his room, he didn't hesitate. He knew why she was doing so. He too had witnessed Diego's retreat. Renaldo was very sensitive to Diego's needs and saw helping him as his responsibility. Renaldo helped Carmen as much as he could with the bills from his check at Allsave. They had hired him for stocking after Frankie's death.

It was nearly midnight by the time the Youth Officer at the Chicago Lawn Station called Carmen. She had been worrying about Diego because he always called if he was going to be late. He had said nothing about going anywhere after practice. She was relieved to know Diego was still alive and not harmed. The Youth Officer told her she would not be able to visit him that night and someone from Audy would call her in the morning to tell her what was going to happen to him. The officer said she may want to consult a lawyer because it was a serious charge and the Public Defender was way over- loaded.

Carmen woke Renaldo and asked him what he thought they should do. He said he would call Brother Mark at St Rita's first thing in the morning. Brother Mark handled all the discipline and problems at St. Rita's and was a friend of both Carmen and Renaldo. Renaldo thought they should talk with him before doing anything else. Carmen didn't sleep a wink. When the lady from the Audy Home called the next morning she said they would not go to court until the afternoon "call" at 2pm. She could come to the Audy Home at 12P.M. to talk to Diego.

Diego rested but he couldn't sleep. His guilt rose as he tried to doze on the hard bed with the very thin mattress. His mind always went to the worst day of his life up to this time. He didn't want to go there. He wanted peace.

Chapter 3

Life without Father

Monday August 2nd, 2010, 4:30 PM, 5611 S Sacramento Ave. Apt#9, Chicago Ill.

He was six but he remembered the exact moment when he learned of his father's death; August 2nd, 2010 at 4:30pm. The moment could not be more deeply emblazoned on his young heart. He was number five in the family, with two older brothers and two older sisters. Isabel was a year younger and they were very close. The Freemans were a big happy family. A new baby was coming in October and they were all excited. New babies were a big event in the Freeman household. When Carmen was pregnant, the family would all talk about the new baby on the way. Diego loved Isabel but she wasn't a boy. He was hoping and praying the new baby would be a boy. But he would be happy no matter even if it was a girl.

Every morning at six A.M. his dad left the house to go to the Chicago Lawn Police Precinct on the south west side where he had been for five years as a patrol sergeant of the Chicago Police Department. He had only five more years to his twenty year retirement but he had no plans for leaving the job. He and Carmen had tuitions to pay and a house to buy. He supplemented his income with four hours five days a week as the security officer at Allsave Foods which was their local market. He enjoyed Allsave better than he did his job on the PD. The owner of the Allsave grocery chain, Mr. Ira Goldman was a Jewish man married to a Catholic woman and he always took a special interest in Frankie because of all the kids. He had two boys of his own but they were grown and out of the house. He would always ask Frankie to see the latest picture of the kids. He was very generous with Frankie at Christmas. Mr. Goldman, who would come to the store every couple of weeks, knew the mayor well and offered to cut a path for upward movement for Frankie on the force. But Frankie said he would rather advance on his own. Mr. Goldman was shocked but very impressed.

The Commander of the Chicago Lawn District was new and everyone knew he had gotten on the list and appointed because of his connections in the Mayor's office. It was rumored that he was a "bagman" for the Ward Committeeman who was the mayor's brother in law. He was universally regarded as a jerk and a lousy commander. He was not well liked and worse, he was from the north side. Frankie had thought about transfer but that could harm his schedule. He had been on the seven to three shift for the whole five years at the precinct and it was perfect, just five blocks from Allsave the security job.

At seven each morning, his mom walked the six blocks to St Rita's where she would work in the kitchen even when school was not in session. She and the other cook, Edwina, had cleaned and stocked the kitchen in the summer, took their vacations and prepared for the session that would start in four weeks. Juan Diego was eager for school to start because he'd be able to go all day. He wanted to be with his older brothers and sisters even though a new baby was coming. He knew the baby would be six years younger than he was and at the beginning the baby wouldn't be much fun as a playmate, even if it turned out to be a boy.

Late in the afternoon when his mom and dad were at work, Renaldo, his fifteen year old brother, answered the door. Filling up the doorway was a big white policeman with his hat under his left arm. Everyone in the house froze except Diego. Was the policeman there to question Renaldo or Jose? Jose was just a year younger than Renaldo. They were the only two old enough to get in any trouble. But the officer had a very quiet approach, especially for such a tall rough looking man. He didn't sound like he was there to arrest anyone. He was red faced with a lot of pock marks. He had a silver name tag. He was Sergeant Costello and he had a silver gun and a holster very similar to his father's.

Diego assumed because he was also a sergeant, that their dad probably knew him. He asked if their mom was home and Renaldo said she was at St. Rita's in the kitchen and would be home about six. The Sergeant asked Renaldo if he was the oldest and when he answered yes, he asked him to step outside for a minute. After they talked, the Sergeant left and said he would go to Carmen at St. Rita's.

When Renaldo came back inside, he had tears in his eyes and went to the bathroom. Diego could hear him vomit. Diego couldn't figure it out. When Renaldo finally came back into the living room, he told Jose that they needed to go outside for a couple of minutes. When they came back in, Jose just sat in a chair with a blank look. He rocked back and forth without saying anything.

In less than half of an hour, Carmen came home and she was crying. She sat in his dad's big chair and gathered all six of the children around her. She couldn't speak for a long time. She was sobbing so hard she looked like she couldn't get her breath. She opened her mouth to speak, but couldn't get any words out. Finally, Renaldo told his mom that he would take over. He looked at everyone through his tears and blurted out "daddy's dead".

Diego remembered when the Robinson kids told him their grandmother died and when the Ortiz' puppy, Chico, had died. But he didn't think dads died. How could he die? We had a party last night for Isabel's birthday. He wouldn't go away before the new baby came. The Robinson's grandmother was old and got sick and then died. Daddy wasn't sick. He was strong. He's alive. Renaldo and mom don't have it correct. They must have misunderstood the sergeant. This is a mistake. He'll be back later tonight or tomorrow. They shouldn't try to fool us.

About half an hour later, Father Kevin, the pastor of the church and the president of St. Rita's High School where Renaldo and Jose attended, came to the house. Brother Mark was with him. While they were there, Edwina, the other cook and a couple of teachers from St. Rita's grade school, Sister Eugenia and Miss Bartlett came. They sat in the kitchen with Carmen. They tried to calm her saying that the sobbing was probably not good for the baby. She told them that if God loved the baby, he wouldn't make her sob.

Everyone knew her Franklin R. Freeman. He and Carmen were a remarkable couple with a remarkable family. Both were very generous with their time. Both were enormously sincere and hard working. They both tried all their lives together to be good and do what they thought God wanted, but Frankie's death was too much for Carmen to take. She couldn't care for the kids alone. She needed Frankie. The kids needed their father. Diego was beginning to sense that something awful was going on. People were acting so serious and different. It may be true that "daddy" isn't coming back. Their house was normally a place of activity and laughter. But now, no one was laughing. There was only crying. For the first time in his life, Diego couldn't go to sleep even though he was very tired and in bed. His dad had put a night light in the room and he lay there staring at the ceiling and wondering what was next.

The Freemans of Sacramento Ave

As a young man, Frankie Freeman was a boxer, a fighter with a future. He played both offense and defense for three years on the Chicago Vocational High School football team. He played at both tailback and the corner back position. He boxed in the Golden Gloves and won the light heavyweight division in Chicago at sixteen. He entered the Marines after graduating and did a tour in Viet Nam. The shrapnel that gave him a purple heart was still located in his left leg. It didn't prevent him from returning to the ring when he returned to Chicago, but by then, he had grown into a heavyweight and it did slow him a bit.

When Frankie met Carmen, boxing began to fade as a career. If he was going to marry Carmen, he needed a regular job, one with insurance and a retirement program, one with advancement. Before they married, he went to work for Sears in the auto parts department. After two years working in auto parts, he applied for the police department, passed the test and he was on his way. He was shocked at how political the department was. But he tried to adapt because he and Carmen had just had their third baby and it didn't look like there was any plan to slow the coming of the Freemans.

Carmen was a "good Catholic". Frankie had converted from his Baptist roots and was interested in the faith and in nurturing Carmen's desire to be a "good Catholic". Whenever the topic of how many children they would need to have for Carmen to be good Catholic came up, he was told that "you ain't wear'in no raincoat in my house" and she meant it. Because of the slang, he had an idea of where she got the term. He assumed it came from the other woman who worked with her at St.Rita's. Edwina Greer, from Jamaica was very religious but had a lot of earthy sayings. Frankie complied with Carmen's wishes. The Freeman family expanded. Both he and Carmen were happy.

Diego inherited Frankie's size and good looks but not his ebony skin, although he always wished he had. His dad's face was handsome with full chiseled features that were enhanced by the shadows provided by his dark skin. Diego admired those looks. His dad's muscles rippled even under his tee shirt and when he would work out, the sweat on his body would make his skin glisten. Even at six Diego knew that he would never look that good. Carmen Ortiz had come to Chicago from Juarez, Mexico. She was tiny by comparison with Frankie and had relatively light skin. Diego inherited her skin.

Thinking ahead, Diego thought that his reputation as a tough guy would have been enhanced by darker skin. He looked slightly more Mexican than black and had less sharp features than his dad. The two older boys got darker skin than Diego, but they didn't get their dad's size.

When he met Carmen, Frankie didn't know very much Spanish and Carmen was limited in her English. Frankie eagerly had learned and spoken Spanish. Carmen quickly picked up English and insisted that all of the kids learn and speak Spanish because she wanted them to be able to communicate with their relatives when they came from Juarez. Most of the relatives would eventually come to Chicago to live with the Freemans for some time.

Not all had Green Cards. But all worked. It was often crowded at the Freemans. The relatives would sleep on the sun porch at the back of the apartment. Diego always thought of it as a bedroom with the best windows, but it was chilly in the winter. Carmen felt blessed to have three bedrooms and the sun porch. She was happy to share them with any of her relatives. Because the Freemans were such good tenants, the landlord didn't mind the extra visitors. They could stay as long as they liked.

At one point, Frankie asked if Carmen thought it was a

good idea for a policeman to have people in the house without Green Cards or visas. She reminded him that before they married she was without a visa and he didn't seem to mind that. She'd say that the Mexicans were the future of the country. Some of the white men and women were marrying the same sex and a lot of the Blacks and Whites were having abortions. The Mexicans were having children. She told him that millions of unborn babies God had intended for the United States were being killed in the womb. So, she would say, there's plenty of room in the country for a few million "undocumented" Mexicans. She'd ask him "who will do the work, if not the Mexicans?"

The wake for Frankie was two days after his death. That night the children were dressed in their best clothes by Sonia and Elena, two of his mom's sisters from Mexico and they all marched to St Rita's basement. His daddy's casket was up toward the front of the room, a long wooden box lined with white satin. All of Frankie's friends and relatives were there. There must have been three hundred people in the dark basement, many of whom were still in uniform. The mood at the wake had lightened a little because not everyone was as close to the family as the people at the house. There was even some laughter in the background as people recounted some of Frankie's bouts as a young man and some of his collars as a cop.

Danny, Frankie's youngest brother, stayed close to Diego. He knew he was the one who would have to take Diego up to the casket. The casket was a very inexpensive looking box. The church was good at making deals with the local funeral home for those who couldn't afford a big funeral. In some cases like this, the church would quietly stand the expense for the funeral and hold the visitation in the basement of the church. But the church always took the least expensive casket available.

They may even have bartered for it, maybe a few

indulgences for the funeral director or some prayers for his soul. The founder of the priests' order was not big on show, having been buried in a wooden box of his own making. The rule of St. Augustine was very much ordered not only to individual poverty, but congregate poverty as well. Martin Luther, a former Augustinian, had eschewed ownership until he left the order and married. Gregor Mendel, an Augustinian scientist was vowed to poverty. In today's world, had he put his discoveries to work as the Father of Genetics, he would likely be a billionaire. The monks were directed to be austere. St. Augustine's followers got the message.

Danny took Diego by the hand and led him to the casket. Danny knelt and Diego stood on the kneeler and looked down at his daddy. He was trying to be brave because he knew his daddy would want him to be. But he couldn't stand it. What he looked at was not his daddy. It was a still gray looking shadow of Frankie Freeman, dressed in his old uniform. His new uniform had three bullet holes and apparently the city didn't buy new uniforms for the deceased. Diego now knew he was looking at death, like the Robinson's grandmother and Chico, the Martinez's dog. He didn't like it and he ran to Carmen and cried like he had never cried. He felt bad because he knew his daddy wouldn't be proud of him and he had disappointed Uncle Danny who he knew was trying to help him to be brave. But Uncle Danny was very kind and hugged Diego until he stopped crying. He hurt worse than ever before. He wanted to go home and go to bed and never awaken. He didn't want to be with friends or family. He wanted to go where "daddy" was.

Six weeks later at school he thought perhaps that would occur. Two young men with automatic weapons broke into the school and began firing weapons in the hall. When they entered the classroom where Diego was, they smiled at the children and then the teacher. They didn't shoot anyone. They fired their weapons at the Crucifix on the wall in the front of the classroom and then shot up a statue of St. Rita of Cascia, the patron of the school. They went to all the classrooms and to the school office and did the same thing. Then, they left the school before the police arrived. By the time the police arrived, there was no sign of them.

No one knew the purpose of the crime until a week later when a note was sent to Cardinal Hurley indicating that the same would happen to all Catholic, Lutheran and Jewish schools in Chicago if they were not closed. The cardinal made a public statement in concert with two leading Rabbis, a Seventh Day Adventist leader and a Lutheran minister indicating that they would not close the schools. The Mayor said he supported their actions but could not afford to provide protection. The city was nearing bankruptcy. The police union stepped forward and indicated that they would work as volunteers if the city would pay for their insurance and provide half salary. The mayor said the city still couldn't afford it. The schools stayed open and each morning prior to the first class, there was a prayer in each classroom for conversion of the terrorists and for safety.

The day after the attack, the principal of St. Rita's came to all the classrooms and said that the children would be safe and they were not going to die. Someone asked if she was sure. She said she was as certain about that as she was that the Cubs wouldn't win the World Series that year even though they were having a very good year. She knew she could get away with that humor because all the people who lived near St Rita's school were White Sox fans. The children were able to laugh. Everyone relaxed.   He would always remember the day of his dad's death and the terrorist incident, each with pain. He was only six, but he had a sense that bad things can happen. At six he had concluded that death was bad and should be avoided.

For the week after Frankie's death, the house was packed with people. Aunts and uncles, cousins and friends, some from Mexico and some from the south side filled the house. They came and tried to console Carmen and the older kids. But the crying didn't stop. The more relatives, the more crying occurred. Diego had never seen so many people in one house or so much sorrow. There was every kind of food; ribs and greens from the south side and menudo, tamales, rice and beans, meals cooked in Carmen's kitchen at the church by the aunts from Mexico. But there was also a very sad feeling to the house. It was creepy. Diego was getting confused, scared and sick himself.

Uncle Danny was from the west side and took Diego under his wing. Sometimes Danny would call Diego, "Juan Diego Ortiz Freeman, my main man" which was his given name and Diego thought that was cool. Then he would say that Diego was just like his "daddy" and it made Diego feel good. He liked his name, Juan Diego Ortiz Freeman. His mom had already told him who St. Juan Diego was and he was happy that he was connected to the Lady of Guadalupe, the woman in the picture in the living room. She reminded him of his mother. He was taken by the picture, the story and the miracle roses. He asked if they could go there to the church when she took the children to Mexico.

Danny and Diego went for some long walks and talked about a lot of things, stuff they saw in the neighborhood, Diego's friends, what position he would like best in baseball and what kind of ice cream Diego liked best. The only important thing to Diego was "when was daddy coming back?" At that, Danny choked a little. There was a tear in his eye. Finally, he said that "daddy couldn't come back but someday Diego would be with daddy" again in what was a really great place to be. Diego asked if they could go there right now and play with daddy. Danny said the only way he could be with daddy for a while was in his thoughts and prayers, that daddy was with God. Diego asked "why? Didn't God have his own friends to be with? Why did God need daddy to be with him"? Danny couldn't go on. He promised Diego they would go for ice cream and talk about this again but for now they needed to get back to the house.

Shortly after Diego's dad died, Uncle Danny, who was not married, went to the hospital and had an operation. He told the family that the operation was successful and he went back to work at the gas company. Later, he got very thin and sick and didn't come from the west side to the Freeman's very often. Diego really missed him and when he died two years later, Diego went through almost the same pain as when his daddy died. Years later, his mother told him that Uncle Danny had been sick and in pain when he was tending to Diego's needs.

When Diego and Danny arrived home where all the relatives were gathered, Carmen was sitting in the living room in Frankie's chair with a picture of him in front of her. She kept telling her sister that Frankie had worked himself to death to support the family. It was ironic. He had been on patrol on the police force in the toughest neighborhoods in Chicago, all over the south side and in the housing projects and had never had an injury. How could he be killed on his second job at the Allsave Foods where he worked security? He was just forty two.

Frankie was a big and powerful man and he didn't take anything from anybody. His manner was powerful and dominant. He didn't have to indicate verbally that he wouldn't take any abuse, ridicule or nonsense from others because his reputation as a feared heavyweight amateur boxer accompanied him in the neighborhood and in the department. When he was twenty two anyone on the south side familiar with boxing or any sport knew Frankie Freeman and they all thought he had a future in the ring. At six foot two and slightly over 200 hard pounds, he had a power package and speed in his hands and legs that gave him his advantage over almost everyone he met in the ring.

He had only one defeat and that was after Viet Nam. Leroy "Spider" Sammons took him out in a fifteen round decision. "Spider" had already won three pro fights when Frankie met him. Frankie knew that he would have to beat "Spider" someday if he wanted to be a pro. Diego learned how his daddy died when Father Kevin gave the homily at Frankie's funeral. He talked about how such a good man had given his life for others just like Jesus did. He was surely in heaven with Jesus. He had fought in Viet Nam and was given a Purple Heart for taking shrapnel in his leg for other people's freedom. He healed quickly and he was able to continue to fight when he was released from the Marine's. But he gave up fighting to be a better supporter of his children.

All he did, he did for others. Diego listened to the words and quietly cried as he sat next to Danny. He couldn't understand why Jesus was more important than he and his mom and brothers and sisters were. Why is it better to be with Jesus? Diego turned to Danny and said "Jesus doesn't need daddy the way we do". Father Kevin said "Frankie died just as he had lived, a real day to day hero, a father who had given his life to his wife, his kids and neighbors". The more Father Kevin talked about what a hero his dad was the worse Diego felt. He died a hero saving the life of another person but it didn't make Diego happy. Derrick, his daddy's killer, "DoDo" Sample was a sixteen year old kid from the neighborhood. Everyone knew he was crazy. He had gone to the door at Allsave with the intention of robbing someone of their purse when they came out with a bagful of groceries. Two older junkies had given "DoDo" the gun and told him they would split the money with him if he went to Allsave and got some money.

Frankie knew "DoDo" from both the neighborhood

and the precinct. He had been arrested a number of times and processed by the Youth Officers. He saw him standing by the front door of Allsave and didn't think anything about it until he saw a gun in "DoDo's" hand. The store policy for Frankie's work was that he was to work inside and protect the cash registers and the customers. The outside of the store belonged to the Chicago Police Department. Most of the time, Frankie would stand near the door and keep an eye on the doors.

He was first a Chicago police officer sworn to "serve and protect" and that was in his bones. He could see "DoDo" talking to a woman with the gun in his hand. Another woman who had witnessed the unfolding of the shooting said that Frankie told the lady at the cash register to call the police and that he was going out to talk to "DoDo" because he was probably threatening the woman. When Frankie went out, he told "DoDo" "We don't want anyone to get hurt here "DoDo", so put the gun down on the ground and back away from the lady". "DoDo" didn't respond except to turn and fire three shots at near point blank range into Frankie's chest. Frankie went down almost immediately and "DoDo" dropped the gun and ran off. People from the store who had seen the incident caught him two blocks down the street and he told them who had given him the gun and told him to do it.

The paramedics reported that Frankie died on the way to the hospital, but considering the location of the wounds, it was likely that at least one of the bullets went directly into the heart and he died immediately. He had always worn a bulletproof vest when on patrol, but had abandoned it when he was off duty in the store because it was just too hot.

Even at his age, the death of his father made Diego painfully aware that things were not constant, that change occurs whether you accept it or not. Pain came calling that day and he became conscious that life is tenuous. He learned that "no one is promised tomorrow" and he lived in that shadow. He began to feel that whatever he held onto was wobbly. According to his mother, every life was sacred and needed to be protected. That was what Frankie did. She told him that only God is constant but at that time he didn't feel at all friendly with God. He couldn't understand how his mother could like God. God was mean and totally unreliable. He harbored a dislike for God throughout most of elementary school and carried it well into high school. His anger at God would not subside.

His anger at "Do,Do" didn't subside, but "Do,Do" had gone to prison and would never be released. He had attempted to "shank" another inmate over a pack of cigarettes. He used a sharpened piece of plastic and didn't harm the other inmate, but "Do,Do" was found dead in the corner of the athletic field two days later, clearly the victim of a 36 inch "Louisville Slugger".

Chapter 4

A Pass for Now

A Mentor

The prosecutor who was assigned to Oscar and Diego's case for processing came to the courtroom with the intent of charging the boys as adults because it was a gun case. Chicago was buried in teen gun cases and teen deaths from guns. If the judge approved, the case would be transferred to adult court. Brother Mark had advised Carmen not to appear in the court for the first hearing with a private lawyer. Accept the assignment of the Public Defender. Brother Mark said that he would come with her and wear his Roman Collar and black suit. The Public Defender assigned to Oscar and Diego's case spent a half hour interviewing each of the boys separately.

He believed them and was diligent enough to a follow-up with the police in the district. He learned that "Hoghead" was indeed a major dealer and had gone after other people who owed him money He had been in prison and was on parole but kept dealing. Apparently, he had been in the back seat of the car that was shot up and he was now in the Cook County Hospital Burn Unit with third degree burns but was expected to survive. The police had recovered the weapons from the car and found that both guns had powder evidence of recent firing and they had no remaining rounds. They would be urging the prosecutor to charge all the occupants with attempted murder, aggravated assault and weapons violations. They were of the opinion that the boys were engaged in self defense, but would have to be charged with weapons violations.

The boy's weapons were being processed for ballistics to determine if they matched any serious crimes. Because it involved guns, the case was assigned to a Juvenile Judge who happened to be new and was eager to take his time to hear all the facts before deciding what to do with the boys. He listened intently to the case presented by the prosecutor. He knew that if the boys went to Adult Court, they could go to prison for more than five years if convicted.

Carmen nearly fainted when she heard what had happened. She simply couldn't believe Diego would carry a gun. When the judge had completed his questioning of the boys, he asked Carmen and Oscar's mother, Evelyn, if they had anything to say. Both told the judge that they couldn't believe what they heard and had no idea of what to do. The Judge asked for Brother Mark's input. He told the judge that he would do anything he could to assist and asked if he could speak to the judge in his chambers with both the prosecutor and the public defender present. The judge asked the prosecutor if that kind of consultation was allowed in Juvenile court. The prosecutor said that it was unusual but not illegal.

The concept on which the juvenile court was founded was designed to give the judge the ultimate discretion in disposing of the case. The purpose was to allow the judge to choose the most positive outcome for a child whose ability to discern and control his behavior was not yet fully developed. The judge was given absolute flexibility in managing the case by acting "in loco parentis", being able to act in the interests of the public, the family and the child. But that concept had pretty much been destroyed by the introduction of an adversarial process back in the late 1950s with a Supreme Court decision that became known as the Gault decision. It came at a time when there was a discovery of many new "rights" and juveniles were not left out of the process.

The case involved a fifteen year old youth sent to an Arizona juvenile correctional institutional for having made lewd phone calls. He claimed they were made by someone who was visiting his house. The youth could have been retained there for six years for an offense which if committed by an adult would result in a maximum sentence of sixty days. Among other things, the youth had not been represented by a defense and the parents were not involved in the process. The case was originally brought by Amelia Lewis, a New York transplant who was practicing law in Phoenix. She was later joined in her effort by the ACLU when it went to the Supreme Court.

The Supreme Court ruled that juveniles had all the rights of an adult except jury trials. From that point forward the juvenile court was on a slippery slope from which both the child and the public suffered. If children could not afford counsel, they were assigned defenders and the good of the child became a contest with formal charges. Plea bargains became commonplace and children concluded that because the lawyer had pled them to a charge that was less than the offense they committed, that they really didn't do what the police were charging them with. Many children developed the same mentality as convicted adult criminal offenders did with a plea bargain.

When they left a juvenile institution, they thought they had "done their time" and could do whatever they wanted as long as they didn't get caught. The discussion in the judge's chambers was frank. The prosecutor acknowledged that it was a case of self defense, but wanted to hold the boys as adults on the gun charge. The judge asked what good the prosecutor was trying to achieve by charging the boys as adults and how would the public and the boys benefit. The prosecutor was candid. Asked what good would come from holding the boys and prosecuting them as adults because of the guns, the prosecutor indicated that it would please his boss and that was his job.

Brother Mark indicated that the boys were normally so involved in classes and football that there was little likelihood that they would be involved in further trouble if "Hoghead" was no longer in circulation and chasing them. While he acknowledged that their judgment was awful, he did note the lack of protection that the police were able to offer kids in the city of Chicago and that neither boy had a father at home to guide them in matters of this sort. Diego's dad had died protecting a citizen from a gun and Oscar's father was either in prison or on the "lamb". He told the judge he would supervise the boys and report to the probation officer monthly if they were placed on probation or some sort of a suspended sentence.

They returned to the courtroom and the judge continued the case for six months under the agreement that Brother Mark would supervise the boys and report to the probation officer. Both Carmen and Evelyn expressed their gratitude to the judge and left the court saddened by the experience but happy to have their boys home safe. Brother Mark suggested to the boys that they would be well served by saying a prayer of gratitude for the judge's wisdom and compassion.

The Mentor

As he had promised the Judge in the Juvenile Court, Brother Mark took a deep interest in both Diego and Oscar. He saw incredible intellectual and athletic promise in both of them and literally prayed for their protection and guidance. The neighborhood was not by any means the worst in Chicago, but kids got killed by warring gangs. About half the killings were accidental. At one time Brother Mark suggested facetiously to Father Kevin that they start teaching a course on how to shoot straight to the gang members in the area in the hope that they would hit only their intended victims.

Both Oscar and Diego had shown skills playing "flag football" in the park district league in seventh and eighth grades. Brother Mark didn't know them well at that point but he had watched a couple of games where Oscar played quarterback and connected with Diego on every pass that he threw. Diego slowed up or sped up according to where he judged the ball would come. It wasn't that Oscar was a great passer, it was that Diego simply was able to grab everything that was thrown. Each of them was six foot one when they showed up as freshmen at St Rita's opening day of the football practice in 2018 though they weighed only 180 pounds each. Head Coach Denning was new at St Rita's and didn't know either of the boys.

Clem Johnson, the junior varsity coach kept a close eye on both boys. He worked them hard and didn't miss any lingering talent that may be there. After the first three days of calisthenics, sprints and passing drills, it was clear that both boys were athletes. When it came to the passing drills, each player was included to determine if there as any talent. Both Oscar and Diego passed and received. They were clearly the best on the field among the freshmen. Coach Johnson was excited about finding they both had speed and skill sets. Later in the week when the pads went on and it came to contact, he found that both of the boys wanted to play the game. They could run, tackle and block. They had the drive to move through small openings and to move others out of the way. They both looked like they enjoyed the contact.

The game of football was changing. Both mothers and coaches were concerned about concussions. In order to keep the game violent, the NFL was slow to move because the owners were willing to pay off huge law suits to former players who were entering early dementia and other conditions. They knew the fans loved the violence. One former college player, who had played before face masks were common, was president of a school board in Minnesota. He was successful in persuading the other members of his board that the removal of face masks would slow the game if all tackles were made by a player without a face mask. No one would want to stick his nose into the tackle if it got broken or teeth got knocked out every game.

In fact the high school games in Minnesota did slow a bit and injuries to the head lessened. But change was difficult. Some people wanted high schools to play flag football only. Others wanted to ban football as an interscholastic sport. There was an increasing feminization of the culture and it was having impact on male athletics. Many mothers opposed both the competition and violence. In many schools across the country, the boards of education ruled that the face masks be removed and the helmets and pads be made of a strong but somewhat pliable rubber. New contact rules were also added that made the game different. A receiver couldn't leave the ground to catch a ball and all tackles including sacks on a quarterback had to be below the hip. There were still concussions but they were fewer and less serious.

Diego enjoyed contact more than Oscar did. Oscar wanted to be a wide out where the most contact was on take downs and the wide out generally had the option of going out of bounds. Renaldo came to a junior varsity game where both Oscar and Diego were playing. He was shocked at how powerful Diego was at running and how graceful he was at receiving. He couldn't believe how well and how far Diego could pass both from the pocket and on the run. Renaldo thought of how pleased Frankie would be to watch Diego.

A problem developed for junior varsity Coach Johnson when Coach Denning watched that second junior varsity game. It was the same one that Renaldo watched. The game was against St Leo. St Rita beat St Leo High 49-0 in a game that the coaches of each team agreed could be shortened after the third quarter. The clock continued to run in the fourth quarter and Coach Johnson substituted a whole team giving St. Leo a chance to score three times. Diego had run for three touchdowns and had passed for two. Oscar had run for two. Coach Denning elevated both Diego and Oscar to the varsity which had already lost three games. They both got playing time, mainly in the fourth quarter when it was clear that they were unlikely to win. Coach Denning had begun to think about building experience among the younger players. Diego was designated the third tailback but was also given some snaps as the third string quarterback. Oscar became a third string wide-out but was placed on the special teams for his speed and abandon. St. Rita didn't make the playoffs. But both boys received enough playing time to letter which was unusual for freshmen at St Rita's. Overall it had been a poor year for St. Rita's. But it wasn't all bad for the boys. Oscar made a long runback on a punt and Diego had thrown five times with three receptions and no interceptions. He had also run nearly ninety yards on twelve carries. They couldn't wait for the next season and started lifting weights and bulking up as much as they could as soon as the season was over. They both played junior varsity basketball but couldn't wait for spring football.

The senior quarterback, one of the tailbacks and two of the five wide-outs were graduating. Diego and Oscar thought that each of them would have a shot at first string at least part of the time. The junior quarterback was shorter and slower than Diego, but could pass better. A lot hinged on what kind of offense was going to be run. Coach Denning had tried the team a few times in practice with the "west coast" offense and if that happened, it favored Diego who could both run and pass on the run.

Coach Denning did choose the west coast offense with the junior quarterback as the starter and he did well for the first two wins. After the court case, Diego and Oscar returned to the team and saw some playing time, but they did not make it to starting positions. After the first two wins, things went south and they lost three in a row. Then they put together two wins and ended the season four and five but with a lot of promise for the next year.

During the summer between their sophomore and junior year, Brother Mark made it his business to keep the boys busy. Brother Mark had developed a relationship with Mr. Goldman of Allsave and "Mr. G" as he came to be known, wanted both boys to work in the store. The store manager had graduated from St Rita's grade school and was interested in their football program. He had been at Allsave his entire career and had known Frankie. He was happy to have the boys work there. Both boys stocked shelves and were "carry outs" when they were not playing ball.

Brother Mark taught summer school and did some tutoring mainly of athletes. Neither Oscar nor Diego needed tutoring, but he put them into a summer reading program at night. He started them out with a lot of biographies of athletes and then on to other leaders and historical characters. He wanted them to see themselves as developing and carving out lives of meaning not just in athletics but in leadership. He introduced them to some saints who led heroic lives and gave their lives for their beliefs. He had some lighter reading, but all of it gave them characters to model.

Diego was struck by a story of St. Francis Xavier. Diego said he wanted to be like him. He would travel to foreign countries and try to help people know more about Jesus. Oscar said that he couldn't see Diego as a priest or wandering the earth. That notion would fade quickly if you couldn't get married. Oscar said he wanted to be a rich CEO or an inventor of some super technology. He would drive a cool car; wear the best suits and shoes he could afford. Oscar wanted to be rich. Brother

Mark was reluctant to introduce them to St. Augustine, the saint after whom his Augustinian Order was named. He thought the boys might get too caught up in the early part of Augustine's life where he caroused and favored prostitutes. He would wait for a couple of years to introduce them to his life and conversion to sanctity.

Brother Mark saw something in Diego that almost perfectly reflected some qualities of Carmen. He hadn't known Frankie well but he thought he must have been a hell of good man from all that was said of him. He did know Carmen and Renaldo well. Diego had something special in his ability to relate to others. He had that rare quality that came to the fore in few young people. He gave the impression that the person with whom he was conversing was the most important person in his world at the time. He was a serious person who was listening and processing every word someone said to him. He wanted the person with whom he was speaking to know that they were special and valued. He was consequently very likable and was always elected president or captain of everything.

Brother Mark found it an unusual trait in an adolescent and even more unusual in an adult. But he thought Carmen had it in spades. Diego's seriousness and profound sincerity was disarming. Carmen showed only love to Diego and he knew that she prayed that all her children would reflect Frankie's virtues. Diego's character was developing in other ways. It was as if each time Carmen, Renaldo, he or other teachers spoke with him, a new layer of depth was imprinted on his character and he grew more mature. He exhibited that character in his studies and behavior.

Mrs. Goldman took an interest in the boys. She told Brother Mark that while she thought it was a good thing for the boys to be so wrapped up in sports, there were other things in life to which they should be exposed. She would take it upon herself to establish an art and music dimension to their development. During the summer between the boys' sophomore and junior year, she and Mr. Goldman took Brother Mark and the boys to a jazz concert and later to an art festival on the near north side of Chicago.

In the late fall after football had finished, they went to the Civic Opera where they saw Carmen and La Boehme. In mid-winter they went to the Chicago Symphony Orchestra twice and heard Tchaikovsky, Mozart and Rimsky Korsakov. Mrs. Goldman did not test their limits of arts absorption by taking them to a ballet. The boys were surprised by how much they liked the music. They weren't taken by some of the acting in the operas. But the exposure to the small bit of culture colored their view of what was enjoyable and it carried throughout their lives.

Often, he and Oscar would talk a lot about their futures and sports fantasies, catching the winning touchdown in the last seconds of a game or running a kick back eighty yards. They were both growing physically and emotionally. Because they were such good athletes and anticipated a positive future, they were secure in themselves. They had great self images and were sliding through adolescence without many bumps after the episodes with "Hoghead". Nobody else bothered them. The gangs respected their athletic ability and stayed away from them.

Watch Out for Brother Mark's Elbows

The warm October day made it difficult for learning. But the school couldn't afford the air conditioning after September. Brother Mark lifted the pitch and the seriousness of his voice to secure their full attention. "It's essential that you learn the difference between what we know as justice, a virtue and what we know as legal, a status in the law. This distinction is a critical matter for all of us. But it is particularly so for those of you who choose law as your life's work.

"The virtue of Justice is an act by which we render to another what is their due. It is important to your eternal happiness. Legality is quality of an act that is allowed by the law. It is important to your freedom in this life. Justice comes from what we know as the natural law. Legality comes from what we call the positive law or man-made law which in turn should derive from natural law. But please, please do not confuse the two. We have a great legal system in the United States based on the United States Constitution which dates to ?????? Anyone want to hazard a guess"?

"Mr. Jackson"

"Brother I believe you will find that to be 1776". "Brother Jackson, Nice try but no cigar. If I were to allow you to look it up, where would you go to find the correct answer?"

"I would Google it."

"And if the internet was down and all the libraries in the world were closed?"

"I don't really know. I guess I would probably just ask somebody."

"Brother Jackson, please open your backpack and pull from it the little pamphlet that I gave you that includes the Declaration of Independence signed in 1776 while the founders of your nation were fighting a war with England for your freedom from tyranny. The pamphlet also includes a copy of the United States Constitution dated 1791. These are the two critical documents necessary for you to understand this experiment that we know as the United States of America, a democratic republic of which you and I are equal members.

"And when I say that we are equal members of this republic, I don't mean you are allowed to sit at this desk and scatter profound philosophical pearls as I do. I mean that we are equal in our origin, our destinies and our natures. We come from God, we each have the qualities that make us human beings, our bodies and our eternal souls and that our destiny is to return to God. In all other matters we are unequal. Do you agree?"

"Yes Brother, but if we are equal, why do some people appear to be more equal than me, they have a lot more stuff?"

"Brother Jackson, I'm not sure you heard what said. We are only equal in origin, nature and destiny. Our equality is not the critical factor in our lives. But it is important. God made us equal and part of our equality is our liberty. It is important to be constantly aware that God made man and that is the reason we treat each other as equals. Each person's life is sacred. It reflects God's work. We treat each person as a child of God. While the sanctity of our life comes from God, our human dignity comes from the commitments we make to each child of God and to the society of which that child of God is a part. We render justice precisely because the other person is a child of God. We offer mercy and charity because the person is a child of God. We exist to demonstrate love for the creatures God has made and the more deeply we demonstrate that love, the more we please our maker. That is what life is all about. Keep that in mind as often as you can. Part of acting justly is acting legally. We don't offend against others' rights.

"That's the answer I will expect you to provide on the test. But more importantly, I pray that that will be a principle you will allow to guide your life. Now, let us return to the subject of our legal system. We are bound by laws that govern our public behavior, our interactions with others and the society. Ordinances and laws tell us what the limits of our behavior are. And we have a system for controlling the behavior of our citizens and for that matter our non citizens. It is the criminal justice system. We call our systems for detecting, arresting, prosecuting and judging those who offend against the laws our criminal justice system. We have a separate legal system for managing civil interactions which we will address another day.

"We refer to those who make the final judgments as to what is legal, what is constitutional in this country as justices, Justices of the Supreme Court. To be perfectly accurate, we should refer to them as legalists. Frequently those who are referred to as Justice this or Justice that may render judgments that are legal but unjust.. Would anyone want to venture an example for us of which we are all aware from our study of history and from which we can all benefit? Lorenzo? Tony? Diego? Anyone care to enlighten this sleepy group?

"OK, turn your attention for a moment to slavery, the institution in which one man could buy or sell another man and keep him in chains. It caused a civil conflict in our nation in which a half million Americans died and millions were wounded. The Supreme Court Justices had ruled it legal as late as 1860. You will recall that slaves were made free as a result of the Emancipation Proclamation, not by the Justices of the United States but by the proclamation of President Lincoln. Was slavery just? Do we all know what justice is? Ladies and gentlemen, this is pretty easy stuff.

"Just think, because of my keen sense of justice, one of you would probably have gotten an A for your effort today just for that easy example. Now would anyone like to add their example? Good grief, what is the most contentious issue facing this county? It's an issue that has been dividing this country for more than fifty years. It divides families, parents from children, brothers from brothers and sisters from sisters. Hey people, it's 2020, we've got issues that don't relate to NASCAR, the NFL, rock or the movies. O.K. let's go at it from another angle. Do you ever look around and wonder if there should be some more folks in this classroom, guys and girls that God intended would be here? Take note of the empty seats. Or do you ever think that the girl or guy that God intends for you to marry was never born?

"That's perhaps the most puzzled look I have ever seen on your faces and I have seen some really puzzled people in this class. Does that mean you are getting it or am I floundering"?

It was clear that Brother Mark was getting upset. His brow would furrow and his body would tense when he knew he was not getting through. They all hoped he would not blow. His six foot four frame covered with 230 pounds of rippling muscle was frightening even under his cassock, even at age 62. The boys had all seen him in the workout room in the basement with the free weights and in a bulging black tea shirt on the football field where he helped with the line. The football coaches, who occasionally would scrimmage softly with the varsity when they wanted to teach them something special, didn't allow him to participate. No one knew why but they speculated it might be a negligence or liability issue if he was to injure someone.

When he was on the basketball court, which he often was, he was careful, but he was also very rough, very rough. There was no doubt that an unintended elbow by Brother Mark could fracture a skull.

The legend was that he had never played football because he came from a very small town in northwest Nebraska and that he had joined the Marines right out of high school, fought in Viet Nam where he received enough injuries to acquire two purple hearts. When he returned home, he joined the Augustinian monastery in Missouri. He showed intellectual acumen but didn't want to become a priest, despite the fact that the monastery made training priests their principal mission by operating a seminary.

After a few years of working the farm, the apple orchard and the kitchen, the Abbot insisted he go to school. In the early eighties, the Abbot sent him to Notre Dame for a degree in

History. The story was that an assistant Notre Dame football coach had seen him throwing the football around one day with another brother from the same order. They were playing catch at a fifty yard interval. The coach approached him, learned he was a monk and asked him to ask his Abbot if he would allow him to play. Brother Mark indicated that he was thirty years old and way beyond playing days. The coach remarked that if he wouldn't play, the least he could do is pray for him and the team, which Brother Mark agreed to do.

"Would it shock you if I told you that over the last forty seven years since 1973, there have been more than sixty million, that's the number six and with six zeros after the first digit, sixty million small human beings killed in their mothers' wombs? Surely, it is likely that one from that number may have been headed for this classroom when they were conceived. God intended those sixty million people to populate this country as citizens, as mothers and fathers moving this country to its destiny. But they never had been allowed to live the life God planned for them, to feel the warm embrace of their mother, see a sunrise, have a coke, dance, sing or even hear a melody because seven quote "Justices" in 1973 were cowed by a minority of hostile women into abandoning their intellects, consciences and sacred duty to interpret the constitution as it was written. That is fact and opinion. They acted in doubt and rendered a judgment that was a death penalty for the innocents. Three D imaging is increasingly demonstrating the obvious humanity of the being in the womb, making it impossible to accept that the being in the womb is anything but human.

"These "Justices" were people who knew both the constitution and the natural law and they knew that both bodies of law forbid the cold blooded killing that they said was legal. The women and the "Justices" lacked respect for the sanctity of human life which is the thing that makes man human. Half of the sixty million killed in the womb were female. These were women who would now be between the age of infancy and fifty five. They would likely have given birth to another twenty five million children who along with their descendants will always be missing from God's kingdom on earth. I am confident that God has them in his heaven, but they and their offspring are lost to us and history. Now, someone take a chance on what I am referencing. Yes, Elena."

"Brother, you're talking about the Roe v Wade case from 1973. We studied that in civics in freshman year. Brother Solomon brought in pictures and stuff. It was awful. One guy got sick. The whole thing is stupid. Everybody knows people shouldn't kill anybody, but especially unborn babies."

"Excellent, Elena. Looking at the matter from the perspective of the being in the womb, abortion is the best example of something being legal and unjust. St Thomas Aquinas, back about six hundred years ago, gave us some insight into the law worthy of our consideration today. He noted that there is eternal law which is sourced and belongs entirely to God. There is the natural law which is written in the hearts of all of us and there is positive law made by man which governs our public behavior.

"The natural law cannot be flawed. Positive law made by man can sometimes be flawed. Stay mindful that legality and justice must be distinguished. Frequently that which is legal is very unjust. One of the reasons why it is essential to note the difference between these two very different matters has to do with our expectations. If we expect justice from the law, we can be disappointed.

"The outcomes of disputes submitted to a court wherein the judiciary follows the positive law and the constitution are quite predictable but not always just. In cases where the judiciary applies their own personal sense of justice instead of the law, outcomes are unpredictable but could be just, nonetheless it can be a bad outcome for society and for the litigant who is treated unfairly. King Solomon was a king, not a judge with a constitution. His judgment concerning the baby whom he was going to order cut in two in order to resolve the issue of to whom the baby belonged was clever but would have been unjust to the baby. The threat got at the truth, but thank God he didn't have to execute his threat.

"Even in matters not as serious as killing, the law has some serious defects. We should note one that you will want to be fully cognizant with because it involves your money. Let's say that Rafael purchases a large block of stock of a very well-known company from which he has a reasonable expectation of realizing a handsome profit. He intends to assign the profit to his six children's college educations.. However the CEO and the accounting department of this respectable firm conspire to embezzle hundreds of millions of dollars in order to fund their yachts. The company goes bankrupt. What happens to Rafael and his children's college funds? Help me with this. It happens a lot and you need to know. Rafael?"

"Well Brother, the tone of your question suggests to me that I may not be treated too well in this venture, perhaps I will lose my investment in which case I will be a very unhappy and poor person. Brother, if my wife and I have six children I am likely to be poor to begin with."

"You are correct, my son, not about being poor. Some of the wealthiest people have large families. And you will certainly be enriched by your children's love. By the same token, some poor families have many children. Children are not causal in matters of wealth. But when it comes to the bankruptcy about which we are concerned, you are in fact likely to be treated very shabbily. The law favors and tends to protect the business section of the community in order to keep it healthy, not the individual lender who may have purchased stocks or bonds or simply loaned money. The company may be allowed to stay in business, reorganize and you may receive a few cents on the dollars you invested. You can hope that the perpetrators of this crime may go to jail, but that is slim satisfaction for your loss. You will be treated unjustly, but legally. Bankruptcy also gives the individual a chance to start anew at the expense of those who gave him credit or loaned him money, a matter that also seems a little light on justice.

"If you had been old enough to see the outcome of bank and insurance company failures in the early part of the century, you would know that at your expense the government will always take care of those large businesses that fail no matter how ill advised or crooked the action of those who caused the failures.

"We are running out of time here. There have been three empty chairs in this room since the beginning of the year. I know that the class has three fewer enrollees than there are openings. I don't know why they are empty. It could be for any of a thousand reasons, positive and negative. For purposes of our discussion, consider the possibility that the three seats were meant for people who were among the millions killed in the womb or their missing offspring. In any event, what I want you to do for your homework is to think about those people who are not here.

"When you come to class tomorrow, you will have a single page typewritten that will describe briefly the imagined life of the person who is missing, what they may have done in their life. Perhaps, during their life, they became a renowned scientist, a military or a peace leader, an inventor, a musician, an artist, a drunken bum or an embezzler. Perhaps they became the mother or father of children; perhaps children with the same accomplishments. Consider too what the consequence of these people missing from our society means to you and to me and our country......... and to God.

"If you would prefer, you can think about these people, the consequences of their missing from society and then make an argument that justifies the actions of their mother who made the decision to have them killed in the womb. In doing so, you would be in the company of the seven "Justices" of the Supreme Court in the 1973 Roe v Wade decision.

"Now, I certainly don't want any of you to think that I am cynical about our legal system. It's the nature of our human condition and the societies we establish that make for flawed systems, but it's clearly the best in the world and perhaps in history. So we should adapt to it and be both prudent and wary. Naturally, if you are dismayed with the injustices in our system, I would encourage you to do everything you can in your life to improve the legal system by making it more just. That may be a significant part of the mission given to you by your God when he created you in cooperation with your parents.

"That's probably enough for today. Naturally I will expect you to be able to make these distinctions between legality and justice and cite examples in a test, pop or scheduled. But more importantly I hope you will apply the distinctions to your approach to life and not be satisfied in your own behavior with what is legal but with what is just. Justice is a noble virtue that leads man to God the Author of all justice. A just man is a strong man. And remember make your paper your own work, do justice to yourself and others. Remember Micah's admonition "Do Justice, Love Mercy and walk humbly with God". One matter that we all need to factor into our daily lives is that life has a binary outcome. Everyone here will go to heaven or hell. Let us pray for each other."

Town Hall

When the class met the next day, Brother Mark collected the papers and declared a Town Hall meeting. That meant that the students were free to ask any question that interested them and was not personal. The first question came from "Chino" Flores who was a serious student. "Is America a racist nation"? Brother Mark paused and asked "Chino" if there was a specific event or policy that caused him to ask the question. "Chino" said that he didn't feel a victim of racism, but that he had read materials produced by the NAACP and LaRaza and other organizations that suggested America was racist. Then Brother asked if "Chino" cared to define racism. He struggled for a moment and then said that it was when people didn't treat you fairly because of your race or nationality.

Brother Mark took him back to yesterday's discussion. Whose job is it to define what is fair? Are we talking about fairness or justice? If people treat someone unjustly, if they don't give them what is due them because of their race, then it is clearly racism. But if someone just doesn't like the other person for some other reason. Perhaps they don't like their behavior, their values, their pushiness, their tattoos, where they wear their pants or their haircut. As long as they treat them justly, then it is not racism.

Brother Mark asked "If a person comes to you with a lengthy criminal record, a lot of homely tattoos, dirty oddly styled hair, pants exposing most of their buttocks and rings adorning a number of places on their person and they have difficulty answering easy questions and you decide not to employ them, it probably isn't racism that suggests you don't hire them as maitre de at your fancy restaurant. It's common sense. "I'm reminded of a young Catholic man who suffered the severe handicap of a stutter. He had applied to be a news anchor at a television station.

He interviewed and when he learned that he didn't get the job, he told his girlfriend that they discriminated against him because they weren't hiring Catholics.

"As Christians we're obliged to love people, but not to like them. To love them we are required to treat them justly and to hope the best for them. I can dislike the behavior of the person in front of me in line because they crowded in line or gave off body odor from not bathing, but I still have to love them.

"As I have aged, I try hard to love everyone, to wish everyone well. But I have begun to distinguish between the people I meet. I find that I divide people into two categories. I know it is a type of unfair profiling but it's a reality for me. It happens. I tend increasingly to be attracted to some people and repelled from others. Race or class has absolutely nothing to do with the distinction that my mind makes. I like and want to associate with people with whom I share values. I want to be separate from those who don't share my values. My basis and bias for distinguishing between those whom I like and those whom I dislike is the single value of how a person appears to me to value the sanctity of human life. I don't deny that for some people, that distinction is complex.

"Our society has become so transformed into a secular humanist culture that it is difficult for many to know how to value human life. To recognize the sanctity of human life is difficult for many because evil disguises itself as good.

"There are a great many people who believe themselves to value human life by killing unborn babies. They don't want to subject the babies to a life of poverty or disability. Or they don't want to subject themselves or others to the inconvenience of bearing an unplanned baby. A lot of people think they value life by assisting the elderly or feeble minded to kill themselves or deny them medical assistance. They don't want them to suffer or they don't want them to use up scarce medical resources. There are people eager to kill convicted capital offenders whose danger to others is controlled for life in an isolated prison cell where they might not ever breathe the air of their keepers. There are those who believe they value life by killing living human embryos in the name of a scientific effort that has yet to produce a single cure after billions of tax dollars have been expended and millions of human embryos have died. "And there are those who are eager to make the first effort to deal with international conflict the use of lethal arms in the interests of protecting others. For me the judgment concerning how to value human life has become easier as I age. I find the command of God embedded in my heart, do not kill, easy to follow.

Joyce Flanagan always asked the Catholic questions of any of the teachers. Everyone thought that she would probably become a nun. But her prowess on the basketball court put that in doubt when both college and WNBA teams started scouting her in her junior year. She had already decided as a sophomore to go with University of Tennessee assuming she didn't break anything before that. She would easily play in the WNBA . If they changed the rules she could probably play in the NBA.

Joyce asked Brother Mark if he thought that the Catholic Church would survive all the efforts of the anti-religion people, the rise in atheism and the cooperation of the courts in banning God from the public square. Brother Mark smiled at her and said she could relax. He pointed out some of the threats to the Catholic Church that had occurred over the centuries both from within and from without the Church. He pointed out the irrationality of the Christian faith and the ineptness of those who lead the Church. He noted the pedophilia scandal and the poor manner in which the bishops managed it. And then, he assured her that God's body on earth would survive anything sent its way. He included the threat of terrorism. The Church would survive the terrorists, the atheists, the agnostics, the incompetent and the anti-Christs. We empathize and pray for them because they have not yet been blessed with faith.

"Joyce, it's important to remember that Christianity is an absurdity. Believing in a god without scientific evidence of his existence is nonsense. Further, believing that God became man, died and rose from the dead is preposterous. And finally believing that he comes each day in the Eucharist and that we will enjoy eternal happiness after our bodies turn to dust is too far- fetched...... unless, unless that God whom we talk about has blessed us with the ability to believe that for which we hope and for which we have no objective evidence. The gift of faith allows us to believe, to take that step into the joy of Christian hope. Look to the good in people and the beauty of existence and consider from whence it comes. The author of that goodness and beauty will sustain his Church".

No one had their hand up for a question and there were still fifteen minutes left in the period. So Brother Mark went off on one of his rants that were equal heat and light. Every day, he read what was left of the print version of the New York Times, the Chicago Tribune and the Wall Street Journal. He would do an occasional review of the Economist. He was always well informed. He was a good source for information. He was rife with opinions. He was comfortable with informed people disagreeing with his opinions. But he couldn't suffer nonsense from the uninformed. His approach to dispute was taken from Aquinas, to rarely affirm, never deny and always distinguish. The members of the class valued the manner in which he presented his opinions.

And he was honest in labeling his opinions as such. He would signal an opinion with putting his index and middle fingers up on both hands to signify quotation marks. He trained the students to do the same to distinguish between what they knew and what they thought.

"I am positive about our future as a Church and as a nation. But I am also profoundly aware of issues that need to be addressed. I sometimes feel I am an old man too familiar with the problems of our country and our world. This is not the country which your parents and I inherited. We have not been good stewards of the world we are passing on to you. I fear your generation is following our path. We are a large, diverse, seriously indebted and conflicted country and subject to much more complex and more serious problems than we have ever before faced. Our manufacturing base has moved to nations with lower, sometimes uncivilized wages and inhumane conditions. Our export import imbalance remains problematic.

Our education system provides neither the humanizing nor the skills necessary to provide a sufficient number of properly trained employees to manage the types of work that remain in our country. And our dwindling youth population doesn't seem to want many of the jobs available that involve muscle and sweat.

"There is an increasing gap in income disparity between the winners and the losers that is occurring. And one of the things that contributes to the problem is the education system. At St. Rita's, we are trying to help you avoid being a loser. I can tell you three things that will help to keep you from being a loser. Don't have sex or children until you are married. Finish as much schooling as you can afford and master. And then work hard and love your spouse, the parent of your children. You know that nearly half of our nation doesn't make enough money to pay income taxes. As citizens they are rightly entitled to vote, but a vote with no "skin" in the game is a form of representation without taxation. Increasing numbers of our citizens are dependent on the government for food, housing and healthcare and some like it that way. We truly pity them. Our borders are porous and our government is conflicted by the level of illegal immigration. Business wants cheap labor and the taxpayers don't want to pay for the educational and social services that illegal residents often require.

"Internationally, much has changed since the nation of your grandparents' and your parents' day. Nuclear capabilities continue to spread to hateful nations, some of whom feel no obligation to honor rules of human interaction and some who view us with distain or worse, hate. We are deeply engaged and committed to nations whom we don't trust, often for good reasons. We engage with them to fight conflicts with other enemies who fight asynchronous battles under no civilized constraints. We face and will continue to face terrorism from this day forward. It will not stop or lessen. Hate and evil is an eternal battle. We struggle domestically to decide on a battle plan to challenge these terrorists. Do we grant total knowledge of our private lives and interactions to the government in the hope of protection? Do we give terrorists citizen rights when they attempt to kill us or do we deny them any rights and consider them dangerous illegal enemy combatants and treat them accordingly?

"Since the nineteen seventies, technology has given us incredible progress and convenience. But it has also created a moral crisis. Technology has outrun our public moral compass. Many of those to whom advanced technology is available tend to believe that because they are able to do something, it should be done. At the extreme is the issue of cloning of human beings. In the near term is something I have already mentioned, embryonic stem cell research which kills the unborn. Technology can be exceedingly dangerous in our international conflicts. We live in a time when the use of an Electronic Magnetic Pulse could destroy the electric grids that exist throughout the world and bring nations to a standstill. We are subject to cyber warfare from individuals and enemies who if not properly defended against are able to cripple our economic, financial and national security systems to the point of total destruction. Cyber warfare threatens our economy and our national security. It's a reality you will be subject to all your lives.

"Despite all the problems that I have suggested, I know that good will triumph because the Holy Spirit will always be in charge. Remember that fact when you feel burdened by the problems of the universe or your own world. The problems will pass. How you react to adversity is the quality that builds your character. Dress yourself each morning with a positive attitude and remember the purpose of our existence is to love"

Chapter 5

Death in the Lagos Vatican

What Sudden Illness Could Be Fatal?

Diego's mind was jolted back to the chapel and the moment by his secretary Bishop Sanchez's coughing. It took a few seconds to remember who and where he was. He had been the pope of the Catholic Church for just over two years and was still having some difficulty adjusting to the idea, the role and the name. He was still Diego, but he was also Pope Francisco Augustine. He had taken the name of Francisco to honor both his father and St Francis Xavier, one of the founders of the Jesuits who spent much of his life as a missionary trying to Christianize Asia. Diego had thought of himself to some extent as a missionary to South America and Africa on some of his travels. He hoped to move the Church to a missionary church renewing the evangelization of the entire world.

Jordan's presence in his life had deepened his consciousness and commitment to the spiritual life. He had tried to emulate both his father and St. Francis in their practice of living for others. He had taken the name of Augustine to help him to stay mindful of just how human he was and of his constant need for conversion and compassion. Diego was mindful also that while he was thoroughly American, his ancestry had African and Spanish blood which was probably a common mix in the North African city of Hippo from which Augustine came.

He assumed that the dinner the night before had been unremarkable. Certainly the portion of the meal for which he was present was un-remarkable. The rolls and salad were served and the grace was said. There was a very small group at the table in comparison with most evenings at Pope Francisco Augustine's table. The table was generally graced with a fairly large contingent. There was most often a mix of notables, theologians and intellectuals from different nations and religions who were visiting Rome. Often, two or three practicing lay Catholics from parishes in different countries around the world were present. Frequently there would be at least two women and one person under thirty years of age. Rarely, if ever, was an elected official included in the guest list. But dinners in the Nigerian "Vatican" had fewer guests than in Rome.

Last night's dinner had been a working group which the pope tried to avoid. He had determined that working and eating was not good for his digestion. Bishop David Sanchez, the Pope's secretary was present along with a Vatican diplomat, Bishop Marcus Stepanovich from the United States and Father Daniel Flores, a new member of the household temporarily assigned. He would soon be assigned to the Secretary of State's office.

After some light hearted discussion about the latest victory of the Brazilian soccer team playing in the World Cup, Francisco initiated the conversation. It was protocol at the papal table for the pope to initiate the discussion. He would normally start with questions for his lay guests hoping that the notables at the table would pick up some information viewpoints that they would never gain elsewhere. Last night he went directly to a more serious discussion. "We absolutely need to bring every resource at our disposal to effect some kind of truce to this country. If the conflict continues, the entirety of the African continent could be drawn in. I fear we don't have much time. If the Chinese believe their oil interests may be threatened, they could persuade the whole of Nigeria, Chad, Niger and much of the rest of the continent to join with Kenya and or Uganda. If China provides the arms, then it would be over quickly with much bloodshed. Father, do you think Cardinal Swarago has done everything possible to exert pressure on the United States, Russia and the European Union to generate a more powerful UN presence here?"

Bishop Stepanovich, the Vatican diplomat with focus on North America was assigned to the Vatican Secretary of State. He lived in Virginia and was familiar with Cardinal Swarago's work at the United Nations. He responded with support for the cardinal "I'm sure he is working on it diligently. I know it is a priority for him, mindful, that his own family could be involved because they are still living close to the fighting in the north. Cardinal Stepanovich was of Serbian descent but was born in the United States and was a frequent guest at the pope's dinner table. They had become friends while working in the Vatican Secretary of State's office which acted pretty much as the Vatican government, the Prime Minister and the Foreign Secretary at the same time. Their meetings were less common after the pope moved his offices and his household to Lagos. Cardinal Stepanovich had opposed the move, but adapted to it having seen the positive response on the part of many of the faithful especially in Africa and South America.

Bishop Sanchez rarely engaged in discussion of Vatican business, but listened intently to each word. He had a flawless memory and was frequently called upon by the pope to refresh his memory of a conversation. Father Flores sat silently at the table, listening intently to the conversation. The pope urged Bishop Stepanovich to familiarize Father Flores with the depth of the Chinese involvement in Africa. "Perhaps Father Flores, having spent so much of his recent time and energies in South America is unfamiliar with the situation in Africa. If you could provide him with some time and information, perhaps we could benefit by his comparative perspective". The bishop nodded acceptance of the assignment. "If it is agreeable with you, Holy Father, I will spend time with Father after dinner on that subject. I really would like to discuss the American situation with you as soon as possible and if it is agreeable I would like to do it now."

The pope moved forward in his chair as a gesture of agreement. The bishop continued "I am fearful that the situation of the Church there is intolerable. The future is jeopardized by any number of practices that seemed challenging in their infancy, but now have become threats to the survival of the American Church. Because you saw it first hand, you know the depth of damage that was done when they lost so many of their people and so much of their assets resulting from the molestation scandals shortly after the turn of the century. It is no news to you that they are troubled. Many who realized that priests, as do all men, can have "feet of clay" justified their departure from the Church. "They seemed almost as bothered by the weak leadership of the hierarchy as by the behavior of the pedophile priests. They couldn't help but notice that not a single bishop lost his job. The scandal was that they couldn't deal with the truth. Instead of relying on the Holy Spirit and addressing the problem, the vast majority of the bishops listened to their lawyers and ill informed psychologists. They concentrated on holding on to their priests and their power, retaining the guilty in service.

"I don't know why, but it seems we have had great difficulty in finding bishops in America who are both holy and good administrators. The holy ones seem to be poor managers and the good managers, assuming their previous holiness, seem to lose their focus on holiness to the demands of business. Upon their ordination to the episcopacy, they seem to change. There seems too much truth in that nasty American joke about the little boy who asked his mother what they were doing while the Episcopal ordinandi lied prostrate. Her response was that "they are removing his backbone". And all too frequently that seemed to have been the case. They seemed to be led away from spirituality and it allowed them to accept anything and everything and call it Catholic. Why they didn't rely on law enforcement to sort out the mess makes no sense at this point. We're still vilified over those matters. Fortunately for now, I think most bishops are using their heads in these issues.

"Your Holiness, you are also firmly aware of the fact that there are a lot of people in the United States and elsewhere who were incredibly excited about an American pope being elected, but are now angry with Your Holiness. This African move was not popular. "There are still many sound churches and still a few Catholic schools, but they are becoming fewer by the year. Father and Bishop, you may know about these units that they call cells. I am sure there are similar units in South America. They refer to themselves as CHRISTIAN COMMUNITIES. Many are beginning to develop some very peculiar characteristics. Some have priests attached, but most don't. They embrace a free form theology that varies from cell to cell depending on the leadership. Some have orthodox theological beliefs. Others are off the map. Some are seriously evangelical and others seriously charismatic. Many are seriously secular subscribing to the "gospel of prosperity". Granted, there was not much that the bishops could do when they were formed. They called themselves *grass roots* organizations and pulled people, the alienated, the liberal, the divorced/remarried and the homosexual, away from the scandalized institutional church, but kept their name as Catholic.

"We were blessed enough to be allowed to sustain some form of the priesthood presence in some of them, even though most of those priests are now married. The compromise under John Paul III, allowing the ordination of the married and separated married priests at least kept us from ordaining women. As you know, some of these communities are more than forty five years old and are not going away. Some have manufactured their own theologies, few of which come close to the Magisterium. Some have adopted bizarre characterizations of Jesus; Jesus as a married man, as a woman, as a homosexual, as a political operative for the Romans, and, not really dying on the cross but brought down before his death and whisked away to Syria. Some outliers have adopted re-incarnation. There are many who regard Jesus as a leading prophet but not God. Much of this started in the "Jesus Movement" where progressive theologians found it too challenging to live with the ambiguity of faith and wanted to rationalize the whole of theology.

"Science and relativism have pretty much led them to believe that there is no such thing as a mystery or a miracle although the scientist's scientist, Albert Einstein remarked that everything is a miracle. Bishop Stepanovich went on "I know Holy Father that you have encouraged Cardinal Suarez' Congregation on Sacred Doctrine to have the American bishops suspend the church relationship with the more bizarre communities and recall their priests for rehabilitation in the teachings of the Magisterium, But little seems to be happening along those lines".

Pope Francisco looked tired and sad, but he reminded the bishop that the Holy Spirit would always be in charge in the long run. He said he would pray over that matter in chapel this evening. He had lost his appetite. Though Father Flores was generally aware of the conditions in the United States, he seemed stunned and remarked "Your Holiness, I don't believe we would have a real Catholic church in the United States were it not for the Hispanics, many of whom came there illegally. God certainly does *write straight with crooked lines* to have brought that about".

The pope was greatly upset to be reminded of the serious

flaws in the American hierarchy. Because of his short tenure, he had named only three American bishops, but they were his bishops no matter who named them. His response was pretty much what Bishop Stepanovich anticipated "I can order Cardinal Suarez to do so, but for now I will pray that God blesses him directly with the wise judgment you urge. Cardinal Suarez is a wise and holy man and I believe he will be guided by the Spirit to make the right decisions in these matters, if he is given time. Right now I feel the need to pray over both the African and American matters. Pleased do not find me a poor host, but I must go. You will find me in my chapel if you require my attention".

Father Flores blurted out "But, your Holiness, you've not eaten a thing and Sister Sophia made the menudo and this special Mexican dinner with your mother's recipe. She worked very hard on it and she will be disappointed".

The lack of air in the hospital chapel was stifling. He was perspiring and removed the cap that he had been given to wear. He knelt on the leather kneeler and started to pray again. Even though he was on his knees, his mind drifted back to a light sleep. Had it not been for the top of the kneeler on which he rested his arms he would have fallen over when his head tipped to the side. He started to pray again. His mind went back and forth from prayer to unconsciousness. Finally, he gave in and sat. His mind tumbled into unconscious dreams. Often he went back to his childhood and the path that led him to this day.

Chapter 6

Football, Football, Football

Stardom Speeds up the Pace

The next two years of high school were a blur for both Oscar and Diego. They both bulked up by lifting weights almost daily and following rigid diets. In their junior year, Coach Denning decided on a "west coast" offense partly because of Diego's skill set. They won nine of ten games, made the playoffs and played in the state semi-final losing to Bolingbrook. For the season, Diego threw for 2200 yards and ran for 550. Oscar made 26 receptions and 12 touchdowns. Diego made 16 touchdowns and was named all city quarterback as a junior. At six foot three and 215 pounds, Diego was slightly larger than Oscar. Both became objects of attention of many college recruiters.

Both boys were in incredible shape. Brother Mark had persuaded them not to waste their bodies or talent on alcohol or drugs. He kept pointing out that there was really no limit to their futures if they stayed in shape and didn't get hurt. He noted that the better their conditioning the less likely they were to be injured. He also kept them mindful that because of their talent, they had responsibilities to use it properly and help others in the process. They were meant for leadership. He impressed upon them the need to study as well. Scholarships came from better schools if there was a good grade point involved.

Both Coach Denning and Diego liked the "shotgun" and he had an incredible talent for rolling out left or right and throwing on the run. He could roll and within a yard or two of the tackler, set his back foot and throw sixty yards with accuracy. No high school coach had seen that in Illinois recently. He was remarkable. Oscar was the most frequent target. Diego was equally capable on the "play action". He could fake twice and with his quick release, throw easily. He could instantly survey and decide which of his receivers was open. Then his release was like lightning.

Neither Oscar nor Diego was satisfied with the year because they had lost to Mt Carmel in the regular season and to Bolingbrook in the championship round. They resolved that they would win state the following year and began to impose their resolve on the rest of the team. They would both be captains for their senior year. When senior year came round, they beat Mt Carmel 21-0 in the fourth game. They all wished that that win could be the end of the season. They went on to an undefeated season and beat Naperville for the 8A Championship. Both Diego and Oscar were named to the fist team All City and All State. Five of the most prominent football universities in the nation had visited with Coach Denning just to talk about what kind of guys both Oscar and Diego were. His comment was that he would be pleased to have both of them as sons.

Before the season even began, Brother Mark knew what was coming for the boys. He gathered Carmen, Coach Denning, and Oscar's mother Evelyn together with a previous graduate of St. Rita's, Dwight Bright, who was playing tight end for the Pittsburgh Steelers. He asked Dwight to sort out how the boys should go about fielding recruiters. He suggested that they talk only to the head coach, no assistants, in their own living rooms with their parents present. He said to ask the coaches to spell out exactly what they could expect on the field and in the classroom. He also advised them to be careful of any coach who promised them anything more than a scholarship and an opportunity to compete to play provided the coach was still employed.

When it came down to the decision, Diego chose Northwestern and Oscar saw his best opportunity at Ohio State where there were no outstanding wide-outs. They both supported each other's choice. Diego saw Northwestern as a place where he could play and be in regular contact on Sunday's with his mom and family. He thought the Big Ten was as good a competition as any conference except perhaps the SEC and he didn't want to go that far from home. He also wanted to pursue his plan to become a Marine and there was a Navy Reserve Officers Training Corps in which he could train at Northwestern. His dad had been a Marine and both Renaldo and Jose had served in the Marines. Jose was making the Marines his career. He was a Lt Colonel. Diego thought there was an outside chance he may want a career there.

While he had given consideration to the possibility of playing in the pros, it wasn't his life's goal at the time. But he wanted desperately to play at the university level.

All American and Then Some

Both Oscar and Diego admired Brother Mark and his classes. They appreciated the guidance he was giving them. Brother Mark was always encouraging them, telling them they would be successful and it made them feel good about themselves. But Brother Mark was tough and demanding. If you were on a basketball court with him, you needed to be alert and tough. He didn't play dirty but he played hard and approaching sixty he could still dunk. He loved competition and he knew a lot about the theory of competition. He didn't belong to the school that said kids should not compete. He liked winners. He saw competition as part of the human DNA and as natural. In Brother Mark's world, team work was essential to developing a whole person. Games and sports, especially the ones that involved team work, were generated in the name of competition and were very important to human development.

In one of his Social Studies classes, he had a lecture that he gave every year and talked about competition and fairness. He observed that competition was a basis for war, for business and politics. But it was best displayed and learned on the field of play. He indicated that not all competition was good for the world. But as long as competitors played by the rules it was generally a positive factor. He acknowledged that not all competition was waged fairly. He did point out that competition was a huge factor in the transfer and integration of civilization in the West.

Brother went all the way back to Aristotle about three hundred fifty years before Christ. He told his students that Aristotle had tutored Alexander the Great in Greek philosophy, the arts and mathematics and that Alexander had spread those critical civilizing elements as part his dominance of the known world at the time. Some historians saw Alexander as a benevolent conqueror. He waged war and conquered in order to achieve that dominance and in the process spread civilizing influences.

Brother Mark applauded the Greeks for having channeled competition into sport, namely the Olympics which the world still enjoys. And, he praised them for generating the co-operation of nations in what is a splendid example of competition. Then, Brother asked if the class agreed with his evaluation of competition. Was it good or bad? It led to an interesting discussion. There was a lot of disagreement. There was competition of ideas going on in their discussion.

He suggested that a lot of people saw competition as a negative aspect of society. They would prefer cooperation as opposed to competition. But he noted there could never be cooperation in some instances and began a serious discussion saying that never could one cooperate with evil. The discussion ended on a note that surprised the class. Brother said that the most important competition that took place in the universe involved the competition for the salvation of souls, the conflict between good and evil, between God and the Devil.

He asked them to observe their own lives. There was often the battle between what they know they should do and what they would rather do, which is not always between good and evil but choosing between competing priorities. Diego hated it when he did anything wrong. If he let an impure thought about one of the girls in the class linger or he told even a slight lie, he felt dirty afterwards. He still had a bit of a guilt hangover from the theft at Mr. Mapes hardware store and having burdened his mother when he and Oscar went to court on the gun charge even though he knew it was necessary.

He also hated going to confession. He knew Father Kevin would recognize his voice and he didn't want him to think less of him. But Brother Mark had told him that Father Kevin was "cool" with whatever you said in confession and always gave him good advice. Brother Mark said that whenever he went to Father Kevin for confession, the first thing Father Kevin said to him was to remember that he was confessing to God, not to him as a man but as God's representative in the box. He would remind Brother Mark that when it came to sinning, he, Father Kevin excelled and had likely out- sinned Brother Mark. So Diego began to relax when he talked to Father Kevin in the confessional and began to think of himself talking through Father Kevin to God and asking for his forgiveness. Whenever he came out of confession, he always felt relieved and ready to start anew with what he knew he should do.

Chapter 7

Transition

Graduation

Diego didn't really want to leave St Rita's. Everything he needed or wanted was there. His friends, his mom, the teachers and gridiron stardom were all he needed to feel happy. He would miss Brother Mark's classes. He'd also miss Mr. Robinson's physics classes. Mr. Rally Robinson was a super guy and a super teacher. One of the students had looked him up on Google when he first came to the school because Brother Mark had told them that he was a former Cubs pitcher. What was funny was that his real name was "Rally". It wasn't just a baseball nickname. He had spent three years in the minors in the Cubs organization. When they first brought him in from Des Moines, he was in the bull pen. But the next year, they put him in the rotation and he won twelve games. Chicago had its own boy on the mound even if it was up north. Too bad the White Sox had not taken him. The following year, Rally won eleven. But in his fifth year with the organization, during spring training in Arizona, his shoulder stiffened and became inflamed. No matter the therapy, they couldn't relieve the pain. Surgery was successful but he could never get the speed back. He was finished.

He never talked about baseball in class. He was too interested in teaching physics to discuss his career. He was an assistant baseball coach and occasionally he would talk about his days in the majors with members of the baseball team, but not in class. He was grateful for his time with the Cubs. He loved the Cubs despite the fact he was from the south side where the

White Sox ruled.

Mr. Robinson was the son of a Baptist minister, the pastor of The First Baptist Church on seventy ninth and Paulina. It was smaller than a mega-church but large with lots of active members, some of whose children attended St. Rita's. Before he became pastor, Rev. Robinson had been a physics teacher himself. He had taught at Wright Community College and continued to do so while he was pastor. Rally was playing for Wright when the Cubs drafted him. When he was let go, he went to Northern Illinois and eventually received his doctorate.

Every year at St. Rita's he gave a lecture in the auditorium to the whole school on a topic of his choice. He wanted to stimulate the interest of the younger classes. Physics was in the senior curriculum. As a result of the lectures, students would have had three physics lectures under their belt by the time they reached his classroom.

Mr. Robinson converted to Catholicism when he married. He did so with the blessing of his father and he became a very active Catholic. When Diego was a junior, Mr. Robinson gave what was almost a three hour lecture with only one break. He talked about the universe, its origin, development, current knowledge of its status and its future. The lecture held everyone's attention and held it tightly. He used a PowerPoint presentation that was so clear that it stunned the whole school. He talked about how the Greeks though advanced in other areas, had thought that the sun went around the earth and how that theory prevailed as conventional wisdom all the way up to the sixteenth century when Copernicus tried to promote his heliocentric theory. Most of world thought that the earth was the center of the universe and that everything in the universe circulated around the earth.

The students found it difficult to believe that people

didn't know that the earth rotated around the sun. It seemed so elementary. Mr. Robinson described how difficult it was for Copernicus to challenge the notion of a earth centric universe. When Galileo demonstrated beyond doubt with the benefit of his telescopic findings, he was castigated by the Church. He wasn't recognized for his discoveries until long after his death. The pope condemned him and wouldn't let him use his information to teach in the universities. Finally Isaac Newton proved beyond doubt how the universe has been functioning right along.

Mr. Robinson began to talk about all the modern scientists, theoretical physicists and others who had won Nobel Prizes in Physics for findings concerning the universe. And, he talked about others who had planets and stars named in their honor. He told the students about how famous and renowned all these scientists were; how important they were to learning and the advance of science.

Then he shared with them the description of the beginning of the universe. "That enormous explosion, the incredible boom that physicists tell us occurred about fourteen or so billion years ago, what they call the "big bang" was God's love become manifest in existence, the beginning of our universe, the beginning of matter, space and time. The physicists cannot tell us the exact nature, the how or the why of the explosion, but they are certain it occurred and are learning more each day about the how of the event. "In 1933, Father Georges Lemaitre, a Belgian priest and physicist described the origin of the universe as the "primeval atom". Einstein labeled Lemaitre's full description of the beginning of existence as "the most beautiful and satisfactory explanation of creation I've ever heard". The event has now become universally known as the "big bang". Father Lemaitre noted that "the fireworks are over and just the smoke is left". The physicists tell us that the "big bang" is still echoing all around us in cosmic microwave background radiation.

Then he talked about all the scientists who taught about

the universe today and the discoveries of planets, stars and black holes. The students' minds were full of ideas about the awesomeness of the universe and how smart the scientists were. He paused for a long time and stayed at the podium. It was clear that he wasn't finished with his lecture but he wasn't saying anything. There was no applause, only quiet, a slight tension.

After a three or four minute pause and absolute quiet, he said "Tomorrow morning at eight, Father Kevin will consecrate a piece of bread and a sip of wine and they will become the glorified body of Jesus Christ, God, the being responsible for each of us and the existence of this universe which I have been describing and in which we reside. It is a universe made by God, the same loving God with whom we hope to spend eternity. I will be blessed to serve as an extraordinary minister of the Eucharist and I will serve his body and blood to nurture your eternal souls.

He stopped and left the podium. There was no applause. The students all left the auditorium in self imposed silence each caught up in their own thoughts.

The Northwestern Wildcat

At Northwestern, Diego's freshman year was tough. Despite Brother Mark's preparation, Diego's study habits were not up to the level required for his course of study in leadership. Northwestern was not St. Rita's. But Brother Mark knew that Diego had the smarts and could handle the material. When Diego was a sophomore at St. Rita's, a three person team of Ph.D. researchers from the School of Education at the University of Chicago proposed a longitudinal study involving a new race/cultural free I.Q. test. They were researching the test in four different schools and neighborhoods in Chicago and needed students of all ages, races and cultures. Carmen was agreeable to Diego's participation and he was tested over three years with three standardized tests as well as the new culture free test. No matter the test, Diego consistently scored 128 or above which impressed the researchers. The researchers didn't openly note it, but Brother Mark thought that they were surprised by the fact that a Black/Hispanic athlete would consistently score that high.

Northwestern offered a leadership curriculum as a minor in the school of business. But the narrowness of the rest of the business curriculum was not attractive to Diego or Brother Mark. Brother Mark suggested that in his freshman and sophomore years, he take history and philosophy along with a couple of business courses, to broaden his knowledge of the world. He was fluent but he also took Spanish on the assumption that no matter what he did in a career, he would have perspective and a disciplined language facility. Brother Mark urged him to take all the leadership courses available.

If Brother Mark saw anything in Diego, it was leadership. He had no idea of what form that would take, but he saw it in Diego. The Spanish and the business courses were not a problem for Diego but the required reading for the history and philosophy courses was substantial and he was having some trouble keeping up. He was disappointed he wasn't able to go home every Sunday because of the demand of his studies. He had to study much more than he had anticipated. He shocked himself when he made the honor role in his first semester. He discovered that he had a facility for remembering a lot of what he read and it made it easier to perform on tests and in writing his papers. He had insight. And he had no difficulty with play books in high school or at Northwestern, which was a seriously complex system.

He had few problems in preparing papers once he had done the reading and research. He knew how to use the internet to do his research and could find almost anything he needed there. Probably because of his athletic skills, his dexterity on the keyboard was excellent and he could type easily. Sometimes he could write a decent paper with the first draft.

A young and very attractive junior cheerleader, a tutor, took a shine to him and helped him with his studies. Heather Livingstone may have been the cutest and smartest woman on the campus and she was all about football. She was on course for Phi Beta Kappa and career in broadcasting. She had made herself an expert on Big Ten football and was hired as a sideline commentator in her senior year. She hardly ever studied on her own. Diego pointed out as politely as he could that he appreciated the help but that there would not likely be anything beyond friendship in the relationship. He was too busy to give time to a relationship.

Both he and Oscar had been warned by Brother Mark to be cautious on the female front too soon. He managed to integrate some information on love and marriage into his social studies class. The Brother acknowledged that he had no experience in the love and marriage game. Then he pointed out that there were a few very successful football coaches who had never played a down and a lot of heart surgeons who never had heart problems. He utilized a text that emphasized the significant role that intact families played in society. He was basic in portraying how marriage and sex fit into God's plan for his kingdom. It wasn't by accident that man has a strong drive to sex that is coupled with a woman's need for love and a desire to mother. He labored to help them appreciate that God had created humans to love, to marry and to engage in sexual union. Sex drew its beauty from the lifelong commitment to union that formed its basis.

Brother Mark was enormously grateful that that relationship had played out is his parents' life and that he was the fruit of that love and he noted the same was true for each of them. While he didn't say it, he knew in his heart that he was sacrificing the joy of that union to a higher purpose. From time to time he would question his fitness for the sacrifice. But he always ended concluding that it was to the brotherhood that he had been called. He knew that he was in the presence of youth whose hormonal development was occurring each day and that it was a challenge for them to check the advance of their sexual desires. He urged the class to follow God's plan for marriage before sex and acknowledged that it was a major discipline to remain virgin. But he had been told by those who did so, that it was worth their while. He suggested that when temptation came around, they simply say they want to turn the situation over to the Lady of Perpetual Help or the Lady of Guadalupe. If that didn't do the trick, think of the next best thing they liked, visualize catching the winning touchdown pass in the last second of the game, making a solo tackle, being at the top of the honor roll, being discovered by a movie producer, winning American Idol, flying an F-15, being a runway model in New York etc. He urged them not to engage in a sexual relationship until they were married when they could support a wife and rear a child.

When Diego cautioned Heather that their relationship would be limited to her tutoring, she told him about her boyfriend who had played tailback at Alabama and was studying medicine at Harvard. She said she was very comfortable in having Diego as a friend. Diego was a little embarrassed for thinking she was interested in him romantically.

As a freshman, he was the second tailback and there were a couple of plays designed for him to throw. He ran for two touchdowns and threw for two. The other tailback and the quarterback were both seniors and they were playing a "west coast" offense. Sophomore year he switched to quarterback and threw for eighteen touchdowns, sixteen hundred yards and four interceptions. He ran for eight touchdowns. One of the touchdowns was an eighty five yard run off a bootleg. He was an excellent faker and he used the fake well on the play action. His tailback ran for nearly sixteen hundred yards and 12 touchdowns. They came in second to Michigan in the conference and went to the Rose Bowl against Arizona State as the default when Michigan went to the Fiesta Bowl as part of the playoff series. Junior year was not quite as good. He lost four of his offensive linemen and it took the new linemen some time to adjust to the offense.

From the summer of his freshman year in high school, he and Oscar worked for Mr. Goldman, initially in the store. Mr. Goldman had both Renaldo and Jose work for him. They all started out in the store. But by junior year, they began to work for Mr. Goldman at his home, working with the gardener, the chauffer and sometimes in the kitchen. Diego and Oscar continued to work for Mr. Goldman while in college. There was a workout room in the house and they were authorized to use it when they were not working. Diego was eating a lot and bulking up. When he reported for the first day of practice in senior year, he weighed 225 and was six foot four and ran a 4.9 forty with equipment.

Two Fronts

For the last three summers at Northwestern, Diego had spent a month each year at Camp Pendleton in California. He loved the Marines as much as he loved football. He applied himself and took his preparation seriously. He assumed that at some point he would be in a war zone if not in combat. His military professors warned the trainees that the conduct of war had changed so radically in just the time of their careers that there was no way of covering all the possibilities. Asynchronous war was new to them when they entered the military and it would change again requiring different skills and different weapons. He could not imagine all that he learned in his policy classes on national defense.

He was shocked to find that the country was not nearly as secure or defensible as he had assumed. After the President pulled the troops from Iraq and Afghanistan in 2011-14, Iraq ignited into a civil conflict which was assisted by the Iranian government. The Taliban flourished in Afghanistan. Both countries returned to chaos and America lost strength in the Middle East and in Asia.

The ordinary American citizen had no idea of just how weakened the nation had become. When the new President came to office, Americans were largely war-weary and the President had promised to undertake a fundamental transformation of the United States. He had achieved success in the role of the U.S. in the world. The United States was globally regarded as a sort of "paper tiger". It had failed to aid the Syrian rebels, refused aid to a weak unelected Ukrainian replacement government, neglected to intervene in the hostage taking in Nigeria and had engaged in useless dialogue as Iran undertook the development of its nuclear arsenal. He was confused and simply couldn't figure out what to do with North Korea. China was assuming much of the American role of military dominance throughout the world and India and Russia were soon to gain posture.

Cuts in manpower and weapons had weakened the country and left the nation vulnerable. Small rogue nations took advantage of the unwillingness and the military was spread too thinly to be a consequential force. Radical Islam had spread terror across all of Asia, Africa and Europe.

The realities of cyber and of electronic warfare frightened him. Back in 2017, Iran obtained the atom bomb. North Korea had engaged in an unsuccessful attempt to detonate an electromagnetic pulse in the sky above the eastern U.S. air space. It knocked out some electronics in Vermont and Maine for a brief ten minutes, but fizzled. It was a foretaste of what could happen unless the threat was taken seriously. Mass destructive weapons were everywhere in the world. American traitors had shared national security data with the world and China long ago had hacked into the Pentagon's and the CIA computers. There were virtually no military or espionage secrets to be protected. When it came to weapons of mass destruction, it was only a matter of who was crazy and inhumane enough to use them. It was estimated that at least twenty nations had the atomic bomb and only ten of them were in any way committed to cooperation with the United Nations or the International Atomic Energy Agency.

There was such chaos when President Benson came to office in 2017 that his entire early energies were devoted to correcting foreign policy and he was only moderately successful.

Diego came back to football and the campus laden with thoughts of national security but his mind switched quickly to the game. It was comforting to address the X and 0 of a pass play rather than worry about national security. He was well prepared for the season having kept in top shape though summer camp.

The coaches and sportswriters were looking for big things from him with an experienced line and he did not disappoint. A Chicago sportswriter had labored to place him on the Heisman watch, but he never rose above the fifteenth slot. They won ten games losing to Ohio State in overtime. Oscar was playing wide out for OSU and caught two touchdowns. When they met after the game, Oscar took it easy on Diego but there wasn't all that much room for a lot of trash talk because

Ohio State had lost two other conference games.

The Big Ten was strong in 2022. Northwestern ranked fourth in the in the early standings for the playoff series and that eventually put them in the Sugar Bowl against Florida State which was number three. Northwestern won in the fourth quarter. With eight minutes to play, Diego hit his wide-out on one touchdown and his tailback for another and then ran up the gut for a two point conversion. For the season he threw for twenty touchdowns, ran for eight and had a sixty three percent completion record. He ran for nearly six hundred yards as a quarterback.

When graduation came around, he was eager to go to Camp Lejeune. It would be the jumping off point for his time in the Marines and perhaps and overseas assignment, but he would also do more leadership training. He was proud of his work and play at Northwestern and he assumed his football career might be over. None of the pro teams had shown a lot of interest in him and the sportswriters were of the opinion that he was good but was not likely to go very high in the draft.

When the season had finished in his senior year, Heather asked if she could introduce him to some of her friends who had admired his play over the four years. He agreed and asked Carlos his kicker and soccer playing roommate to join them. Heather picked them up in her BMW convertible and Carlos who was six foot two wiggled his body into the back seat with his legs stretched across the seat. Diego had to move his passenger seat as far back as it would go and still didn't fit the arrangement.

When they arrived at "Chip's" a university hangout, a lot of people noticed Diego and waved or said "hello". He felt welcome. After about a ten minute wait in line to enter, he was shocked to see himself prominently displayed in a glossy two by four foot picture to the left of the bar. He was shown in uniform with no helmet in a pose that represented the follow through on a pass from the shotgun. It was addressed to "Chip" and signed by himself. But he had no memory of doing so and the signature wasn't his. It was probably signed by someone in the sports publicity department. He hoped the bar owner had not paid anything for the picture.

When they went and stood at the bar, Heather's friends gathered round and she introduced Diego as her "student" in a joking manner. She said she had taught him all he knew about playing quarterback. After a while, Diego began to feel awkward and somewhat claustrophobic because of all the girls crowding in on him. He asked Heather if they could take their beer to a booth or table. They managed to get a table and many of the girls dropped off but some still stood around wanting to ask Diego about this or that game or play.

After a couple of beers, he asked Heather if they could go. She was a bit reluctant and he said that he and Carlos could walk home because it was only about a mile. Heather stayed and Diego and Carlos hoofed it home. Neither was into the bar scene. It held no magic for them.

Da Bears

he was in the Marines, he didn't participate in the "combine" where hopeful NFL draftees demonstrate their skills. So he thought he was out of the running for that year. He would have to wait until after he left the service to participate in the "combine". His agent said there was an outside chance that someone may draft him just to have him in their stable. He had detected modest interest. When the draft day came around, he was in the Marines in South Carolina. In the interest of good media relations, the Marines made him available to the press for the draft by giving him a chance to go home for the day on a red-eye and return the next night. He and Oscar were sitting in Carmen's living room watching the draft on TV and he nearly choked when they called his name in the fifth spot of the third round for the Chicago Bears. The Bears, Pittsburgh and Denver had called his agent, a friend of Renaldo who usually represented baseball players.

The agent had a suspicion that Diego might go in the fourth or fifth round, but he didn't want to raise his hopes. So he kept quiet. But the scouts for the Bears touted him highly and the general manager and coach bought in. He was clearly an athlete who would fit in. They knew he was going to spend three years in the Marines, but they assumed that if they had a strong quarterback in place when he was available, they could use him as a runner, receiver or defensive back. Even though the Bears had been sold out for fifty five years, it would be a good idea to have a local boy in some role. Oscar went to Oakland early in a late round.

The Bears signed Diego with a fitting signing bonus and a fitting salary for a third round pick. He was immediately rich. Brother Mark had told him it would happen and to use his head when it did. He was tempted to make his first purchase a new car, but he decided to keep his old pick-up until he finished his Marine tour. He would not need a new car in Africa. So he made a huge down payment on a new house for Carmen at the edge of the old neighborhood. But he left her with a small mortgage so she would feel she was buying it with Frankie's help. She cried and cried and thanked God. She wished Frankie was with her. When Oscar got picked in the fifth round by Oakland, he signed a one year deal and went to camp. But while in camp he was traded to the Jets. He played in eleven of the sixteen season games and was considered a good trade. The following year he moved up and played four seasons at wide-out but quit in the fifth year when he began to ride the bench more.

Prior to the draft, Diego had learned that he would be

going to Nigeria. In 2015, the Chinese embarked on an aggressive move to tie up all of Nigeria's oil. United States investors had significant holdings in Nigeria, but the United States didn't use much of the oil because there had been enormous deposits of natural gas and shale in the U.S. and the oil companies were allowed to recover it once the EPA was in the hands of rational administrators. The green lobby had lost much of its control over the government in 2017 when President Carl Benson and a Republican Senate was elected and joined a Republican House. The Chinese were contracting for most of the Nigerian oil and had sent engineers to Nigeria to assist in the drilling and management of the oil shipment. The principal interest of the United States was to protect the American interests and keeping Nigeria free of terrorism.

When President Benson assumed the presidency, he immediately pulled all the plugs in Washington. He had confessed to his wife prior to his run for president, that if he won, he would hold the office for only one term and that he would manage the country in a manner that would either heal it or he would be impeached, assassinated or quit. He feared his actions might further divide the country, but he was going to lead anyway. The actions of the last two presidents had divided the country. The divide was not intentional. Their disparate ideologies and policies had done a great deal to divide the country during their terms and there was little chance of further damage.

President Benson eviscerated the Environmental Protection Agency but left it in place. New rules were initiated that would allow America to become energy independent in less than five years. Oil tax allowances for drilling and depletion were substantially reduced and new rules allowed oil to be drilled on both coasts and in Alaska's ANWR. Shale drilling was expanded.

Solar, wind and bio-fuels were heavily promoted but not subsidized or forced on drivers. Canada and Mexico shipped substantially less oil to the U.S. and coal mining expanded. The ethanol mandate was repealed when he and a Republican congress took office. Sugar cane competed with corn ethanol and both became cheaper with the competition. But the big contributor to the energy market was the slowing of the economies in China, India and the U.S. There was an energy bubble that burst in 2018 and the price of oil dropped.

After the President ordered a ten percent cut in all federal government departments, he directed all Secretaries of Departments to have the staff prepare a budget that reflected the most rational cuts, submit the budgets to conference committees of both houses for modifications and approval. He ordered the finished product which came with some bi-partisan support to be executed. He urged congress to cut taxes to five percent on manufacturers and fifteen percent on all businesses and his request was honored. With the same legislation, he proposed and was favored with suspension of all corporate and farm subsidies. Farmers could be supported by some trade tariffs but were not subsidized. Substantial surpluses were bought by government and stored or shipped in emergencies to countries in hardship at cost. Business deductions along with taxes were lessened and revenue rose substantially.

In the second year of his term the federalist President requested congress to deliberate a Fair Tax that represented a value added approach to tax as a trade off for income tax. States became the important government entity because it was there where the tax was collected. The IRS had become so politicized and was held in such distrust that the idea of a Fair Tax was favorably viewed by the public for several reasons. The tax would be added as the product went through its manufacture, development, marketing and sale cycle. Imports would be taxed in the same manner as they came into the country.

The adoption would essentially abolish the historic role of the IRS within three years. But there still needed to be an agency to insure the Fair Tax was being collected by the states and cities and properly passed on to the federal government. The tax passed after three years of deliberation with an iron clad law that it would replace the income tax. Jobs were created, unemployment plummeted and the economy flourished.

The Fair Tax destroyed many of the benefits of the underground and cash economy. When people bought an item or a service, they were paying what replaced their income tax. Yachts got more expensive and it brought the incomes of the cash workers and the "undocumented" into the taxed economy. It did away with most of the K Street lobbyists whose labors were aimed at subsidies and special deductions for the wealthy and those whose businesses depended on government largesse. Gone away were the tax shelters created by congress and formerly enjoyed by big business and the wealthy. A part of the bill that created the Fair Tax dealt justly with the "undocumented". They would be put on the books and at the end of their work life, they would receive the amounts that they had paid into Social Security taxes. This was money that under the old system they would never collect in old age. It placed everyone on an equal footing when it came to tax. The motto of those who promoted it was "you buy, you pay your tax". This pleased the Greens and those who wanted to see a leveling of the economic order.

In 2018, all of the federal education funds were sequestered and returned to the states. The amounts that came from all the individuals in each state were returned to state departments of education under an agreement that required the states to spend that same amount on education as was spent in 2018 for the following five years with no offsets for other current state funds. The consequence was a skeleton federal Education Department that contracted with the National Assessment for Educational Progress to promote but not impose curriculums and testing systems. States vastly increased charter schools and voucher programs. An increased number of states passed Right to Work laws and teacher unions were decimated. Parental involvement was enhanced and student performance began to improve on standardized tests. Charter schools grew. Voucher programs appeared in every major U.S. city and eventually fifty percent of all elementary students were in voucher or charter programs.

The Chinese Problem

President Carl Benson, who prior to becoming president owned and managed the largest minority owned hedge fund in existence, appointed a vigorous billionaire Secretary of Commerce who had spent her life in international trade relations. He commissioned her to do what she determined was necessary. She worked with the Trade Secretary and in effect they threatened to initiate a trade war with China after the Trade Secretary's efforts to generate a new trade agreement were rebuffed. The downturn in the Chinese economy left the Chinese unwilling to remove any burdens from their trade practices. The trade imbalance began to improve after the president urged Congress to ban Chinese electronics unless there was at least one American manufactured part included. The Congress accommodated the initiative by introducing legislation that banned anything that did not have any American part.

The Chinese prevented any progress and chose to continue with their destructive trade and monetary policies. Their exports suffered. But they had more than trade problems. China's one child policy had created a chaotic circumstance where some of their villages had dangerously unequal sexual imbalances with as many as 125 men to 100 women. There was a buildup in testosterone in the cities and the young men were taking on a more bellicose attitude toward Beijing. Young men from the cities went to remote rural villages to seek and in some instances kidnap young women. In some of the villages, the peasants had paid little attention to the one child policy. The consequence was that there were equal numbers of men and women in the villages.

In 2014, the Chinese officials were fearful that the nation would suffer from a labor shortage and a lack of resources available to the aging population. The government undertook a new initiative wherein couples where one of the spouses had been an only child were allowed to have more than one child. It proved less popular than was necessary to remediate the problem. It was too late to deal with the lack of sexual balance in the aging population. The Chinese housing market had gone badly. Whole cities of housing had been built, but the necessary commerce and business was never established in the areas. The Chinese youth population had plummeted and the elderly population that required care and support had soared. But they couldn't support the housing with the slowdown in the economy. In their efforts to employ the young men, the government had developed a massive military but the conflicts they faced did not lend themselves to ground forces. In 2030, there was a Chinese winter in the making.

The U.S. troops had been pulled from Iraq in 2011 and were pulled from Afghanistan in 2014. The President advanced the Afghanistan pull out to please the base of his party in the hope of being re-elected. And he was re-elected in 2012. The pull outs proved disastrous and civil wars of one sort or another ensued in each country.

Over a five year period, U.N. sanctions weakened the Iranian economy but did not end their effort to obtain their nuclear weapons. In the same period, Israel had delayed the Iranian threat to obtain a nuclear bomb by assassination of the nuclear engineers and scientists and by sabotage of ships that carried the necessary raw materials and parts for centrifuges and missiles. Iranian oil diminished and their economy stuttered. The U.S. president labored to draw the leaders of the free world into an agreement to lessen sanctions in the hope that Iran would abandon its bomb plans. It proved a hoax on the part of Iran and the Iranians continued their effort. In 2015 they claimed that they had five nuclear war heads and the delivery systems. The youth population threatened an Iranian spring, but determined that the free world would not support them and abandoned the effort. They had to rely on the mullahs to fail. Israel didn't feel it could wait any longer for the Iranians to fail in their effort to secure a bomb. They undertook an effort to destroy the centrifuges but they were only partially successful and the effort to secure a bomb continued.

Why Nigeria?

In his last term as president, President George W. Bush had established the African Command. The move was prescient. Terrorist groups, including al Qaeda, had found Africa a fertile ground for both recruitment and training. In 2012, the strikes over oil in Nigeria and the religious conflicts between the Muslims and Christians in the north had caused chaos throughout Nigeria. Boko Haram, a terrorist group in the north, was known for terrorizing the Christians and the government whenever they felt disposed. Founded in 2001 by Mohammed Yusuf, they labeled themselves the People of the Tradition for Proselytism and Jihad. They undertook a new insurgency when the government ceased the gasoline subsidy. The occasion gave Boko Haram an excuse to come south, recruit, attack government facilities and kill Christians as they regularly did in the north. Their goal was to turn northern Nigeria into an entirely Muslim area with Sharia law. Millions of Christians fled the north and Boko Haram. At the time the U.S. State Department under the guidance of Hilary Clinton refused to identify the group as terrorists because it would give them notoriety.

In 2014, Boko Haram gained their notoriety by taking nearly three hundred young girls hostage and attempted to use them as trades for the release of their imprisoned terrorists associates. Americans and Europeans responded with tweets about how nice it would be to have them released, but the American President lamented the fact that the most powerful nation in the world could do nothing. The U.S. would need a formal request by the confused, hapless president of Nigeria to intervene and then the President would want to look for approval from the U.N. which equally confused and hapless. It was a habit for the President to procrastinate, but finally sent some "advisors" to assist in the search. He refused to intervene in Syria early on when Assad could have been toppled with little bloodshed and before the rebel forces were contaminated by Al Queada.

Boko Haram took confidence from the lack of action on the part of the U.S. and utilized the occasion for recruitment. The Chinese knew how to use terrorists and had for years invested widely in Nigeria seeking minerals and oil. They also funded business enterprises. In 2013, China decided to take advantage of the chaos surrounding the off and on suspension of the oil subsidy and engaged the radical groups. At the cessation of the subsidy they persuaded and funded the Boko Haram to join with the unions and conspire to stop the shipment of oil to any country other than China. Boko Haram totally shut down the oil platforms and the ports. There were a number of U.S. companies with considerable assets including oil in Nigeria. The U.S. had become an oil exporting nation after the administration left office but U.S. companies still had oil interests in many nations. The U.S. did not have a formal protective status with Nigeria, but when President Benson came to office, he warned China that the United States Marines would be coming to Nigeria whether at the request of the Nigerian President or not. And the National Assembly needed to protect American interests and to insure that the oil would be shipped into the open market.

The Chinese did not respond to the warning. The Nigerian government stumbled and Islamists began to take increased power. Eventually the government agreed to ship all of the oil to China. The navy had been stripped of much of its fleet, but President Benson sent a single warship with a brigade of Marines to Nigeria. Lieutenant Juan Diego Freeman was among the troops deployed. They hoped not to engage in combat but were armed to accommodate it. The oil was being shipped in the north but little was being shipped from the south in Lagos. Local refineries were dilapidated and when a Nigerian billionaire industrialist sought to build refineries and pump oil from the waters off Lagos he met with resentment and blockage from Boko Haram.

In June 2025, Diego had been commissioned as a second lieutenant and was reassigned from South Carolina to a training unit at Camp Pendleton in Southern California. He was attached to an advance company that was assigned the mission of establishing protection for the headquarters' company in Lagos. They arrived in the first part of August of 2025 and set up a perimeter around the pertinent shipping areas and oil fields with multiple platforms and lines. The Marines were in the port, approximately a quarter of a mile from the refinery. Perimeter guards were established and at sundown of their first day in country the Boko Haram attacked. Diego's troops were prepared and repelled the attack easily. They felt comfortable. They were confident and settled in.

After being in country for three months, they had been attacked twice, easily repelling the attacks. The attacks were made by small bands which would hit and run. In two of the attacks a week apart, individual posted guards at the perimeter were killed. At dawn a week later, the Boko Haran attacked again. As Diego joined in the response, he took a .30 caliber bullet in the left shoulder and went into shock. When he awoke, he was both angry and embarrassed. He was wearing body armor but the bullet went right through the opening below the shoulder and exited from his back. He knew immediately that this was not a good start for a person who considered the possibility of a career in the Marines after pro ball.

Chapter 8

All Pro to Politician

Ramstein Air Force Hospital

If someone had asked Diego where he wanted to spend his twenty fifth birthday, Diego would never have thought to mention a hospital room in Germany. But it was so. The doctors, familiar with the fact that he had been signed to be a professional football player, were concerned that their effort to reconstruct his left shoulder might fall short and did not want to take the responsibility for leaving him crippled. The shoulder had been pierced through by the bullet. The orthopedic surgeon assigned called in a couple of German civilian neurosurgeons to reconstruct the shoulder. They did an expert job. So good, that after just five weeks, Diego could have gone back to Nigeria.

But two days before he was to be released from the rehabilitation unit of the hospital, a full bird colonel appeared in his room and introduced himself as a representative of the Commandant of the Marine Corps. He told Diego that the matter of his assignment had gone through the office of the Commandant and that he would be assigned to the Pentagon rather than to a combat unit. Diego resisted saying that he didn't join the Corps to be assigned to a desk in Washington. He had only been in country for three months and wanted to go back to his troops. He had barely tasted combat and he wanted to be in Nigeria or to wherever there was action. The Marine Commandant had played at the Naval Academy and was a huge football fan. He learned that Diego had been injured and took an interest. He wasn't going to be responsible for allowing Diego to end his career before he donned a Bears uniform. He determined not to risk further injury for a big name ballplayer.

Diego was assigned to the Pentagon in the congressional liaison office where he spent the next two years pleading with congressmen to understand how unprepared the nation was for defense. He couldn't understand how un- interested most congressmen were in national defense. The Pentagon could do little to please them. Troops were deployed in Europe, Korea, the Middle East, Southeast Asia, Africa and on the entire border of the United States, north, and south, on the east and west coasts. There were few left to deploy and neither the members of the House nor Senate seemed to care.

Utility Man

Diego had been reared in a household with one person giving direction. The rules and the goals were clear. He played team sports where there was one head coach who gave direction. He served in a military where direction was given by the Chief of Staff and came through his commanding General. He adapted well to clear direction. He remembered the instruction in some of the classes at Northwestern in his leadership courses. The principles taught by the professors conflicted with those taught in his military training. The professors argued that the more participation the members of a group had in the development of a goal and the manner in which it would be achieved, the more likely they would be to participate in achieving the goal. It made sense in some respects. But when it came to the football field, only one person could decide the direction.

When it came to many important matters, only one person could determine the goal. It was up to him to make the distinction between the groups and the goals. He worshipped in a Church where there was a single person whose job it was to lead and inspire. Washington was different from anything he had ever seen or wanted to see. What happened in Washington was chaotic and it made him feel insecure and uncomfortable about the safety and future of the nation. He concluded that there was so much division that there was no leadership, no clear goal or direction that the citizens could embrace.

Every politician brought a different set of values and rules to the congress. Each had their own idea of what the republic represented and what should be the priority and direction of the country. He could not leave Washington soon enough. He promised himself that if he was ever assigned a leadership position he would do all he could to make the direction of the organization as clear as possible. He completed his Marine tour and promised himself he would never return to Washington other than to play the Redskins.

The Bears were elated by his return. He had signed what in his mind was a handsome rookie contract of twenty four million but it was guaranteed for only one year. Renaldo and his agent advised him to defer as much salary as the tax laws allowed until the Fair Tax kicked in and to live conservatively until he had a longer guarantee and larger salary. If he succeeded, he would be in the multi- year hundred million contract sphere and would have nothing to worry about financially. He also needed to be comfortable that he would be with the Bears for more than a year if he was going to purchase a home. He rented a very comfortable three bedroom condo with a view of Lake Michigan in the south loop and bought a one year old Yukon Denali. His older sister, Rosa had established her own interior design business and took on the task of creating a décor fitting an NFL star, nothing too fancy, but nice enough to want to be there.

The Freeman family had to make some adjustments in their lives. Diego played on Sunday afternoon, the traditional time for the whole family to gather at Carmen's for dinner. Most of the family wanted to go to the Bear's games or watch on television to see Diego play. Monday night became the family dinner time with an opportunity after dinner to watch the Monday night games together. Diego would sometimes be coaxed to do color on the plays and players which made for great interest even to his sisters and sisters in law. In his second year after a lot of success in his first, Diego signed a five year contract with three years guaranteed. The sportswriters considered him an excellent journeyman tail back. He wouldn't rival Gail Sayers or Walter Payton but he could keep up with the others.

In his rookie year, the Bears had an All Pro quarterback, a good tailback and a corps of wide receivers, but no tight ends. So they initially used Diego as a tight end. They put in a couple of end arounds and a couple of double passes. By mid-season, the tailback had been replaced for the second time due to injuries and they had gone to their number two tailback. They used Diego as his relief. When Diego ran off a 66 yard sprint up through a strong secondary against Green Bay, they decided to have him start for the remaining four games. He scored five touchdowns and gained enough yards to start the following season at tailback.

Midway through his second year with the Bears, Diego went to the Monday night dinner as usual. The Monday night game was Philadelphia against Detroit which didn't hold a lot of interest for the family. Neither team looked headed for a playoff spot. Diego's older brother, Marine Colonel Jose was posted overseas so he couldn't attend Carmen's dinners. The only other family member unable to attend the dinners regularly was Diego's youngest sister, Angel who attended Florida Atlantic University in Boca Raton.

When Diego received his football ride to Northwestern, Mr. Goldman had been kind enough to rollover the money from the education trust he had set aside for Diego to Isabel's and Angel's funds. Isabel had finished college with an education degree and no debt. In her junior year, Angel at FAU was still debt free due mainly to Mr. Goldman and with some help from Diego. That year, she moved off campus to live in a rented condo with a girlfriend, Sonia Fernandez from St. Rita's.

After dinner, Rosa called Diego away from watching the game to talk about Angel. Sonia had called Rosa in confidence the day before and had shared some news about Angel, who was an excellent student majoring in computer science. She participated actively in the activities of the Newman Center where she attended mass every Sunday and she was part of a youth outreach from the Newman Center. She joined three other girls each week to visit tutor kids in computer skills at a youth center in the poorer section of Highland Beach.

She hadn't had a steady boyfriend until her junior year. She was smitten when she met Denzel Davidson in her African History class. Denzel was a very handsome, very hip and very speedy wide- out for FAU. His personality and smile were infectious. FAU had risen to national football prominence in 2022 when they played for the National Championship in the Orange Bowl against Alabama and lost by one point. The current team wasn't even ranked in the top twenty five. Nonetheless, Denzel stood out because there was a talented quarterback who used Denzel as his primary target.

At most universities, there was a lot of loose sex. FAU was no exception. There was a lot of "hooking up", date rape and drunk rape. As a result of all the loose sex, there were a lot of STDs and pregnancies. As soon as Angel moved into the apartment with Sonia, she was persuaded by Sonia to visit the Health Office and to start taking "the pill", just in the event of some sexual mistake, consensual or forced. Angel had not been sexually active until one night after a party at Denzel's fraternity. The wine had flowed freely and in a state of compromised judgment, she got carried away. The fraternity had no rules against women in the rooms. Once the moral ice was melted and nothing untoward had occurred, sex became a weekly entertainment for the couple. She would go to confession at St. Joan of Arc every couple of weeks rather than confess to the Newman chaplain whom she knew well and who might recognize her voice. The priest at St. Joan would give a light penance and admonish her not to sin again. She would make a resolve. Then, a few days later, Denzel would pressure her by asking if she really loved him. She didn't want to lose him, so she would give in and restart the cycle.

She was scheduled to have her period the week before Thanksgiving. When it didn't come, she blamed the tardiness on the stress of tests and scheduling her trip home for the holiday and the weekend. Three weeks later when there was no sign of a period, she began to panic. She considered the possibility of pregnancy. She didn't want to go to the Student Health Center because she thought they might pressure her to quickly abort the baby and she didn't like any kind of pressure.

There was a brochure at the Newman Center for a Pregnancy Help Center operated by the Catholic diocese located in Delray Beach that gave free pregnancy tests and ultrasounds. She walked in the third week of December and they confirmed that she was eight weeks pregnant. They showed her a picture of an eight week fetus. It was clearly a child. The counselor asked if it was a surprise. Angel said that she had suspected it for about three weeks but it clearly was not planned. They talked at some length about Angel's situation, her boyfriend and her family. She simply didn't know how Denzel would respond. They had never talked about marriage or children. He talked almost exclusively about his chances of going to the NFL. That was his only interest and his only goal.

At the apartment, she showed too much concern, almost depression for Sonia not to notice. Sonia asked if there was something she had done to anger her. Angel told her she was not angry with anyone other than herself and then shared the fact of her pregnancy. Sonia asked what she planned to do and she said she simply didn't know. She needed to talk to Denzel.

When she called him, he said he was tied up Friday and Saturday night but he could make it on Sunday. She was planning on leaving for Christmas vacation on Tuesday night and was very eager to discuss the baby with him. She didn't want to wait until Sunday, but she agreed. He would meet her at a sports bar on the water in Highland Beach at six. When they met, he ordered a beer and asked if she wanted her usual glass of Merlot. She declined. He asked if she had become a tea totaller. She said she had a reason for not drinking and then shared the fact that he was about to become a father. Denzel didn't respond positively. In fact, he was livid. He accused her of getting pregnant intentionally so she could share in the fortune he would make in the NFL. He told her it was all "bull...." and that a white girl from New York had already tried that on him when he was a sophomore. He had threatened her with telling her parents that she was pregnant with a black man's baby. He paid half for the abortion. He would do the same for Angel but he didn't want her telling anyone about the baby.

She cried. He stood up, said that that was the "f......" deal, take it or leave it but we are finished one way or the other". He slammed down a ten dollar bill on the table and left the restaurant. When she got home she passed Sonia without a word and went to her room and sobbed uncontrollably. She exhausted herself and then slept. She stayed home from her Monday classes. When Sonia left the house, she called Rosa and told her about Angel. She didn't know all the details but she was positive Rosa would want to know that Angel was troubled.

Angel called Rosa later in the morning and told her that

she needed to stay in Boca Raton over the holidays. She had a lot of studying and some volunteer work to do. Rosa didn't know what to say or do. She waited until that evening when she would see Diego and ask both Diego and Renaldo about what they thought she should do for Angel. She asked Diego if he thought that she should leave for Florida the next day to see Angel and talk

with her.

Diego suggested that she talk with Sonia before going and ask her to get more information regarding what Sonia thought Angel was planning. If she was not going to destroy the baby or herself, it might be best to let Angel think for a couple of days about what she needed to do. Rosa knew that Sonia would be coming home on Wednesday so there would not be a lot of time for her to assess Angel's state of mind.

Diego told Rosa that the Bears were playing the Dolphins in the Thursday night TV game in Miami. The team would be in Miami on Wednesday afternoon. He could take Angel to dinner Wednesday night after the team had had the run-through of the game plan. Rosa called Sonia on Tuesday morning. Angel was in class and they talked. Sonia told her that she and Angel had spent most of Monday night discussing her condition and Sonia was nearly certain that there was no danger of her destroying the baby or herself. According to Sonia, Angel seemed almost eager to become a mother. She could continue to go to class until the baby came and then use the daycare at the university which was much cheaper than private day care. If she could find a sitter, she might be able to work some. Sonia sounded excited about having a baby in the apartment.

When Diego and Angel went to dinner, she immediately shared that she was pregnant. Diego acted surprised and asked about the father and what his plans were. Angel said she was on her own and didn't even want to talk about the father except to say they had dated for more than a semester, he was a football player and they were through. She said she had "screwed up, but like mom always says, own it and good will come from it if I react properly. It's all in my attitude".

Diego was shocked at how mature his youngest sister was. He was pleased. He thought he would be dealing with a basket case instead of this mature young woman who was facing the biggest challenge of her young life. He suggested that she needed to talk to their mom sooner rather than later. Mom wouldn't want to be left out of the most important matter in her child's life. They both knew their mom would be supportive. One of Carmen's younger sisters had come from Mexico to Chicago unmarried and pregnant and she and the baby were warmly welcomed into the extended family. Diego wanted to be as supportive as possible with Angel. He told her that because she was a Freeman she would never want for emotional or financial support. He and the family would always be there. She said she knew that and that was why she felt secure.

When she came home at Christmas she had a slightly different attitude. She had gone back to the Pregnancy Center for an ultrasound. When she saw the baby in 3D, she became profoundly aware that she would be fully responsible for a new life, a new human being with a life of its own and an eternal soul. She also realized that she was alone no matter how supportive her family would be. She began to think about her future and how things might be six or ten years down the path, trying to raise a child without a husband. Even with the family support it could be a difficult and lonely job. Was she being fair to the child to bring him or her into the world without a father? She felt certain guilt about that possibility. She also felt a guilt about thinking of herself and wondering if she would be severely handicapping herself for marriage. How many men wanted to raise someone else's child? He would have to be very special.

After her dinner with Diego, she called and told her mother about the baby over the phone. Carmen was delighted at how positive Angel was about the baby. When she came home at Christmas, she spent a night with Rosa and her husband Michael talking about her future. After a couple of hours of discussion, Rosa bluntly asked if Angel had given any consideration to adoption. Angel said she had given it some thought but thought it might be too difficult to give her baby to someone she didn't even know. She had taken a couple of brochures from the Pregnancy Center that addressed adoption in very positive terms depicting the adoption as the most generous gift a mother can give. The woman who wrote the brochure had given her child in adoption and had gone on to have her own family. Her view was that adoption can bless the child with a loving two parent family and the parents with a gift only God and a mother can give.

After a week of praying with her mom and enjoying the warm and relaxing comfort of her family, Angel made a decision. She could make the sacrifice. She could see the bigger picture and give her child a better chance in life. On May 22, 2033 Franklin Renaldo Freeman, an eight pound four ounce boy was born at Northwestern University Hospital in Chicago. The new adoptive parents were both teachers, the father a high school science teacher at New Trier High in Winnetka and the mother a law professor at Northwestern University Law. The new parents indicated comfort with an open adoption, but Angel wanted to leave them free to raise Frankie unfettered from a prying birth mother. The last time she saw Frankie was at his baptism where the entire Freeman family said their goodbyes. Angel studied law at the University of Michigan and eventually became a very successful partner in a Chicago law firm. She married an investment banker at age forty. Frankie was her only child.

A Time for Change

After six seasons with the Bears, five of which were Pro-Bowl seasons as a tailback, he had enough. He loved the game and the action, but in his sixth season he suffered a severe hamstring pull that wouldn't heal. He played a sixth season, but couldn't generate the speed or drive to merit the Pro Bowl. Diego knew it was time to retire. He was thirty one and eager to get on with his life. He planned to go to law school and had already scored well on the LSAT and had been accepted at Loyola Law in Chicago. He was encouraged in this by Brother Mark. He wasn't really that interested in practicing private law, but at Brother Mark's urging, he was eager to do something in public interest law. His status as a pro ballplayer and wounded Marine could be valuable in public interest circles.

Shortly after the end of the season, he was approached by Mr. Goldman of Allsave and Mayor Tito Perez. They asked him to consider running for a south side congressional seat to replace a bent congressman who had accepted a quarter million dollars of bribes to his personal accounts to introduce various bills that would benefit his sources. They told Diego he could do the city and a lot of people on the South Side a lot of good and that they would do all they could to make sure he would win. That kind of promise in Chicago from the Mayor was the point at which time one could plan their victory party.

Diego's brother Tony, who was a corporate lawyer and who had some experience in politics managed Diego's campaign. There wasn't much to do. The Mayor's polling company did a poll early on and found that Diego would win with an eighty percent plurality no matter what he said or did. He won big. There was a lot of money in his campaign kitty. Tony didn't want to waste it in case Diego needed it for a future campaign. Tony had spent very little on the campaign. Near the end of the campaign, a representative of the Mayor visited Tony and told him that he needed to spread the money around to the unions, the printers, consultants and precinct captains. They would carry Diego to victory whether he had the votes or not.

His victory was nearly unanimous. He was very popular in Chicago and even nationally. He had it all going for him. He was rich, good looking, all pro and a wounded war veteran. And he was single. There were women from all corners who would like to change that status, but Diego had been so busy and occupied by his work and family that he had never gotten around to thinking about marriage. He had dated but had not met Mrs. Right.

The Congressman

On the second day of his orientation to Congress, he attended a meeting that was presented by the Congressional Budget Office. He was taking copious notes on his I-Pad when a young woman who wore an I.D. badge indicating that she was a CBO staff member pointed out that all the information that would be provided in the orientation was already digitized. He could download it while sitting there. She sat down next to him and helped him by showing all the information that could be acquired at their website. She had introduced herself as Jordan Crawford, an engineering analyst for the CBO evaluating and costing out the construction projects proposed by congresspersons. She welcomed him to Washington where she had been in the CBO for five years.

Somehow she had introduced something into the space when she sat next to him that changed his consciousness. It wasn't just the gorgeous aroma of what was obviously a very expensive perfume. It was something human, calm, peacefulness in her manner. She possessed an aura that was powerful and pleasing. Her presence sharpened his awareness, relaxed him and commanded his attention. When she took the microphone and made her presentation, he was highly impressed with her obvious competence. But that was not what completely overwhelmed him. She was beautiful and her manner was soft but utterly assured. His attention hung on her every word, but his eyes couldn't move from her appearance. She had a soft peachy skin and her hair was a soft blonde, short, curly as if permed and fashionably styled. She was tall and thin but had shapely legs, those of an athlete. Her attire was impeccable and her expensive gray business suit hung on her as it might on a runway model. She showed a subtle playfulness in the way she approached her remarks. She was beautiful, but had cuteness in her personality that could not be missed.

He was taken. His heart beat a little faster, his mouth was a little bit drier and his awareness was as intense as at any time he had had a monster linebacker break through with the intent of rattling his tonsils. This was the beginning of something new in his life. Being newly elected to congress was nothing by comparison. This was a moment that Brother Mark used to identify as the one when you know you are supposed to be here. For some reason, he knew he was meant to be here seeing and listening to this beautiful woman. She was clearly someone his mother would love. She had some of the same characteristics as his mom. That thought shocked him into a moment of panic. God, God, please don't let her be married. He shot a look at her left ring finger and when he didn't see a ring, he calmed a bit, but not completely. This was his future. She has to be single and he prayed "she has to have some slight interest in me, please God".

At the end of the orientation, there was a reception of wine and cheese for the rookie congresspersons. Diego naturally turned to Jordan and spent the remainder of the reception talking with her and another rookie, a female Congressperson from Iowa. He made an effort to be subtle in his attempt to ferret out her marital status. But she was clearly not much given to talking about herself. She appeared to be genuinely interested in learning more about the congresspersons and their legislative interests. At the moment, Diego had no interest in legislation or projects. He was interested only in Jordan, her marital status and her future.

The Iowa congresswoman was interested in knowing about Washington and its restaurants. Jordan shared that there was an excellent Italian restaurant only a couple of miles from the Capitol. Panic set in when Diego thought that when the reception was over, it was possible he would never see Jordan again unless he was on the right sub-committee and she was called to testify. Immediately his mind went to what construction project in his district would bring him into contact with her again.

His heart and spirit soared when Jordan suggested that she would be eager to go to dinner with the two new congresspersons. Was this just an extension of her work or could she have some small interest in him? Dinner would tell. He would surely learn her marital status during the evening. The three went to dinner at an intimate bistro that Jordan pointed out most people in congress didn't frequent. Both women wanted to talk about football and Diego was at first delighted to share a few humorous stories about some of his teammates and in his self effacing manner, some errors that he had made while playing. But that wasn't advancing his agenda. He wanted to talk about Jordan. He wanted to kiss the beautiful face next to him. But that was not going to happen tonight.

He also wanted to kiss the Representative from Iowa who was twenty years his senior and seriously overweight, when she inappropriately asked Jordan if she was married. Jordan responded that she had never even come close to marrying. She was only twenty seven and didn't even have a current boyfriend. Diego wanted to leap up, shout and tell everyone in the restaurant that they should take a good look at Jordan because he was going to marry her.

They had taken a cab from the Capitol. Jordan lived in the opposite direction from the hotel where Diego was registered. The Iowa Representative was staying with a relative in Virginia and had parked back at the Capitol. She said that she had enjoyed the evening so much that perhaps all three should stay in touch. Perhaps they could meet at the same restaurant next week at the same time to compare notes. Jordan at first demurred but with some encouragement from the Iowa representative, she agreed. Again Diego wanted to kiss the representative.

A week later, Jordan and Diego returned to the same restaurant. But the Iowa Representative had called Jordan just before she had left her office and told her that she had to be at a family function in Virginia that night. She would be eager to meet another time. When Jordan told Diego that the Representative would not be coming, he feigned mild disappointment, but he was overjoyed. He had had enough of Congressperson talk in his first week. He wanted to be the best representative he could but he was eager to talk about anything but politics tonight.

She shared with him that she had tired of Washington and preferred not to talk about her work which had turned so political that it was difficult to be fully professional. Because they had talked about his football career the last time, he said he wanted to talk about her, her family, her schooling and how she ended up in Washington. She wasn't eager to talk about herself. He probed a bit about her life with appropriate questions, what an analyst does, how she came to engineering, where she studied and then got a little personal with what she did with her leisure. Diego was interested in who she was and asked about her life before Washington. She indicated that she had attended public elementary school in Omaha and had then gone onto the Catholic High School even though she wasn't Catholic. Her parents were not religious nor were they anti-religion. But they wanted her to get the best education available in the area and that was at the Catholic school, St Joseph Prep. She breezed through her first two and a half years with great teachers. Her math and physics teachers were both Ph.D.s. Her math teacher had published a book on calculus and was a brilliant teacher.

She told him that she was required to participate in the religion class, but there was little theology discussed. It was more like a civics class where the object was to encourage the students to be tolerant and broad in their thinking. She had been instructed in those areas at home and so it was not offensive. The teacher was a lay person who had only elementary knowledge of world religions and limited interest. Jordan never decided if the teacher was a practicing Catholic or just a baptized Catholic who used her religion to secure a job at what was considered a prestigious high school. Jordan gained the impression that no one else on the faculty really wanted to teach religion, so it was assigned to the newest member of the faculty who was Catholic.

Both the math and the physics teachers urged her to go into math or engineering as a career. When she went to Iowa State, she studied both. She took engineering as a major and math as a minor. She had used all of her electives up to her senior year to study economics. It was a five year program and it led her to the analyst role as a natural outcome. She had thought about staying in Nebraska, but her mother and father both urged her to spread her wings. So she chose Washington. Her parents knew the local congressman and he suggested the CBO, rather than his office because he said "it will be less political". She liked her boss and the work was interesting even though very political. She was shocked and a bit disgusted by politics and the waste. A lot of the projects were really about jobs and less about structural or civic needs. She felt for the taxpayers. She told Diego that she was surprised by the amount of travel involved with her work. It was an element of the position that she had not planned but she found as a bonus. She shared that congresspersons take an incredible number of trips to foreign countries. They are accompanied by someone from the CBO if the trip involves research into projects in other countries. She had become something of an infrastructure specialist and had been to Egypt, Russia, Brazil, China and South Africa. She laughed when she said that on the trips, she had taken, she had been "hit on" by congressmen ranging in age from 29 to 75. The irony was that not one of the projects they had requested had been approved by Congress. Her reports had little to do with the rejection of the projects. They were simply not viewed as priorities for the budget and were dropped.

Diego wanted desperately to ask about "Mr. Right" but thought better of it. He needed to be patient. The evening passed so rapidly that he was shocked when she said that she was an "early to bed and early to rise" girl and it was past ten. She had to be going. "Wait, I haven't proposed yet" was what he wanted to say but that would come another day.

He had moved into a rental condo and had paid an unemployed friend to drive his car to Washington. He asked if she had a ride home. She said she would take a cab. He insisted on driving her home. She acquiesced. On the way home, he secured another dinner date for the following Wednesday which was short of a week. She said facetiously that she would do so if it was considered an appointment with a congressperson. She didn't date business associates. But she agreed with the understanding that she would have to recuse herself from any research on any projects he might propose if they went to dinner again. He was agreeable to the arrangement.

For the next week, when he found himself in meetings or on the floor in congress and someone was droning on about some matter that was consequential only to some self interested group, he found himself thinking of Jordan. He hadn't mustered the courage to go to her office just to see her, but he wished he could. When Wednesday finally came around, he couldn't wait for dinner. A congressperson from New York was in his office seeking support for a new sentencing bill that would aid his brother who was going to prison for drug peddling. Diego abruptly stood and said that he hoped his brother would gain insight into his behavior while in prison and told the congressman that it was a drug peddler who cost him, his six siblings and their mother the comfort, love and affection of their father.

Diego had agreed to pick Jordan up in front of the Union Station. They went to the same restaurant they had visited twice before and sat by a window that opened onto a well lit courtyard with a number of potted plants and a couple of ornate but cheap looking Italian sculptures. He asked how her week had been and she indicated that it had been uneventful except for a blowup in a committee hearing in the Senate Finance Committee when a Senator from Florida was castigating her boss for some tax and revenue figures that proved totally inaccurate. Her boss took the criticism and indicated that they would try to do better in the future. She could feel her boss's pain during the hearing but commented that that was why she was paid the "big bucks". She had always thought the Senator to be a decent human being but he was under a lot of pressure in trying to reform the tax structure and needed accurate information.

Diego listened but really had no interest in political discussion. He wanted to know more about Jordan, what her parents were like, her likes, dislikes, what she read and other than

Italian food, what she ate. He was eager to find out how she spent her spare time because he wanted to do the same thing as long as he could do it with her. She looked him directly at him, engaged his eyes and smiled, then said "peanut butter sandwiches with lots of jelly and occasionally, a hamburger. I am a very sophisticated gourmet." Then, she said "why do you want to know about me. You're the congressman, high school football star, college star, pro star and war hero". He looked at her and said "Wait a minute. Where in the world did that come from"? She said "It was easy" and asked if he had ever *Googled* himself. He acknowledged that he had done so in his first year with the Bears, but not since then and had not thought to do it as a congressman. He was flattered until she said that she always *Googled* anyone who asked her out. It was a matter of safety in her mind. Then he said "Jordan, what would I find if I *Googled* you"? She said "nothing, I've done it before and I have never put my profile up on Facebook or any other site. I am essentially a private person and you have pulled more out of me and know me better by now than many of my friends."

What an opening he thought and went ahead "Jordan, I've never said this to anyone, but I want to be more than your friend".

"Whoops, that was a little unexpected, two dinners and you are talking more seriously than I had bargained for. Isn't it a little early in the game, we are barely into the first quarter". He leaned back in his chair and took a small pull on his wine and was quiet for a few seconds. "Frankly, yes, it is a strong and sudden interest and if it had happened to me before, I would be worried. I've been out with a lot of women for dinner, but this is different. I don't know how I know but you are different, at least different to me. I think about you a lot and I want to be with you. Enough said for now."

She sat not entirely surprised because she had had some of the same thoughts and that was why she had *Googled* him. She really wanted to know if he was as good as he seemed. But she simply was not ready to get serious with anyone no matter how wonderful he was. She leaned in with candlelight brightening her lovely facial expression and said "Diego, I'm flattered that you are interested in me. You are a terrific guy and any girl in her right mind should be absolutely ecstatic about being on your dance card. But frankly, I'm not ready for romance. I'm caught in a state of confusion and it wouldn't be fair to bring you into it. I don't know what I want to do with my life. I've got a terrific job, good pay, excitement some days, travel, a great condo and I'm sitting here with a famous handsome man who is interested in me and I can't respond. It's a very long story and you really don't want to hear it. It's only my problem and one that I've been trying to work out with the help of a wise counselor. But I am not there yet and until I am satisfied that I am ready for a relationship, marriage and children, I can't burden you. You don't deserve that. I'm glad you brought the matter up because we really shouldn't go further in this. I know it can't be just friendship."

Diego was stunned. He felt like he might drown. No blindsiding linebacker had ever hit him that hard. He just sat, looked out at the courtyard and fought back the tears. He didn't have a voice. He had nothing to say and he didn't know what to think about. His mind was frozen. Finally, he turned to Jordan and said "What in God's name could be so much of a problem for you that I can't help you with it?" She responded "Indeed, what in God' name. Do you think you want to give me a ride home now or should I grab a cab?" He drove her home mostly in a painful silence. He couldn't think about anything other than he could not lose her.

All the way home, Diego wondered what she could possibly mean by "Indeed, in God's name". When they got to her apartment, she opened the car door, stepped out and leaned in saying "If I ever get myself on the right track, you will be the first to know". He smiled and drove off wondering what he could do to help her. He could not let her go.

He was devastated that his dream which was less than six weeks old, a dream he had built of blissful thoughts and intoxicating romance had faded in the moment when she said she was simply not ready for romance. He was in love and he had seen how his older brother, Renaldo, had blossomed and developed as a man by virtue of his love and marriage to Sharon. Her love for him had clearly complimented and completed Renaldo as a human being. Becoming a father had furthered his already developed sense of responsibility and he was a wonderful father to his four children. Renaldo was happy and that was exactly what Diego wanted. He wanted marriage and fatherhood more than anything. The woman he had hoped would be the mother of his children was confused and burdened and he wanted desperately to be of help to her, but he didn't know her burden.

He had had burdens himself, but other than his father's death they didn't linger or affect him deeply. He got over them quickly and moved on with his life. Diego had told Jordan about the one time that he had been deeply burdened. In Nigeria, one his men was killed by a sniper. He was overwhelmed with grief and anger. He had to write the letter to the Marine's wife and child. He was tied up in frustration and indecision for two days because he couldn't think about how horrible it would be for her and his son to know more about his death than just the fact that he had died for his country.

The Marines would have informed her of the death, but he had to write the personal letter as the one who was his leader. He struggled, but had to write. There was no chaplain attached to the unit to whom he could go. He discussed the problem with a guy whom he knew to be serious about life. Sergeant Tom

Wilson, a career Marine was single so he was not bringing up something that was in the sergeant's immediate future. The sergeant told him to write about hope. He knew people couldn't live without hope but he didn't know exactly how to phrase it. Diego had been given instruction in OCS on what to write, but it seemed dry and not at all consoling. He wanted to say that he was absolutely sure the soldier was with God because he had given his life for others. He had made the ultimate sacrifice. He had loved his fellow man totally. Then he thought "what if she didn't believe"? That might not console her.

He remembered how angry he was with those responsible for his dad's death. People kept saying it was God's plan. He didn't like the God with those kinds of plans. He had no idea of what the Marine's wife believed. But he wrote what he thought was right and that was that the soldier was surely at peace in heaven. He had made the greatest sacrifice. That night he thought about what he hoped someone would write to his mother if he had caught a fatal Nigerian bullet in a vital spot. The bullet to his shoulder came three weeks later but because he survived there was no letter about his death written to Carmen, his mother. He told Jordan that the night he wrote the letter to the soldier's wife, he thought about his own dying and what it would be like after that. He simply couldn't imagine what it was like after he died. But now the loss of his love was enough.

Gotta Try

Coach Denning was famous for his saying "Gotta try". If a man got past you on the way to the end zone or if you thought you couldn't reach the pass or block the beast across from you, you still had to try. He had to try to heal his relationship with Jordan. Perhaps he could call her and try to talk of hope. He believed in the value of hope and he thought it might move her in the right direction. She had briefly commented that she simply didn't know what her life was all about. He thought initially that she was joking, but it turned out that she was dead serious. He was happy that he had not laughed when she said it. Here she was the most mature, confident and brightest woman he knew and she said she didn't know what her life was about. Perhaps that was her burden.

He drummed up the courage to call two nights later. She said she would be happy to talk with him on the phone but it would have to be about him and not her. She needed time to consider matters on her own. He called three more times, each time asking if he could simply see her for a walk or a coke, nothing consequential. He tried to subtly probe concerning what was bothering her, but she said nothing. After the third call, she said she didn't think it would be a good idea to continue talking and asked him not to call for at least a week or so. She shared a few things about her life but didn't go deeply into what might be bothering her.

One night when they were talking about their teen years, she told him how she had transferred in her junior year from St. Joseph Prep. After the beginning of the second semester of her sophomore year, one of her girlfriends shared with her that she had had sex with the priest who was the president of the school. She indicated that it was consensual. Jordan pointed out to her that it couldn't be consensual because she was not old enough to give consent and he was in a position of power. She pointed out to her friend that it was de facto statutory rape. The priest was a rapist. Jordan couldn't stand anyone who took advantage of others because of their power position. Jordan encouraged her to tell the police, but the girl's parents had told her to keep it secret until she graduated and they would take care of it then.

Jordan was incensed but was hesitant to tell her mother

who was a friend of her girlfriend's mother. Jordan told Diego that she went to the public library created a new e mail account and sent an e mail to the bishop's office at the diocese indicating that they needed to look into the matter of the sexual behavior of the president of the school. She didn't specify the girl's name. There was no reply to the email, but the diocese must have done some investigating because, at the end of the year, the president was sent to the missions and she never heard of him again.

At the end of the sophomore year, she told her mother that she was not going back to the Catholic school. Both of her parents insisted she go. She was getting a good education and that was necessary for her admission to a good university program. But on the opening day of school, she went to the public high school and enrolled. She called the Catholic school and told the registrar's office that the family was moving out of town and she wouldn't be re-enrolling. When the registrar at the public school told her that she needed parental approval to enroll and transcripts, she indicated her mother had passed away and her father was a traveling salesman. He was out of town overseas for two weeks. He would not be home until the next week. She would bring a note of approval from her aunt for the present and from her father upon his return. She faked the note and told her parents a week later that she had enrolled in the public school.

Her parents were seriously disappointed but were pleased to be raising a daughter who knew what she wanted. She shared the whole story of her enrolling with her parents, but she didn't mention the priest and the sex to her parents. She felt she had taken care of that on her own and didn't need to involve her parents.

Diego had already formed an opinion of Jordan's

strength of character. She was indeed a person who knew her own mind. No one was going to shape her destiny without her acceptance. She was strong. He loved hearing anything about her. He enjoyed exploring her fun side. She had a dry and acute sense of humor that he delighted in. He was always in need of lightening up. He had been accused of being too serious about life, but it seemed to come with his sense of responsibility. He had been told from childhood that he was gifted and needed to use his gifts for the benefit of others. Brother Mark had pounded that into both Diego and Oscar and they took it seriously. He pressed himself too much and was not enjoying being a congressman as much as he thought he would. It was a serious, complex and challenging business.

And it all seemed to be all uphill. Not many in congress thought like Diego did and not many wanted to move in the direction he wanted to move. Was this where he needed to be?

Chapter 9

The Discontent Grows

Conspiracy

Eight year old Patricia Ann Pascuzzi stood beside the white grand piano on the patio of her parents' River Forest mansion, dressed in her $800 first communion dress. The crowd was gathered in the massive garden where the celebration was taking place. There were one hundred and fifty of their friends and relatives present to hear Patricia, accompanied, by her mother, sing four verses of "This Little Light of Mine". The fifth verse appeared on a six foot television screen and the crowd was urged to join in. They did so in full voice. Many, including her uncle, Dominic, had imbibed sumptuously at the bar and he was prepared to sing anything and everything. Most were in comparable condition.

Patricia attended St. Luke's elementary school in River Forest which was one of two remaining Catholic elementary schools in the Chicago area. She was a member of the 2059 First Communion class. Most of the Catholic schools had closed years earlier in 2030s. Catholic bishops had foolishly struggled for decades to keep the Catholic schools open for the ten percent of the baptized while neglecting the education of the ninety percent and then wondered why the pews were empty of the young. When the schools closed, some Catholic parents home schooled and others formed private schools. A number took their energy and concern for their child's education to improve the public schools and challenged the teachers' unions. St. Luke's was kept open until Patricia graduated from the eighth grade because of the generous gift of her father, Angelo.

The Pascuzzi family had been in the liquor and uniform rental business since prior to prohibition. In its early days the company's services were not always the first choice of the customers because they were nearly twice as expensive as the competitors' prices. But visits by the company's salesmen known in the community as violent men always resulted in a sale. When Angelo took over the business, he had taken the muscle out but in the minds of the customers there was always the possibility of a return to normal.

After his fourth Chivas, Uncle Dominic who was seated at a table near the front of the patio, initiated his favorite rant concerning the pope. "You had to know the day those ass.... cardinals put that "n....r" in the pope's chair that the Church was gonna f....g fall apart. Now there's not a single one of them sh......s who would waste more than one bullet in that b......d's brain to put the son of b...h down. They just should'a taken him out before he moved to Africa with the rest of the n....... Who would'a ever thought about this crap when he was runnin around Soldier Field? I don't know who's gonna do it, but I'll put a grand into the project".

Uncle Mario asked him if he was serious about doing away with the pope. Dominic responded "damn right, f...... a". Mario commented that it would take a hell of a lot more than a grand to get the job done and Dominic agreed.

Sam Scarletto, a distant cousin, who was sitting next to Mario, said that he had heard the idea of an assassination of the pope at his club. One of the members of the Society of Italian Artists, a euphemism for a generally non violent element of the "outfit", had told him that there was a very high ranking and very angry cardinal in the Vatican who still resided in Rome. He was eager to advance the project. He didn't know the name of the cardinal, but he was told that he would have easy access to the pope in Nigeria.

Two years after his election to the papacy in 2058, Pope Francisco Augustine announced that he would move the offices of the Vatican to Lagos, Nigeria. He thought it was appropriate for the pope to be in a country where the Church was both respected and persecuted. He felt comfortable in its environs. St. Peter's Basilica and the Vatican Museums remained open and many of the functions of the Church still occurred there, but the pope wanted to be in Africa where the Church was flourishing. He promised that after five years in Africa, he would move the Vatican to Rio where the Church was also burgeoning. The number of Catholics in Italy who actively participated in the Catholic Church had dropped to less than two million. Ironically, the Italians still baptized their children and buried their dead from the churches that remained. Those who took the time and trouble to marry also used the church. But the Italians had thought of themselves as owning the Catholic Church and had managed it for so long that they came to think of it as Italian.

The Church was a monument to be admired but not a factor in their lives. Its universality mattered not to the Italians. It happened that Rome was the center of the power and culture at the time that Christ founded the Church but Jesus had never set foot in Rome, only his Church had gone there. Peter and Paul must have been led to Rome by the Holy Spirit because that was the center of power. The confluence of Greek culture, Roman law and order and Jewish theology and tradition came together in Rome at the time of the apostles. Both Peter and Paul met their violent ends in Rome and the Church stayed on and grew.

But in Francisco's mind there was nothing sacred about Rome in his time. Rome was as secular as any city in the world and Francisco felt like he needed to be where the people of God were. So he moved to Africa. Beyond the location issue, there was a recognized and worldwide split in the Church between the religious Catholics and the secular Catholics. The seculars substantially outnumbered the religious. The split was not a split concerning holiness. There were secular Catholics who were sincere and holy in their own sense, but they didn't grasp the theology of the natural law. They had slid sideways into the relativism of secular humanism to accommodate the conventional wisdom of the modernist culture. It never occurred to them to challenge the trend. Toleration ruled. Their desire was for the Church to be modern and popular and live up to the times. At one point a Pope was asked his view of unnatural sexual relations and the Pope responded "Who am I to judge"? What he meant to say was that he does not judge the sinner, but if there is unnatural sex involved, it is a sin. The problem was that from that point forward every Catholic politician based his vote for same sex marriage and a lot of other unnatural matters on the Pope's comment.

By the same token there were religious Catholics, traditionalists who were more religious than they were holy. Their moral compass made it difficult for them to embrace the mercy of toleration. The seculars had a much easier time of dealing with the chaos and the deteriorating behavior in the stumbling culture and confused Church. They were comfortable and could live and let live. Some of the secular Catholics took their theology from the bargain basement where there were discounts on most of the Church disciplines and moral standards. They reasoned and relied on the fact that as children they had participated in some activity led by the nuns, a novena, the nine First Fridays or some magic bullet that guaranteed them a ticket on the heavenly express. So there was no need to continue to worship. Sin was outmoded, a silly notion. God was all forgiving and they were saved.

Something comparable had happened at the beginning of the Enlightenment when science and measurement turned man's attention from the spiritual to the material world. The Church authority was jettisoned and the influence of the Church was almost obliterated, but the Church survived. The modern secular/religious split involved both beliefs and practices. Less than half of the baptized Catholics practiced the faith in any way. Mass attendance ranged from five to twenty five percent in Western countries. Research showed that even among that group, only about half believed in the true presence of Jesus in the Eucharist. Substantially more than half practiced artificial birth control and about the same number supported politicians who favored abortion, embryonic stem cell research, the death penalty, euthanasia and gay marriage.

The Catholic bishops in the U.S. lacked vision. They maintained a religious instruction program that focused ninety percent of their efforts and funds on an elite fifteen percent of children whose parents were conscientious enough to sacrifice to afford to send the kids to Catholic schools and provided a program that involved thirty hours of volunteer instruction for the eighty five percent of baptized kids. The problem was that only about fifty percent of those parents were conscientious enough to get the kids to the program with any regularity. The consequence was that the vast majority of baptized Catholics came to adolescence and adulthood knowing nothing about church doctrine or morality. They went to the work place, the voting booth and to marriage and the family without the Church's adornment. The Church failed badly to involve youth in the faith.

Catholics voted for the politicians who represented what Pope John Paul II labeled "the culture of death". There had been a point at which six of the nine Justices of the Supreme Court were nominal Catholics and a large number of Senators were Catholic were but the "culture of death" prevailed lead by Catholics.

A few years after the turn of the twenty first century, it

became apparent that because of a drop in the birthrate, some European countries could not survive without immigrants to do the work and tend to the aging population. Asian and African Muslims rushed into the European cities. Over the years, many of the smaller churches throughout Italy had been turned into Muslim mosques. Only one of the great cathedrals in Italy, St. John Lateran, in Rome, was used for Muslim worship. It was still the Arch Basilica of Rome, but because it was not used often enough for celebrating mass, the Muslims simply occupied it one day and began worship services on a regular basis. The pope asked law enforcement to remove the worshippers and they did so on a number of occasions, but the worshippers kept coming back and breaking in and occupying the church. No one was prepared to put them in jail. In some countries, the law would have supported their occupation through "adverse possession" an oddity of law. It was not the first or last Catholic church in Italy or Spain to be made into a Muslim mosque. It happened as the Islamic conquest in Europe established the Ottoman empire.

Cousin Sam turned to Dominic and asked him if he was serious about being a part of the project to kill the pope. The cardinal with whom the Arts society was in contact was of the opinion that he could secure the necessary resources in Africa to make the project work without any evidence to lead to the sponsors. But it would take some time and some money. Dominic said he would need some time to think about it. It was a big step from complaining about the pope to killing him. He still believed in heaven and hell, but it might be worthwhile. How could he go to hell for cleaning up the mess that the cardinals made? He wondered what would happen once they took care of the present problem. Could the devil they know be better than?????

A lot of the hierarchy in the Church felt that they and

their offices were being diminished by the new pope. Contrary to precedent, when the new pope celebrated liturgies in St. Peter's and elsewhere they were directed to sit in the rear and the laity were seated in the front where they could see. Prior to this, the laity was always looking at the back of the bishops miters and could see nothing. The pope was eager to go directly past the hierarchy to address the people. He would provide the theology directly. The modern communications tools that were available to Francisco and were enhanced every year were perfect for communicating his message directly to the people. He was readily familiar with their capability and he was convinced that the Holy Spirit was behind the technical developments of the age. He would use them to the advantage of the Church in the service of Jesus.

The Italians were not the only national group upset with the pope. There were others, advocates whose methods for dealing with the problems of expanding population, the aging, the expanding costs of health care and the seriously disabled was to "terminate" them. The groups campaigned to put pressure on pregnant mothers to abort and on the aging to engage in suicide or active euthanasia. The death movement had literally taken over the world thinking in a materialistic naturalism. The Catholic Church was the principal opposition to the "culture of death" throughout the world. The irony was that they were sometimes joined in their opposition by the Muslims whose antipathy for Christians and Jews was intense. The population control efforts of the elite were in full force, but they had moderate resistance. In the United States, the war on the sanctity life had its ebb and flow.

When it came to the sanctity of life, the great unity of belief among Orthodox Jews, Muslims and conservative Christians was inconsequential to the political order because most Catholics left their religious beliefs outside the voting booth. The Church was opposed by the secularists and growing body of active hostile atheists. The incredibly sophisticated methods of preserving life that science and technology had provided at great cost to the taxpayers provided an existential paradox. The medical profession had the ability to save the life of some newborns as early as twenty weeks while the Supreme Court's criterion for killing the unborn was set at the third trimester, the twenty fourth week with Roe v Wade. The incongruity was lost on court and the Democratic party a principal plank of which was abortion on demand. Medical technology had exploded and there was a battle of the forces particularly in Africa and South America.

While one group was trying to save people from disease and death, others were trying to make certain that the unborn, the weak, feeble and elderly did not survive to consume the limited natural and medical resources. Some of the Non Governmental Organizations (NGOs) were working at odds with themselves. One day an organization was killing the child in the womb, the next day providing surgery for the newborn with birth defects who managed to avoid abortion. Incongruity ruled the behavior of many do-gooders.

In 2013 the President and a Democratic congress committed the nation to a disastrous governmental run health care system. It was a costly mistake and nearly caused revolution and depression. The ultimate goal was a government provided health care system that was by historical definition inferior. In the run-up to the disaster, people lost their existing insurance and many were left without coverage or coverage they could not afford. There came a point post the establishment of the program where insurance companies raised their rates to unconscionable levels indicating that they had a fiduciary responsibility to their investors and that they would not cover the healthcare until the government would agree to reimburse them at the higher levels. There was a shortage of doctors to serve the general public and a plethora of concierge doctors for the well healed.

Taxes had to be substantially raised to cover the cost of the program and much of the payment was deferred by borrowing. It created a serious burden for the young and began a downward slide and accelerated the process of the young abandoning the aged. In the mid-twenties, the youthful working and tax-paying population favored measures that amounted to an embrace of the "culture of death" as no previous generation had. The value of human life had been on a slippery slope for sixty years and young people had unconsciously absorbed the moral slide. They were weary of the tax burden necessary to support the expanding elderly population whose lives were being extended with new drugs and costly medical technology. The medical technology and the interventions were being developed and paid for by the increasing taxes on the dwindling number of young tax payers.

Less than half the country was working. The young were seriously asking "who needs a ninety year old, for that matter, who needs an eighty year old. They've had their time and we can no longer afford the luxury of their extended lives".

Government controlled health care, what care there was and to whom it would be given. Congresspersons were pressured to act and responded by excluding some of the more sickly elderly from care. The government was no longer willing to provide replacement parts, knees, hips, shoulders etc for those over seventy five because of the cost. The harvesting and sale of black market body parts both human and manufactured to assist the aged had expanded. They were purchased by the rich. Black market surgeons were available in the larger cities. Occasionally, poor families pooled funds to purchase a part for a loved one. The government was aware of the practice, but could do little because it was government that created the need.

One commentator noted that the problem with America was that it was not sufficiently socialistic to support a government run health care system. Socialized medicine worked in countries where pervasive socialism preceded universal government funded care. But Americans still retained an appetite for freedom and a measure of the independent spirit that shaped the country.

There had been some breakthroughs with adult and umbilical cord stem cell therapies that cured some diseases. But after billions of dollars spent for experimentation with embryonic stem cell research and development, the effort had been largely abandoned for failure to produce. It turned out that adult stem cells taken from a person could be changed to mimic embryonic cells and could match the DNA of the recipient. The promise of cells taken from unborn embryos went largely unfulfilled. Millions of unborn humans had been destroyed in the process. Again, it was a case of government subjecting people to the will of a few enlightened elite with influence over congress and the executive branch. The Supreme Court regarded themselves as the illuminated elite able to see principles and concepts invisible to the masses.

The U.S. government had assumed both the funding and management of health care and had turned a first class system into a disaster. People were dying while waiting for appointments for diagnostic purposes and greater numbers were dying while waiting for treatment. Rationing became so extensive that it was tantamount to euthanasia for anyone over seventy five whose health was threatened. Abortion and artificial birth control were provided by the federal health care program and became so widespread that the birthrate dropped to the point of no return. A return to a replacement population was impossible. The whole of Europe including Russia, Japan and China had reached that point in the early part of the century. The United States reached it in the late twenties.

The Cry of the Poor

In the first year after the pope had arrived in Nigeria, he was visited by three of his cardinals. All three were relatively young for having the "red hat" of the cardinalate and all three were known to be somewhat liberal. Each had been elevated to their positions toward the end of the reign of Francisco's predecessor. They were each bright theologians, holy and pleasant men and not given to bluster. Bishop Sanchez had interviewed the cardinal from the Sudan to elicit the topic about which they wanted to talk to the pope and to prepare him for their visit. The cardinal's response was that they needed to talk about the poverty of their people and what the Church could do to remedy the problem. That was as far as the cardinal wanted to go in identifying the topic.

During his time in the Vatican State Department, the pope had traveled to areas of enormous poverty where the contrast of the impoverished with the wealthy was sickening. He was ever conscious of that condition and frequently prayed for wisdom in how the Church might help to ameliorate poverty. He was equally aware that in most countries, not only the United States, where inequity was an obscene and vulgar reality, the rich were becoming richer and the poor, poorer. He had known impoverished people from his childhood on the south side of Chicago. He had seen enormous and dismal poverty in Washington D.C. Money in the U.S. was plentiful but not well distributed. Millions of people in cities throughout the world where he had visited were impoverished and dependent and always accompanying the poverty there was a plague of crime, violence, human trafficking, drugs and black market body parts.

There had been a time in the history when nearly all

charity came from religious motivation. Generosity had been a touchstone for Judaism. Jesus had continued the tradition as a central principle of faith. As Christianity informed the development of Western Civilization, caring for the poor began to be insinuated into governments because the people governing were Christian. Francisco had been exposed to enough American and Church history to know that most of the helping institutions in the United States and Europe had begun as religious efforts. The hospitals, many of the schools and universities and nearly all of the social service agencies began as church or synagogue sponsored institutions. As the services provided by these religious organizations began to be fostered and undertaken by well meaning politicians eager to encourage dependency on the political process and government , they came to be regarded as a government responsibility.

When these services began to be funded by taxes from individual's paychecks, taxpayers naturally began to think that the tax for social welfare discharged their individual need to render charity. The taxes that funded social services and welfare programs were sufficient in their minds to qualify as their personal works of charity. When the services became government services, they became secular activities carrying secular values some of which were contrary to the principles of the religious bodies that had initiated the service in the first place. They also became the quid pro quo for securing votes. Eventually, people eager to avoid taxes while fostering their own values initiated tax deductible foundations.

The pope's knowledge of the poverty of South America and Africa was as great as anyone's and his empathy was equal to his knowledge. In both the Senate and later in the Vatican Secretary of State's office, he had worked with the U.N. and the United States Association for International Development. He had pushed Catholic Relief Services and other religious charities to greater effort. He had worked with Non – Governmental Organizations to relieve the poverty of nations. So, assuming that the young cardinals had some imaginative proposal, he was eager to embrace them and their ideas and hear their suggestions.

Ameliorating poverty by loving service was a linchpin of Christianity and he wanted to do all he could. He hoped cardinals who were coming to visit may have some relatively inexpensive apolitical steps that his people and their political leaders could support. He thought of all the incredible good that had been done by people like Norman Borlaug to whose work Jordan had introduced him. He was fascinated by the accomplishments of a single Nobel Laureate whose work in plant genetics and plant pathology had earned him the title of "Father of the Green Revolution" and the unofficial label of "the man who saved a billion lives". His work revolutionized farming in arid impoverished areas, first in Mexico, Pakistan and India and later in Africa. His efforts helped to stave off de-forestation by multiplying yield and obviating the need to claim more forests for agriculture.

Jordan had become familiar with Borlaug by virtue of the lecture series at Iowa State University which honored the Iowa farm boy and brilliant plant geneticist. She became a big fan and followed him as he continued to further his work in Africa from his post at the University of Texas. One man's work had led to proper nutrition for billions. He faced stiff opposition however from organizations which one would imagine and hope would have been eager to support his work. Greenpeace and the World Wildlife Fund opposed him because his work led to profits by agribusinesses. And for some, profit was evil. Francisco thought clearly that in Borlaug's work the Holy Spirit was in play.

Francisco was not opposed to people making a profit. He prized the value of employment that provided dignity for the individual and hope for families. He worried about the changes that were being wrought by technological advance. But he had also seen what good people with imagination and ambition could do to create employment. He had moved to Nigeria knowing that more than half the two hundred fifty million people were earning only four dollars a day. He could see how the terrorists were able to recruit from among the poor who had no stake in peaceful labors.

Diego's knowledge of economics made him aware that income inequality came from a number of things over which the Church and frequently the government had little influence. Some causes of the inequality were under no one's influence. The creation of the microprocessor and the discovery of oil and minerals were major factors in the wealth of individuals. These developments caused a certain oligarchy in some nations and exaggerated the wealth gap between individuals and countries.

While he deplored materialism, he knew that the availability of jobs came from an economy grown by consumerism, a consumerism dependent on population growth and innovation. He had studied enough economics to be an alert witness to the changes, sensing how the roles of capital, labor and resources had morphed as the world moved to the information and technical age. There was still plenty of backbreaking labor left for people to engage in but farming, construction and factory work had changed. The availability of inexpensive transport of goods and developments in countries with inexpensive labor had changed the employment picture in both the developing nations and the developed nations. The computer and the myriad communication devices had revolutionized work and employment. Labor markets were unstable. Robots and search engines had changed business, learning and living. The electronic gathering of data took the tedium from research and accounting while it provided enlightenment for the masses. But much of the work that was not being performed by computers was being outsourced to developing nations where worker's wages were less. The change left those in the developed world suffering unemployment. Technology had replaced too many jobs too quickly. He fully recognized that globalization had become an irreversible reality, a juggernaut that could not be stopped. It was a force that raised the standard of living for some and crushed others. He prayed that those who benefitted the most would find ways to give capitalism a soul, a way where profits could be more equally shared without government intervention. He knew that government had a role. But he also knew that when the balance of private and government employment is tipped to government, it was the road to chaos. Governments would borrow money to generate jobs and the interest paid on the loans could reverse a country's economic growth.

Francisco had experienced great personal wealth and knew that properly earned and managed wealth could benefit society and the Church. As an American, he was proud of the nation where the people whose culture and ethical lives had been informed by the generosity of Judeo/Christian message stood as the most generous in the world giving billions of dollars each year to their charities. He was mindful that while the rich donated more totally, the more generous people were the people who had less. He often wished that was not the case. He was well aware that it took money to spread the gospel and was painfully conscious of the inequity in income and wealth that was rife throughout the world.

But he had seen the disastrous impoverishment of the people that had resulted from state managed economies. He had read widely and witnessed firsthand the failures of socialism and communism. He had studied economics as part of the leadership courses at the university and in his military training. He knew the shattered lives of people who lived in dictatorial nations. He knew the harm that came from the denial of freedom and from the state directing the lives of families.

He was not ignorant of the fact that there was a period in the 1960s when the Church of Rome had given closer cooperation with communist regimes in order to take pressure off the Christians in communist countries. But he had seen how aggressively and successfully St. Pope John Paul II had dealt with the communists and he favored that approach to tyrannies. As pope, Francisco didn't want to error in overstating his position on the distribution of wealth. He preached charity and hoped for both justice and charity. He thought it proper for a pope to judge outcomes of economic life and he was fully prepared to do so. But he was not prepared to back a specific system, though, he did regard himself as a capitalist having seen it function under a free society. He just hoped that the "invisible hand" that guided capitalism had a more generous heart and spirit controlling it. He had participated in enough legislation governing economies to know he did not know enough to judge the way economies should be managed. That was a prudential judgment best left to experts who knew the dynamics and history of economies.

He knew for certain that man needed freedom to work out his eternal destiny and any economic or social system that diminished man's freedom was wrong. He hoped and prayed that the efforts of free men who operated economic systems yielded justice and charity. It was his role to seek the welfare of all from whatever system the leaders chose. He felt obliged to point out problems anytime that their systems came up short of serving their people.

Christianity's core value, love of neighbor, frequently led to an economic ideology on the part of many priests, bishops and popes which was biased to the point of thinking that government should force distribution of wealth. Francisco thought that was a mistake. It was the job of priests and bishops to inspire Christians to share. He knew that some popes and bishops had stepped into the economic arena without sufficient knowledge of the dynamics. Some popes, the victims of insular thought had been urged by the input of advisors who were ill equipped with knowledge or experience in the real world economy. He had watched the Church suffer the damage of people who knew little about banking nearly manage the Vatican bank and consequently the Vatican into bankruptcy.

The Rich Man

When he was a child in his early years at St. Rita's there was a nun who often cited the biblical admonition concerning too much wealth. She would often bring up the story of Jesus telling his disciples that it was "more difficult for a rich man to get to heaven than for a camel to pass through the eye of the needle". Diego would frequently bring ideas and facts that he had been taught in school to Carmen's table for explanation. It was common for her table to be a place where she dispensed philosophy, theology and a bit of economics in children's language. Carmen believed that fostering the spiritual and emotional development of her children was as important as their physical nourishment. She made them aware that their souls longed to be with God; they longed to love and be loved and that that longing was only satisfied by their giving of themselves to others in service. It was there at Carmen's table that Diego learned that God had made the world of his love. God wanted to manifest and share his love with creatures, his children and he wanted his children to experience giving and receiving love prior to coming to God's eternal love.

Carmen knew her children were conscious of both their race and their economic status. They were a minority and not very well off financially. She wanted them to be proud of both their blackness and they Hispanic linage and she worked to make them aware of how much they had been blessed with and how much they could contribute. She admonished them not to ever think of themselves as victims or to feel sorry for themselves. They had lost their dad but he was an advocate for them with God. They were blessed with freedom, good health and faith. They had what they needed to do whatever they wanted to do in life.

She warned her children at a young age not to seek or to keep too many possessions. She taught them that having too much to preserve or protect could distract them from their most important purpose in serving others for the love of God. Diego listened to his mother and adopted her advice. Carmen lived simply. After Frankie died, she never owned an automobile. Renaldo was too young to drive. She had never had a driver's license and she preferred to walk. It gave her time to think. Times when she was walking the children to school were moments to spend with them alone and listen. As a result of her advice, Diego tended to travel light in life. Even when he served in congress, he never kept more than four business suits or pairs of shoes, never more than one watch, television or car. It was just his way.

After Carmen died, Brother Mark shared a couple of anecdotes that illustrated Carmen's common sense theology that she suggested to Father Kevin for consideration. He told Diego about the times when Carmen would gently challenge some comment that Father Kevin had made in his Sunday homily. One time Father Kevin had indicated that man could not in any way contribute to the greatness of God. Carmen told him to take a good look at all the people in the pews who were responding eagerly to God's wishes. God's greatness was certainly enhanced by their worship and he had to be more pleased with them being there than if they were home nursing a hangover. She was of the opinion that no matter how people were dressed, how they behaved in church or how loud the kids may be, they were there to worship which is all God asked.

Then she added he should take a good look at her kids to see how God's greatness was being manifested and expanded. Another time she disagreed with Kevin about the idea that man would not receive a glorified body until the resurrection. She was confident that Frankie already had a glorified body because his perfect happiness in seeing God could not be added to at the resurrection. She couldn't see how his perfect happiness could not be made more perfect. Brother Mark said that on both of those occasions and others, Father Kevin would just say "I'll have to think more about that" and he would.

Carmen shared with her kids that man's purpose was to demonstrate love for God by caring for and helping to meet the needs of others, their brothers whom God created. Her notion was that man comes into life dependent on others as an infant. He needs to be rendered nurture and education as he grows. As he matures he becomes a giver of help to those in need, his spouse, his children, his parents and those in his community. In his maturity, he expands his sense of generosity and concerns himself with the needs of others who are his contemporaries and those in need in the future. He shares with those in need throughout the world, those who suffer malnutrition, poverty, war, disaster.

She emphasized that God gave man the freedom to choose to help or not help, to do good or fail to do good. She often told the kids that God would never force them to do good. It was up to them. In God's plan for man they could choose good freely when they cared for the needs of others. Their freedom would be shattered if God or any government forced them to go beyond justice and render charity to others. She believed that the government that governs people's behavior but excludes God from the public square had no moral claim to force the virtue of charity, a spiritual act. She used to say that's God's job.

Diego carried that theology of man, charity and justice with him throughout his life. It was his motivation as a child when he would work with his friends to meet the needs of one of their friends or some neighbor in need. It was his motivation in sharing his considerable wealth from his successful football career. He carried Carmen's theology of charity into the papacy and wanted to share it with his flock. He often promoted charity among his fellow athletes especially those with big contracts who could afford it. He saw both the good and the evil that could come from people having and sharing wealth.

He witnessed foundations supported by the wealthy who received valuable tax benefits by contributing to activities that he knew were harmful to man and society. But the tax structure was such that they were free to do so. In the twenty teens and early twenties, billions of tax deducted dollars had been spent in countries with people of color to limit births by providing artificial birth control devices. It was pushed on women who opposed artificial birth control and they were made to feel guilty about having more than one child. The funds came from an American computer billionaire whose feminist wife wanted to direct the people of Africa. The program was a form of unofficial foreign policy that spoke the wrong message to the minority women, "there are too many of you for our good". It was Francisco's job and that of his fellow believers to evangelize and convert them to see the sacredness of life.

On the other hand, activities like Norman Borlaug's were a very positive foreign policy message. Subsequent to Borlaug's considerable progress other programs helped in challenging malnutrition. Discoveries that mapped the DNA of plants led to genetically modified (GM) foods that increased yield even further. But that progress too was fought by tax deducted foundation funds used by people who feared that the foods were profitable. On flimsy science, they believed that the GM foods were dangerous because they were unnatural and could lead to disease. There had been no hard research after many years to demonstrate it but people continued to believe.

Diego found it incongruous that the people who seemed to run the world had walked away from the natural law in every other area of endeavor, but some well fed elitists were worried about genetically modified food. It resulted in less food available to the mal- nourished. The elites made every effort to stop its progress by false claims. Uninformed politicians followed their lead and scared the people.

Francisco Augustine hoped a positive outcome may result from his meeting with the cardinals. They met for a light lunch on the reclaimed open air patio atop the garage of the abandoned psychiatric unit where the pope lived. They enjoyed a glass of an inexpensive African white table wine. The pope toasted them with his usual "thanking God for faith in Jesus, for family, friends and freedom and for those who provide our food, those who nurture our faith and those who protect our freedom". The lunch was light and they didn't linger over it. When they had finished eating, the dishes were cleared by Brother Juan and they were served the pope's stout Columbian coffee.

The cardinals had come to talk poverty. They first mentioned a proposal that had had many different versions over the years. They discussed what a splendid display of charity it would be for the Church to divest itself of all the many holdings that made the Church the object of much scorn especially by the socialists and communists. If the Church sold its art treasures it would be evidence of its lack of attachment to materialism. The pope shared with them that nearly every modern pope had had a quiet commission of one sort or another which had explored that very topic. Often the commissions included patrons of the arts, curators, investment bankers, artists, lay people and a cardinal or bishop. Invariably they came to the same conclusion. The art treasures would not yield the fortune that some assumed they would and that some splendid treasures, many of which were of a religious origin, could fall into the hands of commercial interests or museums some of whom may have no respect for their spiritual value to man.

The example used in the last report was a bit preposterous but stated the problem realistically. He told them to imagine the Pieta sitting in the Brooklyn museum next to the <u>Piss Christ</u> a project sponsored by the tax funded American's National Endowment for the Arts. The sacrilege would be awful. Further the commissions had always determined that the art motivated by the spirit and designed to lift the spirit should always be displayed for all the people in a spiritual setting. While it was positive that spiritual art is displayed in public, it was still necessary to maintain spirit lifting art in the Church lest all that was in the public became commercial and restricted in an effort to make it more valuable for the few.

When it came to the other commissions that addressed the idea of disposing of the vast land holdings of religious organizations, it was determined that most of the holdings were in the hands of local dioceses or parishes and varied radically in value. While the pope could suggest to the holders that they could sell the land and give the money to the poor, the he couldn't sell the land. In too many instances the land was in places where the value of the land was less than when it was purchased.

The matter that the cardinals believed was the best hope for dealing with poverty was touchy and as a consequence was mentioned last in the discussion. The remedy would require an act of much greater theological significance than the distribution of money from art or land. The cardinals were blunt in saying that they thought that the best hope for the relief of poverty was for the pope to find some accommodation in order to endorse artificial birth control.

Francisco was gravely disappointed that they didn't bring to the table some idea or knowledge of some important scientific or cultural breakthrough that would increase employment or increase agricultural production. That was the hope he had brought to the discussion. Secular governments and non-governmental organizations had for years been providing shots and devices for artificial birth control everywhere in the world, especially in the developing nations. Francisco thought the practice had a tinge of racism because most of the Caucasian "do-gooders" work to limit populations was undertaken in neighborhoods or countries populated by people of color. He had seen it happen in Chicago, Washington and Rio. The enlightened activists were under the sway of population alarmists and eugenics promoters such as Margaret Sanger, founder of Planned Parenthood who thought that there were too many minorities and feeble minded in the U.S. Many in the developed nations thought there were already too many people of color in the world and had set out to lessen the birthrate in those countries.

Much U.S. and European tax money and tax deducted foundation money was spent to limit births in undeveloped third world countries. But the officials of those countries didn't interfere because they agreed there were too many poor people of color. The Catholic Church had vigorously opposed the effort and it had not gone well in areas where the Church exercised influence. The cardinals didn't come right out with "please

change the natural law and approve of artificial birth control",
but they were stating obvious secular arguments attacking the
barriers and trying to break down the hedges that Pope Paul VI
established in "Humanae Vitae" back in 1968. Many theologians
had challenged Pope Paul's principle. For nearly a hundred years,
each challenge employed some slight twist about how God
would want people to use their heads and exercise scientific
discovery. Each advocate of the effort to forsake the natural law
had been met with the same natural law argument that the
Church had embraced as the foundation of all morality. The pope
listened attentively and respectfully making only occasional
comment.

When he was certain that they had made all of their
points, the pope sighed and gave a brief smile to each of them.
He told them that they had certainly done their homework and
that their arguments were reasonable if they were proposing
their solutions to a court, a government or a teacher none of
whom were bound in their work by the natural law. But their
arguments could not overturn what had been the Church's
standard from its initiation, the natural law given by God. He
indicated that in his own chapel, he had prayed to God that he
would be given some illumination that would allow him to go to
the poor of the world and say to them that God would exempt
them from the natural law and that artificial birth control was
moral and acceptable. He told the cardinals that he would not
have enough priests to baptize all the people that would cheer
and return or join the Church. He would also delight in telling
all those, who, though they may not be poor, suffered by trying
to be faithful to the Church teaching on the natural law. He was
concerned for the group of people who loved others of the
same sex. He said he would personally be eager to dispense
them from the natural law. But he said that neither he, nor the

Church had made the natural law that governed behavior and he couldn't find his way to suspending it no matter how attractive or pleasing it would be.

He reminded them that God was the one who designed man and woman differently in his desire to propagate his children, to generate and sustain his kingdom. He had planted the natural law in the heart of man. Man knows when he acts naturally and when he departs from the natural law. The cardinals knew that what they were asking was for the pope to violate God's law. Francisco promised the cardinals that he would pray and do everything possible within his capability to advocate for the poor, but he couldn't change the natural law. They went away saddened but knowing that the pope was correct.

The "Incarnation Initiative"

The pope had been concerned for a very long time about the extremes to which materialistic secularists had pushed what one of his predecessors, St John Paul II had labeled the "culture of death". During his second year in the papacy, Francisco determined to address the lack of appreciation for the sanctity of life. He wrote an encyclical of which every word was his own. He titled the encyclical, The Birth of Jesus Christ, God. The secular media labeled it the "Incarnation Initiative".

The focus of the encyclical didn't specifically address the birth of Jesus; those were just the first words of the encyclical. After publishing the encyclical, he began regular "tweets" on the same subject in order to communicate directly to his flock. He marveled at the development of communication devices and was taken by the technology that allowed his tweets to be received in the language of the user. In his mind the spirit was active in the ether enlightening man in unusual ways and spreading the gospel. Somehow Jesus direction to the apostles to share the good news with all the world was being undertaken in wondrous ways. The encyclical spoke to the reality that God had become man in the most human of ways, through the womb of a young Jewish woman. The central point of the encyclical spoke to the incarnation of God when the Holy Spirit miraculously overshadowed the Blessed Virgin Mary and she became pregnant with Jesus. Francisco emphasized the fact that the incarnation was the point at which the salvation of the world and for each person began.

The other events of salvation history, the birth, the ministry, the miracles, the teaching, death on the cross and the resurrection were essential to salvation, but the incarnation was the beginning. Jesus became man. Salvation began in the womb of a teenage girl in Nazareth. The being whom St. Anselm referred to as <u>That than Which Nothing Greater Can Be Thought</u> became man in order to sanctify life and provide the opportunity for all to live a joyful eternal life face to face with him. He had created in love and furthered his love in coming as man.

In an effort to stress the sanctity of each being in the womb, Francisco urged his flock to focus on the fact that the Virgin Mary was pregnant with Jesus for nine months. He pointed out that Jesus was at one time a blastocyst, a zygote and a fetus, an unborn human from the moment of his conception, before his birth at Christmas. Though he is God, he is fully human as is every fetus. The pope did not intend to make the thrust of his papacy exclusive to dealing with moral issues to the exclusion of social issues but he was painfully conscious of just how radically the world was being affected by the killing in the womb. History was being robbed by mothers who were acting in the place of God when they determined to kill their off- spring.

Mothers were acting as God determining who would live and who would die, actions that would have meaning over the centuries. The people of the world were being denied. God's plan was irrevocably altered and generation after generation suffered the loss. Each person suffered loss of some of the people who were supposed to be the angels in their lives. Generations of families whom God had planned to be part of his kingdom on earth were missing. Whole nations, cultures and economies were being seriously harmed.

Though the astronomers of the time put the birth of Christ at the rise of certain star in the east, the time of the year when Christ was born was not significant to the reality of God becoming man. The fact that Jesus was God and man was what mattered. History did not recall the date. It had become tradition based on the gospel story. To further the focus on the sanctity of the life in the womb, the pope introduced an initiative to shift the celebration of God becoming man from Christmas to the feast of the Incarnation on March 25. He encouraged people to celebrate spiritually the arrival of God on that date with gifts, given not to those in their families and circle of friends, but to those who were unable to reciprocate, people in the third world and those impoverished in their own countries. He accepted the fact that there would be those, even among the religious Catholics, who would be so wed to traditions of Christmas that they would not respond to the initiative.

The accidents of the celebration of Jesus birth, the presents and partying had become more important than the spiritual significance. He thought that the initiative would generate a more spiritual celebration. It would please Jesus and would contribute to building the kingdom of God. He was so dismayed with how secular and commercialized the celebration of Christ's birth had become, that he felt a need for a radical shift of the focus from the birth of Christ to the initial manifestation of God among his people. It was important to shift from materialism to the spiritual celebration of God among us. He was comfortable that there might just be a few who would follow the initiative.

He was accused from within and without the Church of trying to destroy Christmas for the children, destroying what the beloved St Francis of Assisi had established with the crèche. Ironically, the initiative met with acceptance in the thoughts of many, even among the secular Catholics and even among some non- Christians who felt oppressed by the demands of the increasingly secular Christmas. Christmas had become a winter holiday and was not really a celebration of Jesus birth. Shopping, skiing and consumption were the focus of the period. Expectations of some great emotional lift from celebrating Christmas too often resulted in the pressure of spending and trying to choose the perfect gift. It often ended in a letdown of a forced celebration that had no spiritual boost. Depression was common among those who thought their happiness was found in a new handbag or an "I" this or that.

In the second year of the initiative, the acceptance of the idea of shifting from December 25 to March 25 and celebrating the Incarnation became so popular that there was a significant drop off in the Christmas shopping season. Even some of the Catholic priests became conscious of the need to recognize and promote the sanctity of life. People, including the children were participating in special liturgies that Pope Francisco designed and uploaded to the web for the Incarnation. Homilies addressed the sanctity of all human life and that love was manifest in the sharing with people unable to reciprocate. Some shopping occurred in March, but by and large, gifts to the poor throughout the world were made in financial contributions to non-profit charities that could make direct pass through of financial assistance to the individuals in third world countries. A considerable amount of the gift giving was in the donation of universal credit cards where the card could be put in the hand of a poor person anywhere in the world and could be used to purchase what they needed or wanted. Clearly, the Holy Spirit was involved. Merchants in the developed nations tended to suffer the most. In the third year of the Initiative, Black Friday fell short of the black in the developed nations. Manufacturers and trade nations shifted their marketing to the underdeveloped nations where the money was being sent and spent. Overall, there was a huge drop-off in the manufacture and trade for the Chinese economy and among many Western merchants. In the underdeveloped countries, necessities were purchased.

As the trends developed further, the Chinese felt a need to somehow halt the process and the central government began to look at the most vulnerable spot in which to attack the problem initiative. They began to identify the problem as the pope. They needed to address the issue. The pope was too young to let this initiative progress any further. But how best could they approach and rid themselves of the problem without detection and eventual international sanction? It became a major issue. The last assassination attempt on a pope had been in the last century by a young Turkish man. When caught, he said that he was assigned his mission by the Bulgarian mafia, but no there was no evidence and no sanction was visited on Bulgaria. So far as any investigation was concerned the assassin acted independent of government. In the end, the pope went to the assassin's jail cell to forgive him. Could the Chinese pull off the same without appearing to be involved?

By the twenties, China and India had emerged as the lenders to the world but their own economies had begun to falter. The pope's initiatives were consequential to their economies. China's economy depended on the American and European "black Friday". They needed that to continue growth. Both countries were not only the financiers to the world; they also owned much of the developed world despite their roller coaster economy. The United States had indebted itself to the point where funding the interest took nearly have the revenue and the country was dependent on China for further funding. China and Chinese interests were making an effort to own greater and greater interests globally but especially in U.S. including the means of production. It had worked out exactly as the Chinese had planned.

The World Bank had become the default backup in the event the Chinese did not buy in. The European Union had fallen on hard times early in the century and never quite recovered. The International Monetary Fund suffered a major wide spread financial fraud involving a dozen countries in which tens of billions were lost. While all of the monetary fumbling was underway, there was a powerful group of international financiers who were pressing to establish a single world currency. The weak dollar had given way back to various currencies for trade purposes and it was difficult for the financiers and the governments to rely on as a single stable currency. Along with those who longed for a single world court, the financiers wanted a one world currency.

President Benson, late in his first term, declined to rent additional money from China to support the Fund and to fund the U.N. leaving the European Union with China as their banker. The role of NATO was damaged when Russia marched on the Balkans and the outskirts of Eastern Europe. The young male and female Russian population had fallen so radically that the President of Russia needed manpower more than land for his attempt to reclaim world status. The outcome left Europe without much of a voice in the international community. Britain and France still held onto their veto vote in the Security Council in the U.N., but the U.N. was toothless. Earlier, they had lessened their commitment to any effort to defend democracies and the United States had pulled significant numbers of troops from Europe, leaving Europe largely toothless.

A part of what the media referred to as the "Incarnation Initiative" was the establishment of a formal ceremony to aid women who had lost a child to in the womb to a spontaneous death and a formal Church sponsored blessing and program for women who wished to become mothers. Francisco selected a woman whom he had known in Brazil while serving as a brother to serve as the vice-Prefect of the Congregation on the Liturgy. She had had three mis carriages as a young woman and had the sense that the Church, its higherarcy and priests had little appreciation for the fact that a child of God with an eternal soul had come into the world and happened to die in the womb. She advised Diego that in those instances when the child was sufficiently developed to show a body capable of being seen and handled, there needed to be a formal mass and burial. Francisco agreed and such a mass was initiated celebrating the short life of the child. He was certain that the children never having sinned qualified for membership among the saints. This induced the common practice of naming the child and of aiding those who had lost children to see them as heavenly advocates for the family. The Church became a little more human.

Pope Francisco began the substitution of "Conception Cards" for Christmas and birthday cards. While still a seminarian, he had designed a series of "Conception Cards" that celebrated a person's conception, the day on which a person received their DNA, their body and soul. He sent the cards to his cardinals and bishops. The cards were sent nine months before their births reminding them that they had been given their soul at conception and that they had existed as human beings in the womb for those the nine months prior to their birth. He urged them promote the cards among their priests and people to recognize the sanctity and humanity of the being in the womb. After a couple of years, the practice became more common and the greeting card companies began to print and distribute the cards. A couple of artistic card designers and some of the staff members in the humor divisions in the greeting card companies became well known with truly imaginative cards. Who could argue with the celebration of becoming a human being?

Prior to leaving Rome, Pope Francisco had cleared the Curia of the dead wood, the cardinals who found it difficult to accept change. His theology flourished among those who felt a need for a renewal but was regarded as heresy just as often as it was praised.

Chapter 10

Celebration

A Different World

The celebration in the Ishmala home in the valley of Dammaj was to honor Abdul the eldest of the five Ishmala children. He had recently completed his studies at Thamar University, one of the newest and finest universities in Yemen, the nation he loved. He was the 2040 honor student in Islamic studies and intended to teach all that he had learned, to teach the truth from his elevated perspective. A handsome youth with dark deep set eyes, a sculpted physique and curly black hair fashionably coifed. He was possessed of a smile that melted the resistance of any female within view. He was confident and religious, conservative and disciplined.

His parents couldn't be more proud of their first born. His father, Muhammad, was a teacher in a middle school and expected Abdul to go on to further study, but both Abdul and the family would need to save to fund his further studies. Perhaps he would be able to teach for a while in the middle school with his father. The family was proud, religious and tight knit. They had made a pilgrimage to Mecca together two years before.

Abdul wanted to teach in the local madrassa that was founded by Shaikh Muqbil bin Hadi Al-Waadi'I, the renowned Sunni Islamic scholar. This was the school that was the seat of wisdom that constituted the majority of his study at the university. It was the center of Salafist ideology and that was

Abdul's focus. But the ideology needed to be updated, to become more aggressive in its relations with infidels. Wadi'i was a vigorous and vocal opponent of Osama Bin Laden. He disapproved of his radical actions. But after the Waadi'i's death, the madrassa was taken over by s Salafist Sunni with a radical agenda.

Abdul's parents were patient and peaceful Muslims, but Abdul had developed an edge in his schooling that made him impatient to convert the entire world to Islam. It was time and if it had to be done by violence and domination, then so be it. He would be a part of it. He didn't however share his vision with his parents out of respect for their views.

He secured a position at the madrassa and associated with the most radical element of the faculty. After less than two years he became leader of a faction that took over the philosophical direction of the curriculum and practices. Only those who were of his belief were considered for faculty positions. After five years of leading the radical faction in the school, he became restless. He had accomplished what he could at the madrassa and needed to move on to something more radical. He viewed Osama as the visionary who completed only a small part of what needed to be done to stop the negative influence of Western civilization on the world. Things had to change and he would be a part of it or he would die trying.

He left the madrassa and moved to Islamabad in Pakistan where he was welcomed by a madrassa more radical that his previous one. He became a lead teacher. He brought a new energy and was recognized immediately as a leader in the school and the associated community. He became part of a cell that promoted radical activity against those elements of the government who were trying to liberalize and secularize the nation. He had known from childhood that Pakistan had the

[Type text]

bomb and he wanted to find some way to form a group that could obtain at least one bomb. It would change everything if just one bomb could be smuggled into the United States or Israel. Exploding an atomic bomb in New York City, Chicago or Los Angeles or better, Jerusalem or Tel Aviv would change a lot. Death and fear would be rampant in both countries.

This would be rewarding like nothing else in his life. This became his mission. He felt compelled to finish Bin Laden's work. But he needed to be a part of those who controlled access to the bomb. He needed to be a part of the government though he hated all those with power. He had always had a problem with authority even though his parents weren't in any way authoritarian. He would bide his time until an opportunity appeared. Then he would become famous dead or alive. It mattered not.

In the meantime, he would engage in less significant challenges to the infidel. With a colleague, he would fashion a half dozen teenage potential suicide bombers, kids who attended the madrassa. He had learned from those who had set suicide bombers on their missions, that the best candidates were youth who were exceedingly religious and not too bright. They could be shaped in secrecy and prepared for missions that had limited means of detection. Initially, he had considered becoming a suicide bomber himself and to undertake a mission that would be noticed by the entire world, something with great religious significance.

His dream was to go to Jerusalem and stand at the "wailing wall" with hundreds of Jews praying and to explode himself and them. It would be noticed and remembered. He would be noticed and remembered. The other dream he held was to stand at the main altar in St. Peter's in Rome or St. Patrick's in New York during a ceremony and destroy the symbols of Christianity for the entire world to see.

His colleague at the madrassa had persuaded him that he was meant for bigger things than to destroy himself with a suicide bomb. He could have impact by using the teenagers as bombers. But Abdul needed to be assured that they could have impact sooner rather than later. He could bide his time but only for a while. He needed action. He needed to be needed by the larger jihad.

Chapter 11

Another Death

It's Definitely Murder

Dr. Bender, the pope's personal physician entered the chapel and came directly to the pope's side. He indicated that the deaths were from poisoning and that under the circumstance, they were obliged to call in law enforcement. They had called on what they believed to be a secure line which would not alert the press. But the press would learn soon enough. The pope motioned to Bishop Sanchez in the back of the chapel to join them when the doctor had walked in. The pope told Doctor Bender that his staff would handle the press if he would join them in explaining the cause of death. Francisco couldn't imagine what could have happened. Prior to making any press statement, he hoped to learn more of what had led to the deaths. He sat in with the Chief of the Swiss Guard while the police questioned Bishop Sanchez and Brother Bruno about what happened after he had left the dining room the night before.

No one could find Sister Sophia. They searched the entire complex hoping that she was not sick and fallen somewhere in her illness. He recalled that when he left the dining room the night before he said to Father Flores "Father, I know you will do your best both to eat an extra portion and to thank and congratulate Sister Sophia for me for her extra effort. A little fasting cannot hurt me. I have found the excellent meals here in Nigeria to be a temptation to which I too readily give in. I would see it as an act of charity and not as a matter for the confessional if, without direct prevarication, you should somehow lead sister to the assumption that I have eaten and enjoyed her meal. Good night and God bless the remainder of your day. And Bishop, please ask Cardinal Sardino to come over tomorrow at 10AM. Fathers, please pray tonight for both the Africans and the Americans."

He later learned that when he had departed, his Secretary Bishop Sanchez stayed on at the table but did not eat the menudo. He went straight to the chimichangas. Bishop Sanchez reported that Bishop Stepanovich had asked Father Flores if he thought the soup was saltier than usual. Father Flores, who had grown up in Brazil and was much given to spice, responded "I think it is just right for my taste, but then I can't be given too much spice. I thought it could use more pepper, a condition that I remedied myself."

Bishop Sanchez remembered hearing Bishop Stepanovich say that the menudo made him very thirsty and that the bishop had taken a long pull and drained his glass of Chianti. Then he left saying "I'm going to go to my apartment. Thank Sister and tell her the dinner was excellent. And, please come to my apartment in about an hour and a half and I will bring you up to date on Africa. If we have time, perhaps you can bring me up to date on South America where I understand wonderful things are happening in the Church". As he was about to leave he drank the remainder of his water, poured another glass and also finished that.

Father Flores was a large man, over six foot tall carrying more than two hundred fifty pounds. He enjoyed his meals. He finished the meal and walked into the kitchen where he hoped Sister Sophia might have a left over piece of the raspberry cheese cake she had served at the noon meal. Instead, he found Brother Juan, the assistant cook whom Father Flores had been certain had coaxed Sister Sophia to cook the Mexican dinner and who undoubtedly had coached her through it. He was from Mexico

[Type text]

City and loved his native land and food. When allowed, he would sometimes return to the kitchen after it had closed and prepare a Mexican meal which he would share with Father Flores when he was available. They had become good friends.

Brother Juan indicated to the police that Sister Sophia had gone to her room early and had left the clean-up to him, which he didn't mind at all. It gave him the opportunity to arrange the pots, pans and shelves and spices for easy use. On occasion, he would take something small to his room for a late night snack while he read or prayed. He took the position that if it was ok to pray while you eat; it was certainly ok with God to eat while you pray.

Father Flores told Brother Juan that the Bishop thought the meal was very salty. Brother Juan remarked that Sister Sophia and he had eaten their meal early. Sister Sophia may have added additional salt after they had eaten. He saw her add something but he was just leaving the kitchen to the storeroom when she was doing so and he was too far away to see if it was salt. He noted that she ate almost nothing herself and assumed she didn't feel well. She returned early to her room, a rare occurrence. Father Flores asked Brother Juan to tell Sister tomorrow how much they all enjoyed the meal.

At 10:15 pm the telephone rang in the make-shift infirmary that had been set up in the Nigerian "Vatican". It had been established only six months ago. When the pope moved his offices, the Secretary of State, the Office of the Prefect of Sacred Doctrine, the manager of the Vatican Bank and some canon lawyers to Africa for the five year period, he did so too quickly in Sister Agnes view. Sister hoped he didn't do so that quickly when the move was to Brazil. The phone rang five times before Sister Agnes answered. She had already retired and had dozed off. She heard the fifth ring and picked it up very surprised that anyone would call her at that hour.

She could see from the caller id system that it was Bishop

Stepanovich's number. He could barely speak, but she concluded that he needed help quickly. She called his Secretary Monsignor David Bloom and asked him to go to the bishop's room immediately because the bishop needed help. She then called Doctor Bender who lived just outside the compound and asked him to come to the infirmary. Monsignor Bloom called Sister five minutes later after entering the bishop's room. He indicated that he found him unconscious on the floor having regurgitated with a show of red blood. The bishop was gasping for air and couldn't talk.

Sister called Brother Bruno the assistant infirmarian to the bishop's room and she pushed a gurney to the room. She knew little of the bishop's
medical history. She was trying to think through any health conditions that might be present in the compound and could think of none. No one reported the flu or a serious cold. When she saw the bishop, she knew they had to hurry him to the infirmary and prayed that Doctor Bender would be there. She knew that it was a matter well beyond her skills.

Doctor Bender came into the infirmary at nearly the same time as the bishop was being wheeled in. He took one look at his face and concluded that he was either in serious shock or going into a coma. He knew immediately that the bishop was in need of care far beyond the capability of the infirmary and needed to be moved to St Monica's Hospital, which happily was located next door to the pope's facilities which were located in the abandoned psychiatric wing. He needed to stabilize him first.

As he was doing so, the phone rang again. The doctor told Sister Agnes to continue to help him. It was unlikely there was another emergency and that the orderly Brother Bruno could handle it. In thirty years at the Vatican, Doctor Bender had never had two emergencies on the same day let alone in the same

[Type text]

month. He hoped things would remain calm in Nigeria where there were far fewer members of the pope's household. A Swiss Guard had entered the infirmary and was observing. Brother Bruno looked at the caller id and knew it was Father Flores. He answered the phone and his face turned colorless. Brother knew he was going to be called upon to do something beyond his training and skills. Father Flores could barely whisper and was gasping. He said he needed help quickly. The doctor told Brother Bruno to go to the room with the gurney and if Father Flores was in bad shape to bring him to the infirmary. The doctor could not leave the infirmary and could not spare Sister Agnes.

Doctor Bender and Sister Agnes had given no thought to the pope. They had not thought of a food connection only of disease or trauma. They had done all they could to stabilize Bishop Stepanovich who was now definitely in coma. He ordered Brother Bruno and the Swiss Guard to take the bishop to the emergency entrance and to tell the ambulance attendant that the doctor would follow as quickly as possible. They were to tell whoever was in charge in emergency room to undertake whatever was necessary and that Doctor Bender would be there momentarily and would share what little he knew. He then turned to stabilizing Father Flores who was in virtually the same condition as the bishop. His efforts at stabilization resulted in the same outcome, a comatose patient.

On his way to the emergency room, he called Doctor Helmut Gutmann, a German gastroenterologist who practiced in a charity hospital in Lagos. He asked Doctor Gutmann to come to the hospital as quickly as possible. He shared the symptoms and indicated that it was serious matter. Doctor Bender's first fear was that his patients' condition could be contagious. He knew that both of them were widely traveled and may have been contagious for a while. He was told that both Father Flores and Bishop Stepanovich had eaten at the pope's table but did not immediately consider that a cause. The guard had shared that he had asked his superior to have someone check on the pope's condition and when informed he would let the doctor know if the pope was OK.

Doctor Gutmann was used to little sleep and almost welcomed the call. A bachelor, he spent most evenings trading stocks on the American exchanges and he found the market was too wobbly to trade. He indicated he would be there in about fifteen minutes and that they should prepare both patients for surgery in the event it was needed. Doctor Gutmann then called his associate Doctor Scarcello, an Italian gastroenterologist who was helping out at the charity hospital and urged him to join him. Dr. Scarcello had a charming new young bride, with whom he had planned an evening, but duty was duty. He was a physician and he would go.

When the other doctors arrived in the emergency room, Doctor Bender had Fr. Flores connected to a respirator, but he was failing. He had not entirely stopped breathing on his own, but he was struggling and he wanted to keep him in as good a condition as possible in the event he needed surgery. They were preparing him for surgery when the lab report came back indicating poison. After a conference, they concluded surgery would be futile. And indeed it would have been. When they re-entered the emergency room Fr. Flores had already expired.

When the police had finished their interrogation, Bishop Sanchez met with the pope's spokesman who prepared a press statement as quickly as possible. The pope was barely awake when he approved the statement. Dr. Bender had urged him to sleep. Prior to his leaving the room however, the Lagos detective who had been assigned conferred with the Chief of the Swiss Guard and indicated that based on what they had learned, the pope should not be without immediate security until they learn more of what happened and why.

[Type text]

The detective didn't like the fact that Sister Sophia was missing. He would secure some help and undertake an immediate facility search for Sister Sophia along with the help of the Swiss Guard. He also indicated that he would return to the complex at eight the next morning to continue the investigation. He would leave two detectives to work through the night on the case. He advised the Chief of the Swiss Guard that if either of them learned anything in the meantime, they should inform each other.

Dr. Bender accompanied the pope to his apartment where two Swiss Guards were posted at the door. The pope prayed briefly and retired. As he closed his eyes, he prayed his traditional prayer telling God that he believed, he trusted and he loved God and asked God to bless him with divine mercy as he drifted to a fitful sleep. He was back in the Marines. He had been frustrated by both the brevity and the unsuccessful end of his Marine career and turned to that frustration sometimes in a fitful sleep. He was always frustrated by unfinished matters. He never chose to visit his worst frustration concerning Jordan when he was trying to sleep.

Chapter 12

Reunion

Some Basic Inquiries

After two weeks of communication with Jordan limited to the phone calls, Diego was frustrated. He wanted desperately to see Jordan. He called early one evening after he had stopped on the way home for a couple of beers with his administrative assistant. He was more relaxed than he normally was. When he began to talk with Jordan, she said that she had just arrived home after stopping with one her co-workers for a glass of wine. He could tell that she too was more relaxed than normal. He told her that he was really missing her and would do anything to see her. She relented on her commitment not to see him.

She said that she could fix something to eat at her place but that she would rather go for a hamburger if he could get there quickly. She said she was starving and slightly loose. He rushed over and they walked to a nearby sports grill, more of a greasy spoon than a yuppie bar. But there was food. He had a draught beer and she had a merlot. They were both more talkative than they had ever been. He thought and likely she thought "in vino, veritas". But he didn't say it. He asked how she had been doing and she said she was fine and busy, both at work and in her personal life.

[Type text]

For her to be busy in her personal life did not sound good to Diego because her business did not include him. He pursued the topic a bit and learned that she had been reading a great deal of material related both to her employment and her personal development. Congress was about to recess and she was busy wrapping up project details that had been proposed. Diego was looking forward to the break, but that was when a lot of congresspersons liked to travel at taxpayers' expense. She told him that she had been assigned to travel a week out each of the next three months, Argentina, Europe and India.

Diego didn't have any trips planned. He wanted to spend as much time with his mother and the family as possible. Carmen had been diagnosed with cancer and was taking chemo treatment. Renaldo had said that she was failing.

He asked Jordan if she had made any progress in dealing with her dilemma, knowing what her life was about. She said that she really didn't want to seem cryptic about what was bothering her but that is was personal and to some extent spiritual. She said it was not a "dilemma". She simply wanted to know more about what her life meant before she became involved with the life of someone else. If she was going to spend her life with someone, she wanted to be on the same page as the person in matters that were important to her. She acknowledged that she was confused, but searching. She valued her life and she wanted to make sure she was using her time and energies to the best ends.

Diego had early on observed that she was as bright and as confident as any woman he had ever met and very open in her thinking and sharing her thoughts. She was brilliant and yet humble about what she knew and what she knew she didn't know. She had come to her knowledge and thoughts by dent of serious study and was proud of it. But she was aware of her blind spots and wanted to shed light on them. She simply wanted the comfort of knowing that there was meaning in her life.

Diego bluntly asked something he would never have asked

except for the fact that he was on his third beer of the evening and had not eaten anything. "Can you share what it is that's bothering you?" She said that she wasn't really troubled by anything. She was just unsettled in what she thought may be the most important matter in life. "It comes down to what does it all mean? I'm trained as a scientist. I measure things, look for causes and rely on data. I studied physics and math. As an engineer, I know that everything is caused". Diego gave her a somewhat puzzled look. He didn't know where she was going with the conversation. She stopped and asked if he was following her thought process. She said that she had had two glasses of wine with her friend and maybe she was too loose to talk seriously about anything. He assured her he was on track, but surprised that she, of all people he knew, would be confused.

She let her hamburger sit and nibbled on the french fries. She told Diego that her interest in pursuing what life was about probably came as a result of her engineering study. She had enjoyed the study of physics when in high school and again at Iowa State. But physics, especially cosmology left her with questions. The subject matter of her cosmology class had caused her to think a great deal about the universe. And for her it was impossible to think about the existence of the universe without thinking of why it came to be and its cause.

She knew pretty much how it came to be but that wasn't enough. In order for her to know the meaning of her life, she needed to know the "why" of the universe. At Iowa State, she had had a physics professor who was superb in his observations about the universe and made thinking about it as exciting as anything she had ever pursued. His course addressed cosmology and she was fascinated by the material. She was so taken by the study of the cosmos that she almost switched to astronomy as a major, but she thought that engineering was

[Type text]

more likely a career at which she could make a living. She could learn more about the physical world if she stuck with the hard sciences. She was taken by the fact that science was still discovering much about the universe. Some new understandings contradicted previous thinking. That in itself was exciting.

She had had a precocious roommate at Iowa State who was also in engineering. Prior to entering the university, she had already thought about a few of the matters that interested Jordan. Her observations stimulated Jordan to think about "some important answers". In her words, "the truth about what is and why". The two roommates had spent a great deal of time discussing eternal verities over warmed over cheese pizza and cheap red table wine, "two buck chuck". But they had never come to any firm conclusions.

She said she started thinking about spiritual matters as a college student because she felt empty with little purpose to her life. She found it ironic that, as an engineering major, a person committed to measuring the physical world, she found herself with an interest in philosophy, some of which was pure theory that defied measurement. Science was leading her somewhere, but she didn't know where. For scientists, it pretty much came down to a case of whether there was or was not a way to prove a reason for existence. She knew that if she landed on a high probability that there was a reason for existence, there would be a lot of other questions that would follow and require a yea or nay response. There would be serious implications for her thinking and her living.

If there was an intelligent being powerful enough to create a universe, did the being have anything to do with man? She was very familiar with the tenets of the monotheistic belief in a creative God and wondered about it. But she became so busy with the demands of her engineering studies and following graduation, with her job, that she had just drifted until now. And that is pretty much where she found herself, drifting uncomfortably.She said she really wanted something to hold on to but it was eluding her.

When they finished the conversation, Diego was full of thoughts about his own life and what he believed, a place where he didn't often go. He had always been a believer. Other than when he was in Nigeria and at Ramstein, he had never given much thought to the meaning of his life. He had lived his life vigorously in the manner that his mom and Brother Mark had urged. Since his mother's terminal diagnosis he was thinking more about both life and death. He had always been conscious of the reality of his mom's mortality, but he always put off thinking about his own reality. From the time of his father's death he had always wanted not to think about life and death issues. His life was so fast that it was easy not to think about the most serious matters.

He thought how odd it was that he had been given his belief at birth and was nurtured in it throughout his life. Belief was easy and uncluttered for him. But it didn't occupy his life to the degree it seemed to be occupying Jordan's. If she was to believe, Jordan was coming to faith the hard way. She had to work for it. He thought that the depth of her faith would probably be much greater than his if she was graced with it.

They ended the evening with coffee and sherbet and headed home. When they reached her door, Diego leaned down and kissed her softly on her lips. It was clear the kiss was more than welcome, but after a moment, she backed away and looked at him with a deadpan expression and asked just who he thought he was. They both laughed. She turned and opened the door. She gave him a huge smile and said "good night big guy, thanks for the burger."

Diego danced to his car and sat for a few minutes just

[Type text]

to enjoy the feeling of having kissed the woman he loved. He was ecstatic and more hopeful than he had ever been in his life. He was renewed. He felt empathy for Jordan. She was confused. She wanted to know who she was. He wished she had had the blessing of a mother like his. He was sure that because Jordan was such a terrific person that her mother and father were wonderful people, but they had not been blessed with the same sense of purpose of life that had pervaded his family and his life. Apparently they had not been blessed with faith. Diego could not figure out why such a wonderful person as Jordan was not blessed with faith. He wanted it for her as much as she did. But it made no difference to him. He was in love. He would do everything he could to make her happy. Perhaps just having love would free her to feel the blessing of faith.

He thought about all that had transpired at dinner. It was by far the most interesting night of his life. It was even more interesting and exciting than the night the Bears won the Central Division playoffs and he had scored three times. The wine no doubt made Jordan free to tell him that she was asking the really basic questions. Was there a God? If so, was Jesus God? If Jesus is God, how did he become a human? How did he rise from the dead? If he did, is he now somehow in communion with the people who believe in him? Are all of the things that he said, true? What's its meaning for me?

Jordan agreed to dinner that Friday night. Diego took her to a new Italian place in Arlington that he had been told was excellent and romantic. After a lot of talk about what a disaster the legislative session was and what bills didn't pass, Diego went back to Jordan's quest. He was sincerely interested. This was his life partner and he wanted to hear what she thought. She said that she had read a great deal. She had sat alone at home, in the park and on the subway contemplating what she had read and tried to sort it all out. But she was deadlocked. She acknowledged that the incredible complexity of the universe, including the complexity of the biology and the psychic dimension of man, the longing of the heart and the beauty of love pushed her to the probability of there being a rational intelligent cause of existence.

She had dismissed those who called life a farce long before she even began to read. She rejected the Beckett and the "Waiting for Godot" school. She said that she kept coming back to the concept of an uncaused cause. Some fourteen or so billion years ago prior to anything physical, prior to space and time, somewhere, somehow there had to be a something that caused existence to be. Armed with an acceptance of the existence of a cause, she was lead to the probability of there was a being of unbelievable substance that served as the cause of existence. She told Diego that just arriving there was a relief. She knew she believed in God.

When the word "unbelievable" stuck in her mind, she knew she was somehow on a path either to "faith" or "non-faith" because she couldn't reason any further. She still didn't have a full answer to her quest. She couldn't figure out the "why" of existence. She thought long and hard about what kind of being the cause might be and "slowly and somewhat grudgingly" concluded that the cause was very likely the God that had been pressed on her by friends, relatives and television preachers over the years.

She told Diego she had initiated an exploration of Catholicism, but she had serious issues. She simply didn't like the God that she had heard that Catholics worshipped, the one her friends talked about when she was a child. He sounded vindictive. Even those who promoted that God seemed not to take him very seriously or have much regard for the people that God caused. She thought that if indeed, there was a God that had caused everything, he was truly an awesome God and he needed to be taken more seriously than he was being taken by

[Type text]

the believers, especially the Catholics she knew. She said that even present company needed to take God seriously. If God caused everything and everyone to be, he would very likely want the beings he put into his world treated better than they were being treated. He would want his planets preserved and would want people to be kind to one another and treat each other well.

Diego regularly practiced his faith. He was a regular Catholic. He went to mass on Sunday and prayed because his mother had wanted him to and he wanted to please her. He was surprised by the idea that this young woman, fashionable, attractive and intelligent, whom he loved had given such a substantial measure of thought and effort to the why and how of existence. He found it interesting that she had almost reasoned to faith. The concept of salvation had always been a part of his life, his home, his family and his culture. Every room in the Freeman household had a crucifix and a holy water fountain was located at the front door. The Lady of Guadalupe graced the living room and watched over the family. Catholicism was in his DNA. He thought to himself "I'm religious. But I think the woman that I love is holy. That's interesting".

Chapter 13

Diego, the Legislator

A Drug Free America

Diego had signed on to a dozen or so pieces of legislation in his first year but had not introduced any bills. He managed to keep very busy with committee work, constituent needs and some speaking dates. People wanted to know more about the Bears and the NFL than politics. Because the Speaker of the House was from Illinois and a good friend of the Chicago mayor, Diego received two unusually important committee assignments. The Speaker placed him on both the Armed Services Committee and the Intelligence Committee. He knew Diego would take both assignments very seriously and he was correct. A lot of his colleagues were jealous of the assignments, but they figured he was a wounded veteran and that gave him extra points. There were only a half dozen military veterans in the House. Diego was so likeable that they didn't complain. They knew he would be valuable to the committees.

A couple of national Hispanic groups were pressing him to introduce a new immigration law that would allow what was effectively an open border that would allow Mexican and Canadian citizens to pass from Mexico to the United States and vice versa as people passed from one state to another. In 2015, a comprehensive immigration reform bill had been passed which for practical purposes, was an amnesty program. The irony was that the conservative Republicans had pushed the law to foster a work force and to try to lure some Hispanic voters. It permitted seasonal workers to have work permits and technical workers to have Green Cards. Those who had come to the United States illegally under certain conditions were allowed to become legal and eventually attain citizenship. The Republicans had used an economic argument to gain the support of the nation to promote the bill.

Opponents of the bill indicated that they were in favor of having an additional eleven to twelve million Mexicans in the U.S. but they wanted them to be the eleven million who were on the waiting list in Mexico so they could come legally. The argument meant little because there was a need to deal with those already in the U.S. and there was no will to deport them.

Diego thought it ironic that among the groups that were pushing him was the Catholic bishops. The bishops were supposed to be paragons of virtue but had winked their eyes while supporting the illegal immigrants because they made up a good portion of their flocks. The bishops argued that despite having broken the law the illegal immigrants should be allowed to stay because it would not break up families. They chose not to recognize that many of the illegal immigrants had their families back in Mexico to whom they were sending a part of their earnings and to whom they hoped to return.

At a time of very high unemployment, there was a serious labor shortage in the entry level and the high tech job market. The produce, restaurant, hotel and the packing house industries were short of workers. The tech industries were equally short of staff. A lower birth rate and a stumbling education system had generated a work force that was often unmotivated to work and not adequate to the demands of business and agriculture. For the immigration debate, the Republicans argued that the nation was aging and entitlements were mushrooming without sufficient numbers of workers to support the tax burden. Further, they demonstrated in great detail that a youthful population who did not require immediate entitlements was necessary to a growth economy in terms of both consumers and producers. That youth population in their view needed to be immigrants. Their position was that despite illegal immigration, the country was still short of population because the birthrate had fallen. They made no account for the sixty million people who in the last fifty five years had been conceived but never made it out of the womb alive.

The arguments supporting young immigrants became the basis for their approach in dealing with the large number of illegals in the country and to push to expand work permits and immigration. Their frequently quoted comment was "We need these immigrants now if we want to support our elderly and sustain our economy." Out of fear of constituent uprising, the Republicans initially rejected the plan. But they knew that in 2030 the Hispanic population would become nearly thirty percent of the nation. They mustered the public support to pass the legislation on both sides of the aisle.

In his second year in congress in 2038, Diego started to develop more confidence as a legislator. He had come to congress with a passion for a single specific mission. The nation was falling apart for lack of leadership. Too many potential workers had dropped out of the workforce simply because they could. The government would support them at a certain poverty level which for the unmotivated was sufficient and better in their mind than a low wage job. Many others had made themselves useless from drug use. He felt compelled to address the drug problem. Even if he was wrong in his proposals he needed to bring the life and death facts to an honest public discussion. Congress could no longer hide from the issue. He felt he would be doing something positive for his family, his neighborhood, his congressional district and for his nation as well as for other nations if he could somehow lessen the drug problem.

He had lost his father at the hands of drug addicts. He had watched his neighborhood die, he had seen some of his constituents and friends become addicted and waste away. He had seen the damage that had been done to the families and the culture of his mother's native Mexico and other South and Central American countries. He had seen able bodied young men, some of whom were fathers, use and deal drugs. Too many had died and too many were wasting in prison. If America was going to survive, someone had to do something. The problem had been neglected by congress and the presidency for a very long time. America could no longer stand the status quo, nor could it tolerate legalization of drugs which was being suggested by some as a means of taking the violence out of drugs.

He was angry about the whole drug mess, the dealing, the abuse, the failed policies of control, failed rehabilitation programs and the horrid international implications. He wanted desperately to do something to fix the problem. He hated the actions of the people who were wreaking all the destruction and wasting their own lives in the process. He blamed the addict population of the United States and the flawed efforts of the government to resolve the problem. Tens of billions had been spent to solve the problem and it continued to grow. Whenever he had the chance, Diego reminded his colleagues that the government had spent a billion dollars in Afghanistan to curtail the poppy production. Their efforts to eradicate it had made the growers wealthy by the rise in price. Each time a crop was destroyed, the price of poppies increased. The poppy growers used some of their new found wealth from the rise in prices to aid Al-Qaeda and the Taliban. Finally, it dawned on the military that they were fighting a losing battle, and they simply let the poppies flow. Once they took the stimulus out of the equation, the price of poppies dropped and the farmers had to grow more to keep up.

The State Department and the Drug Enforcement Administration were not as smart as the military. Drugs were informing many of the diplomatic relationships with Central and South American countries. The DEA had agents assigned to every country south of the border attempting to interdict the flow of drugs, but as they put pressure in one country, the problem ballooned from one spot to another. The southern border of the U.S. was like a sieve.

The drug problem was not limited to sources outside of the country. Drugs flowed freely and demand continued to grow domestically. Meth and "crack" were still present and impossible to control. The problem of the "black market" in prescription misuse was enormous and expanding. Prescription abuse had mushroomed and was complicated by the fact that prescriptions had to be available and the control came under the Food and Drug Administration and involved the medical profession.

The U.S. had spent outrageous amounts of money in Colombia to move the problem to Bolivia and beyond where it flourished for years. Diego pointed out that it was as if they were intent on proving the U.S. government was idiotic, "doing the same thing over and over and expecting different results.

The image of America in much of the world most especially in the Islamic world was a nation of violent, drug addicted, sexually obsessed infidels bent on destroying their culture. It certainly was not realistic or intended but it was not an image entirely un-earned.

Diego spent a lot of time discussing the problem with Jordan. She acknowledged that she hadn't given much thought to the problem and that she knew very little about it. Drugs were not popular among her associates or friends. Engineers needed clear heads. She bought Diego's observations because he knew the problem well and painfully. He asked how she would approach the problem. She indicated that if he was serious about her input, she would need some time to read and to think about it. But she agreed that something needed to be done.

She observed that maybe the government was not the right organization to address the problem. She tried to put herself in the middle of the issue in the persons of the counter parties. How and why do people become addicted? How do their opposites formulate the law enforcement response? She was entirely unfamiliar with the drug culture except how it was portrayed by the media. She had never known an addict.

Demand, Demand, Demand

Both agreed that two propositions were the reality. America couldn't tolerate the legalization of more addictive substances and America couldn't tolerate the current circumstance of the war on drugs. The problem was getting worse. She thought about what might be in the mind of someone who used drugs often or gets addicted. She was convinced that someone with a positive self- image, hope and sense of purpose, a sense of why they were, a positive notion of who they were, an idea of what they could be, what they could do with their life was not likely to become addicted. Some might use drugs recreationally, but they were unlikely to become addicted unless they were psychically predisposed. They certainly were a part of the problem because they created demand and their drug use had to be addressed.

In order to deal with the demand side of the drug problem, a purpose in life seemed to be the key for Jordan. She took notice in college and in her work of people who showed their sense of purpose. She had purpose throughout her life. She wanted to please her parents and to have a career. That required discipline. Her current search for expanded meaning in her life gave her additional purpose. She hoped that finding answers would give her even further purpose. She asked herself how some people have purpose and others don't. If parents don't plant purpose in a child, can someone else do it? Can a teacher, a coach or a preacher plant purpose?

She was convinced that somewhere in any legislation

there had to be some provision that would establish a program, the goal of which was to trigger purpose in the lives of very young people. They would need to see their life as a valuable and sacred gift to be lived with great care, with planning, goals and direction. She also concluded that to give them purpose, it was necessary to aim at their soul. She was thinking of a quotation from St. Matthew that she had recently read. He noted that the soul is where hope thrives. Hope was a habit of the heart and the earlier it is planted, the deeper the roots grow.

Her reading about drugs made her aware of all the programs and all the clichés that had been addressed to the drug problem over the years. She knew that none had been successful with sufficient numbers of young people to be considered valid. She wanted to avoid being too clever in her thinking and to be realistic. What can be done to generate rejection of drug use? And who is best prepared to help young people to do it? The material suggested that there were those who maintained that only rehabilitated drug users could have any impact on kids. That school of thought subscribed to the position that those are the only people that kids or users would listen to. She thought "Well, maybe. But what got those people off of drugs and alcohol".

There was evidence that Alcoholics Anonymous worked for a lot of alcoholics. There was a fellow in her office who was "a friend of Bill Wilson". And while she didn't know the full dynamics of AA's success, she did know that two of the first three steps involved recognition of a higher power and turning one's life over to God. This was acknowledgement of a need to rely on the help of a higher power, some transcendent being. She thought how logical and profound that step was becoming as a part of her own life, not from her need to exit an addiction but as part of her search for meaning. It seemed to her that that was fundamental to addressing not only drugs but purpose in any life. Inherent in that acknowledgement was the existence of a being powerful enough to heal the spirit. Bill Wilson was really providing a spiritual GPS for more than just alcoholics.

She spent nearly two weeks researching and thinking about the issue in her off time. She dealt with the data which often was contradictory. She read studies by libertarians who wanted to legalize all drugs, liberals who wanted to legalize some drugs and conservatives who wanted to maintain the status quo. None of these approaches was acceptable to her and she knew they would not be acceptable to Diego. The status quo was what got his dad and a lot of other innocent people killed. She spent three nights drafting her notes. In the end, she went spiritual and suggested that kids had to be made aware that their lives had purpose because they came from God and would return to God. The moment she concluded this, she knew that any legislation that Diego would propose was doomed to failure. God was banished from the public square. Ironically the more she thought about it, the more it strengthened her own belief in God.

It was apparent that government couldn't be the answer. and that was what she and Diego had to face. She had seen the disaster of government and the innumerable programs that had been attempted, failed and still operated often to the detriment of the victims of the programs and the taxpayers who supported them. She remembered President Reagan's comment about government programs being the closest thing on earth to eternal life. They never end. She had experienced the catastrophe created by the national socialized healthcare program which nearly destroyed the nation. She concluded that government simply was not capable of offering important services at the scale required. Government had more on its plate than it could handle.

She had always vigorously supported the separation of church and state. She was frustrated by the knowledge that the needed program could never be offered by government. But she also knew it could never be done by government in a country that had become so secular that God couldn't even be considered in the process. God had been successfully banned from even mention in conventional wisdom. She knew too that the ACLU, the Freedom from Religion people and others would not accept anything that would encourage kids to think spiritually and consider the purpose of their lives if it in any way led them to consider God. Putting God in the game would be unacceptable for any federally funded programs to help kids. But somehow kids needed to know that life has a purpose. How to mount that hurdle was a problem.

She concluded that any effort to deal with demand would have to be offered by faith based organizations and limited in scope lest it lose its focus. It should be aimed only at those under twenty one who were still malleable and most still locked in delayed adolescence. She also knew that any program would somehow have to be linked delicately with law enforcement and prosecution, with authorities that dealt with the supply side.

In her notes, she urged Diego to include a provision in his bill that would require law enforcement to demonstrate evidence of their success with hard statistical evidence that would pass the smell test in the amelioration of the problem in order to justify funding and continued support for interdiction. Law enforcement had to be driven to do better. There could be no more reliance on anecdotal fluff, so many pounds of this or that taken off the street worth so much. "We're winning the war, you are all safe and you no longer have to worry. Trust us" would no longer satisfy.

Diego had spent too many hours listening to professors lecturing on the role of the iron clad law of supply and demand. If the DEA took a million pounds of cocaine off the street without cutting the demand, it necessarily raised the price of cocaine and brought more dealers into the market. When a product becomes scarcer, costs elevate. The buyer, who in this case requires the product to live high, needs more resources to procure the product. In the case of illegal drugs, scarcity resulted in more theft, more robberies and more violence. Those providers attempting to corner the market or prevent the competition from doing so in Mexico and the other South and Central American countries caused thousands of deaths, often of innocent people. Chicago, Diego's home, was the prime American example of the failure of law enforcement.

The drug lords destroyed whole communities and corrupted and intimidated law enforcement in all drug producing nations. When arrested and prosecuted, they crowded the courts, jails and prisons and then returned to the community more crime prone and better trained criminals. And many returned with an attitude of self pity that allows them to justify more drugs and more criminality. Over the years there had been attempts to incarcerate only the offenders who committed violent crimes and release others to the street. But recidivism rates and poor classification methods had failed the efforts. Diego wanted to intercede prior to any drug use to help kids use their heads to avoid even experimentation. He and Oscar had been surrounded by drugs but never even considered their use because they had developed a discipline prompted by their parents, Brother Mark, coaches and teachers.

In the matter of curbing drug traffic, the challenge had to be to press law enforcement to" think outside the box" and to be honest about whether they had an effective battle plan for winning the "war" on drugs. The DEA and related groups would have to prove their effectiveness. Based on the data from the multiple studies she had reviewed, there seemed to be little effect from interdiction. The big issue was whether it was indeed counter- productive. A couple of respected "think tanks" had researched the outcomes of law enforcement and concluded that the problem was often made worse by their efforts. Law enforcement was doing the job it was assigned and was doing it well in their view, but it did not help. They were frustrated, confused and fumbling and they knew it. They were being asked to solve a social problem that didn't lend itself to law enforcement.

The problem for law enforcement was one that Peter Drucker, a noted author of business and management had once observed. No matter how well an organization did the job assigned, it made no difference if the job was the wrong thing to do. Law enforcement knew the reality of the failure of the Volstead Act and the disaster associated with trying to prevent alcohol. But something had to be done and law enforcement had to be somehow involved. The Marines had taught Diego that generals liked to fight the last war. In the case of drugs, the war was being waged in the same manner that prohibition had been waged. And it was equally unsuccessful.

Jordan concluded that the only people under 21 who should be processed in the criminal justice system should be those who dealt drugs. If use was the only issue, offenders under twenty one should not be processed in the criminal justice system. She recognized that there was a post interdiction, arrest and prosecution point at which there could be some good done. When it came to the problem of crime, the police were the ambulance drivers, the courts were the intake people who triaged the patients and the prisons were the hospitals. But the prisons had to be used to control the dealers, not the users. Prisons were too expensive and too hazardous to the users. Perhaps the prisons could get to the dealers, but it had not been successful yet. It was enough to take them off the streets for a period.

Users under twenty one who had not dealt needed a different path, a path with some authority but not the criminal justice system. The further a youth penetrated the criminal justice system, the worse off the community and the youth would be. But where would the authority come from? In an effort to get to a major dealer, too often law enforcement gave a pass to the small dealers. The program that she envisioned would not work with people who had a dealer mentality whether large or small. If a youth was comfortable hurting another person by dealing, they didn't belong in the program to diminish demand.

Addressing the problem of the users who were not dealers required an entirely new paradigm. Perhaps all those good willed people coming out of the universities who wanted to go to foreign countries to help the poor should stay home in the U.S. and become an American Drug Corps taking up a challenge that plagued the nation, a problem that fractured lives and families. They could help by laboring to persuade kids and their peers to keep their heads straight, cut the binges, cut the heroin, cocaine and meth and wait until they were of age to knock down a beer or two. How could young people be persuaded not to waste their lives on intoxicants? Was it possible? Was it worth the effort?

A lot of progress was being made by the business community where there was great incentive. It was nearly impossible to run a business with drug users. A large number of companies had already established drug- free workplace screening with pre- employment and random testing. Even the pro sports leagues had found it in their best interests to get serious about drug use. Businesses provided some promise of safety. And there were some companies that were developing reliable finger touch and pupil scanning technology to determine drug use. Some schools had put in place "zero tolerance" for participation on their athletic teams and that was sloping down to the younger teams as well.

Is Government the Answer?

Diego agreed with Jordan that to lessen demand it would take a program that taught children to see purpose in their lives and that it necessarily involved their relationship with God. Beyond the role of God in kid's lives, one of the things on which they strongly agreed was that there had to be a campaign to generate some social shame on users. Diego pointed out that for years, educators had spent boodles of money and had stolen class time from math and science to castigate people who produced carbon dioxide in their work, their transport and their play. Kids taunted parents who did not demonstrate a "Green" stripe in their lifestyle. "Green" initiatives pervaded the culture and while he supported most of the initiatives, he believed it slowed economic progress. Diego was more concerned about jobs in his district than trying to put up windmills on the south side of Chicago.

The "Greens" had used up a lot of the emotional energy and taxes of America without enough payoff. They stopped just short of prohibiting people from breathing out the CO2 from their lungs. Why hadn't the media devoted the same level of energy and ink to castigating the people who were killing today's young people's initiative and destroying the culture with drug dealing and use? Why hadn't they chosen to castigate the gangs or the drug addicted celebrities and entertainers? The media needed to show the violence done by the gangs throughout the world. Young people needed to know that the former head of the Mexican "Zetas" the source of their drugs boiled his enemies alive in oil and those who used his drugs were responsible for making and keeping his kind wealthy. Those who used drugs needed to be somehow ostracized.

Jordan and Diego considered just how difficult it would be to shame the kind of people who were prone to drug use. Could they be shamed into abstaining from drugs? That was surely a part of the challenge. There had to be a public campaign to identify them as enemies of society and the common good. Like cigarette smokers they had to be ostracized. Even the weekend users had to be shown the damage they were generating in their families and in other countries.

Diego and Jordan realized that there was very little shame left in America. Many of the traditional values and controls inherent in the civilized culture had been abandoned. Toleration was taught as the first virtue in schools and churches. All behavior was morally equivalent no matter how destructive it might be to the society or the individual. Former taboos were now conventional behavior. Children no longer learned behavior from parents, but from television, magazines, Hollywood and rappers. Co-habitation was the norm, out of wedlock births had become the majority, obscenity was integral to entertainment and public language, work was outmoded. If one could qualify for support by the "nanny government", it was used for all it was worth. Those people would be hard to shame.

Illness from smoking was the only self inflicted disease that was recognized in media reports. AIDS was viewed by the media as mystery disease without a cause and obesity was unmentionable. There couldn't be a "nanny" nurturing young people every minute of the day though some in government thought that was a good idea. Young people had to take responsibility, come to their own conclusions about making a drug free life for themselves. They had to have a stake in their own behavior. No one else could do it for them. Any participation in the proposed programs had to be voluntary or at least an alternative to some more restrictive status.

For those users who would not enter themselves into programs because they had not "hit bottom", there would have to be a point when help was imposed. This would necessarily occur at the time of their first encounter with their own discomfort in an emergency room or with authority, principals in schools, bosses on the job, parents, coaches or pastors. There had to be a sort of missionary corps similar to AA to urge kids into the programs. That meant there had to be some back up for those too far gone to care for their own future. That was a problem to which Jordan knew no answer. But she wanted to see a program that would be voluntary and would somehow teach people that their lives were valuable, worth cherishing and protecting.

But, if they couldn't lessen demand, what was the alternative? Let demand play out? Let people use drugs as they do alcohol? Legalize the whole shebang? That may be the reality but Diego was not prepared to be a part of a government that allowed that to happen. He wanted to prevent drug use plain and simple.

One high ranking law enforcement official told him that it would be preferable to leave well enough alone. Just let the drug gangs destroy each other and let the dealers and users destroy themselves. If you take drugs out of the picture, the next thing for gangs to engage in as they do in some countries is kidnapping, smuggling, protection for common citizens, small businesses and neighborhoods. Law enforcement had proven it had little control. He was also advised that because of the rise in the cost and the rationing of medical care especially joint replacements for the burgeoning elderly population, the gangs might give serious attention to providing body parts. He told Diego that there will always be things that people need and criminals who will provide them.

The Bill

A number of very liberal and libertarian groups, some well- funded had pushed the legalization of marijuana for medical purposes for years. A lot of states allowed medical marijuana. The Justice Department played at the edges and did not enforce the federal laws prohibiting use. "Marijuana Clinics" that provided recreational drugs had flourished in those states and law enforcement looked away. Some of the pro-drug groups were regarded as bizarre and not interested in a comprehensive approach. They were largely interested in personal use for their own purposes and half dozen states accommodated them. They legalized recreational marijuana with limited immediate effect. But that did not take into account the long term health consequence of inputting the smoke of weeds into the body and brain, a practice which had negative health impact. A lot of people were still around who remembered the serious downside of the sixties when drugs took the futures of some very promising young people and effectively made them zombies. By the same token there were presidents who had used drugs and proudly acknowledged it in their campaigns in their effort to identify with the young folks.

Diego thought Jordan's ideas were spot on. No wonder. She was a professional analyst and saw the problem and a response objectively and clearly. She was even right about how interest groups would respond. The opposition would demagogue the issue. He wanted to pass the legislation and the thirty per cent support that he seemed to be getting from his colleagues would not get the job done.

Diego worked with his staff to draft a bill which he labeled The Drug Free America Act. He was aware that it wasn't comprehensive and wouldn't solve the problem of drugs, but he had to do something. He had to make an attempt to keep kids from ruining their lives, their family's lives and the life of their nation. He considered the possibility that it may initially result in more drugs and more addicts, but the long run was his focus. He believed firmly that the paradigm had to be changed. The focus had to be on getting young people to stop even experimenting with drugs. If young people could only see the sanctity and purpose in their lives, they might use their lives productively.

He wanted to do more than initiate a conversation about

the drug problem. He wanted to do something concrete. If ever there had been an innocent family that had been victimized by drugs, it was Diego's family, his mother and siblings. It was now 2037 and he had spent thirty years mindful of the damage done by one feeble minded kid with a gun acting at the behest of addicts. Diego knew that the stakes were high for him to introduce such a bill. Because his dad was a cop, he always had a soft spot for law enforcement. But law enforcement wasn't getting the job done and wasn't going to like the pressure of proof of value that he hoped to put on them.

Diego felt obliged to do something to address the problem that had worked so much pain on the nation. He didn't care about his own career or what people would think of him. He was compelled. Jordan advised him to secure buy-in from as many stake holders as he could identify before he introduced the bill. He went to Brother Mark for his advice and spelled out his plan. He would propose turning all drug policy that addressed demand over to the states. The bill would appropriate a billion dollars to the states to distribute to faith based agencies that would be required to provide programs that fostered purpose in the souls of youth. The bill allowed expenditure of the funds to address the prevention and rehabilitation needs of people under the age of twenty one with twelve step programs that acknowledged the role of a higher power.

He chose not to address the matter of people over twenty one. They were on their own. States had found that they were already free to take the chance of legalizing drugs, but still had to face the possibility of the Justice Department intervening. States would be free to decide if they wanted to decriminalize any drugs or keep them illegal. More than ninety percent of the drug prosecutions and incarcerations occurred at the state level. So drugs were really a matter of state importance. If a state legislature and governor decriminalized heroin or cocaine, neither the DEA nor the Justice Department could intervene under the law he was proposing unless it involved a separate federal offense. While the federal government had supremacy in legal matters, most drug offenses were of state laws. States could determine how they would utilize their freedom to make laws and would have to deal with any negative consequences. The focus of the bill was to cut demand.

Under Diego's bill, the Drug Enforcement Agency and the State Department would require congressional approval for any overseas expenditure dealing with interdiction. Drug interdiction would no longer be a basis for foreign policy.

Brother Mark read the bill and then urged him to consider a little lighter version of his plan. He suggested that he not allow states to decriminalize hard drugs. He urged him to visit some mayor of major cities, the Roman Catholic cardinals of Chicago, New York and Los Angeles, at least a couple of governors, the national president of the chiefs of police, the president of the AMA, the president of La Raza and the NAACP and to share his plan with them. He advised him to stay away from lawyers and psychologists. Both would find ways to make things more complex than they needed to be.

The American population was now nearly thirty percent Hispanic and he needed the support of the Hispanics and the Blacks to promote the plan. They were disproportionately into the drug business as users, dealers, prisoners and victims of crime. They were the ones being criminalized by their use. Whites were using and dealing but their dealing and use was more private and often overlooked by law enforcement. There had always been a double standard especially in the suburbs where cops were more likely to know families of users and dealers.

Diego proposed that the cardinal engage the Catholic bishops in the prevention and rehab programs. He tried to impress the cardinal with the fact that it was in many respects a pro-life issue. It involved the preservation of the sanctity and integrity of human lives. Diego thought the Church should be at the forefront of the issue, but the Church had shown little interest in addressing it. Cardinal McHugh was non-committal but indicated he would take the matter under consideration and discuss it with the other cardinals and some other bishops at his convenience. But he told Diego not to count on much support. The Church had its own problems and had limited energy and resources. The bishops and cardinals had never had much success in the political field.

The president of the national association of chiefs of police was outraged and indicated he would fight it. He didn't like the measure that would require law enforcement to prove their worth at interdiction. The Mayor, Tito Perez, told Diego that he would discuss it with his staff and his chief of police and the County Justice Council and get back to him.

The Speaker of the House liked Diego. He initially laughed at the idea of the bill and asked if he wanted to end his career in his second term. Then he thought about it and said "You know, Diego, my guess is that a lot of people don't really give a hoot if the junkies waste themselves. People are tired of the whole thing, the junkies on the street, the murders, the property crime, the need and the costs for a Nanny to incarcerate and rehab the jerks. Maybe parents will begin to realize how costly and dangerous their neglect is to their kids. And maybe some kids will get the message that they are on their own out there.

When my son started smoking pot, I told him that he needed a new place to stay and that he was on his own financially. No more tuition or spending money. He moved out because he was angry. His mother cried. And he was back in a week saying that it wasn't worth it. I didn't laugh at him, but I wanted to.

"You'll have your hearing. You can tell your colleagues that the assistant majority leader and I will be neutral. But I urge you to share your rationale for this with the same words you used with me and to share it personally with them. They will all have to step out on a limb to support you, but the more sponsors you have, the better off you will be. And I suggest you go to some conservative Republicans to sign on. A lot of them will tell you the same thing I have about how tired people are of the problem. If any of them are on the edge of Libertarian, they'll join you. This is a left leaning proposal. But I've found that the further you go left, the closer you get to the right.

And I urge you to pray. You'll have to be hard to challenge law enforcement. They are a crafty bunch. They'll say the sky will fall. From time to time I've thought that we might be safer if the crap is sold in drug stores just like other mood altering drugs that are manufactured. But I'd never mention it in public like some of those guys in the South American countries have. The reality is people just don't want to face reality all the time and they want to alter their moods. Alcohol is one thing, but cocaine and heroin, those are a bigger deal".

Chapter 14

A Challenge

Let's Keep Things
Just the Way They Are

Three days after Diego introduced the bill, a meeting was held in the forty fourth floor offices of The Frankfort Financial Services Limited Liability Company in Chicago. There were seven men and one woman at a large conference table in a room that overlooked Lake Michigan. They gathered over a luncheon of crab salad and some four hundred dollar bottles of white French wine. No one was dressed in an outfit that cost less than a thousand dollars and there was at least fifty thousand dollars worth of gold adorning the wrists, fingers, ears and necks of those present. A fifty year old well tanned and well coifed man with medium build opened the meeting with "Well, at least a couple of you helped to put this son of a bitch in Washington. So perhaps one of you might suggest a response to this stupid bill. The guy has to be the dumbest s… we have ever sent to congress. And we have sent some pretty dumb ones".

The woman responded first. "Mr. Gleason, I acknowledge that I gave him some money precisely because I thought that he was dumb and that we could handle him. But he has enough money to win elections without us. So it was no big deal. Frankly I had no idea that he would come up with a bill that would aim directly at our foreheads. Not that it would make any difference, but he probably doesn't know about the flow of money to this business. I suspect that he assumes that each of us earns our living from the banks we represent. We are best served to insure that that remains the case. The less he knows the better. I suggest that we do not deal with this head-on and further, I urge that there be no violence involved.

You may recall that more than once when politicians get killed, it's very easy for other politicians to use their death as a motive for passing some half- assed legislation that would not pass in normal times. The fact is that is how we got Medicare. President Kennedy was killed and President Johnson could have passed a bill to make the sun rise in the west if he wanted to as long as it was in Kennedy's name. He probably would have totally destroyed the country if he hadn't stepped on it when he pushed the Viet Nam thing. Then that other Bozo right out of our streets upped the costs with that national health crap. Do anything but not violence".

A very large Hispanic man opposite the head of the table stood and started to walk around saying "Let me make it clear. We don't have time to wait to see how this thing pans out. This f...ing thing has to be stopped and if you can't come up with something soon, I have people who can take care of it."

When the man next to Mr. Gleason leaned in and whispered something to him, two person conversations broke out around the table. Mr. Gleason coughed loudly and the conversations stopped. Then he said "Mr. Hernandez, you have not been with us long, but it is important for you to know that we are not inclined to violence and we certainly wouldn't condone or even countenance any person in this room taking the matter into their own hands. This is a corporate matter and your organization is just one component. We are grateful for your successful management of the flow of your funds to our banks and to our individual accounts, but we need to approach our business professionally. Violence is out of the question." Mr.

Hernandez gave a look that added hostility to his hurt appearance. He didn't say what was on his mind, but he wasn't used to being told how to manage matters that were of concern to him.

Over the last two years the cartel that he represented had successfully processed over two hundred million dollars through their banks, ten percent of which went to their personal accounts in Switzerland. If they wanted that money to continue to flow, they would need to stop this move to de-criminalize or legalize drugs, whatever the shit the stupid bill proposed. Their products were being replaced by other stuff. They were already suffering from the meth labs and the over prescribing of legal drugs. Business was lagging behind last year's profits. When people got hooked on things other than cocaine and heroin, it was costly.

Nothing was decided by the end of the meeting. Other matters were discussed concerning the management of the money and whether there was sufficient accountability to make the tax man satisfied. The group determined to watch the progress of the bill and intervene when necessary by spreading some funds around congress if and when necessary. Mr. Hernandez left frustrated. Later that day he went to the night club that his boss owned on Rush St. and reported the results of the meeting. His boss said "f… those punks" and told him to set up a hit that would place a bomb under Diego's car if it looked like the bill was going to pass. That would make things slow down and the jerks in the FBI wouldn't have a clue who was behind the hit. They would think that it was some Republican.

Fortunately, Homeland Security had set up a program for all officials in Washington that involved using a chip in their car keys that would sense an explosive device in or under the car when the congressman or any other government official came within fifty feet of the car. The system automatically set off an alarm. One morning at six A.M. a month later when the bill moved to Appropriations after passing Judiciary, the alarm on Diego's car went off when he left his front door to go to work. Homeland Security disarmed the bomb, got prints, entered them into the National Criminal Justice database and came up with Mr. Hernandez's brother's prints. He was arrested and prosecuted. Mr. Hernandez was found in the Chicago River a week later with two forty five caliber bullet holes in the back of his head and two large openings in the front of his skull.

The Vote

Diego had introduced his bill with bi-partisan support with three Republicans among the twenty one sponsors. He wanted a lot more sponsors but he was satisfied with the twenty one willing to put themselves on the line for a somewhat radical proposal. There was much ballyhoo prior to the introduction of the bill with a lot of mis-information likely given to the press by some of those with whom he had shared his idea, but opposed it. But this was Washington and that was the way it worked. There were only about fifty members in the house when Diego rose to introduce the bill.

Anger had fueled much of his life for some thirty years. It drove much of his success. When he rose to speak the anger welled up. He let the anger flow to his hostility to the drug users in the United States, the inept law enforcement, congress, the confused diplomats and the administration, even the American people for putting up with the drug problem. He gave a stem-winder with greater passion than he had ever mustered.

Prior to standing, he thought about the moment he learned of his father's death. He prayed briefly to his father to ask God to bless him in his work and especially in this speech. He started by describing his mother's and the family's pain that came from his father's death. He spoke about the funeral, the hole in the life of the family that has lasted all their lives and the impact. He literally begged his colleagues to think about the last fifty years, the destruction of the culture of America and Mexico and the money spent that could have funded education and rehabilitation and finally the failure of the effort to curtail the problem.

He then demanded that they think about how unsuccessful the policies have been. The representatives who were on the floor of the house listened, an unusual event in congress. There was positive response in the house, but C-SPAN was the vehicle for support and the speech went viral. The Speaker arranged to have the bill go to the Judiciary first and linger until some members could interact with constituents about what they thought. He spent time with the chair and urged her to take the bill seriously. It would go to Appropriations later. He had heard that there may be more Republicans in favor of the bill than Democrats. He didn't like the idea of a Democrat introduced bill passing with a majority of Republican votes. It didn't look good for the Speaker.

The day it passed the Judiciary, Diego was as surprised as the day he was selected in the second round of NFL draft. He was pleasantly stunned. It would go to Appropriations in April. Exactly a week before Appropriations considered the bill, there was a gang war at the Nogales/Arizona border crossing. A shipment by the Bernal cartel was about to cross the border in a furniture semi and their principal rival opened fire killing the driver and his partner. In the exchange, two U.S. Border guards and one Mexican guard were killed.

In all, ten children lost their fathers that day. A week earlier, a shootout had occurred in Phoenix with two gang members on each side killed. The media used a lot of face time and ink asking whether the passage of the bill would make things safer or more dangerous. Appropriations passed the bill with all the provisions and there was a quiet celebration in Diego's office. It was the first time he had relaxed in three months. He went to dinner with his staff. Naturally Jordan was included. She was delighted with the bill's progress. While he worked on the bill, they hadn't been spending as much time together as Diego would have liked. They did see each other at least once during the week for dinner and a lot on weekends. The relationship was flourishing. They decided to go to the zoo the following Sunday where they were comfortable among the occupants who were honest, forthright and loving, qualities sometimes missing in their world.

Chapter 15

Hidden Threat

Start of a Bad Papal Day

It was not the normal four A.M. when the pope arose. His bio clock had kept him asleep until six. Upon wakefulness, he realized that he had already missed the time when he normally celebrated the mass for his household members. He assumed that Bishop Sanchez had done so as he normally did if the pope was scheduled to celebrate a later mass for another group. He went through his normal prayer, meditation and exercise routine and then went to the chapel where he con- celebrated a private mass with Bishop Sanchez, his second mass of the day. At breakfast, Bishop Sanchez indicated that neither the Swiss Guard nor the police had been able to locate Sister Sophia.

However the Swiss Guard who was on the front security gate at seven p.m. said that she had been picked up by her brother Michael, a teacher and another man. They had left in a car. She had not reported to anyone in the household that she intended to leave. When the Swiss Guard asked her to sign out, she said she would be right back in. She said she was just going to go to her brother's car to say hello to his children. However, the outside Swiss Guard said that she entered the rear seat of the large old black Lincoln automobile in a manner that suggested she was frightened. But she didn't say anything. Her brother sat in the front seat and the other man got into the back after she did. The bishop said that the police went to her brother's home and there was no one there.

Chief Bito Mebimi, of the Lagos department accompanied the investigating detective to the pope's rooms along with the Commandant of the Swiss Guard. They met in a conference room. The Chief of the Swiss Guard had informed the visitors that the room where they were meeting was a secure room and had been swept by his staff earlier that morning in anticipation of the meeting. The pope opened the meeting with a prayer to the Holy Spirit for guidance and turned the meeting over to the Chief of Police. The Chief indicated how pleased the city of Lagos was with the pope's decision to relocate the Vatican to Nigeria and how positive the relationship was between his department and the Swiss Guard. Then he indicated that they were at a loss to explain the poisoning, but noted that they were not making any assumptions. It was possible that the poisoning was accidental, but they were going to treat it as a double murder until they could find Sister Sophia to learn how what they presumed was rat poison could end up in the menudo. They had made no progress in their search for her.

The Chief then bluntly asked the pope if he had any enemies. The pope chuckled slightly and indicated that the devil was always on his case and that the devil was so clever that the pope sometimes couldn't determine who his enemies were. The Chief told the pope how important it was to the investigation for the pope to think about anyone who was upset with him for any reason. The pope said that he had a joyful relationship with Sister Sophia who had been a member of her order for more than twenty five years, was a very holy woman and a great cook. He could sense her joy in the food she prepared and he assumed she was happy about being part of the household. The pope had also met her brother who was a mathematics teacher and his wife and four children. He doubted Sister would do anything to harm him or the other priests. He thought for a moment.

Then he said "It's been reported to me that there are many people in the Vatican who are still very upset about my having moved to Nigeria. I spent a great deal of time in prayer asking God how to persuade them that it was best for the Church, but many were resistant to change and I believe still hold ill feelings. I don't know which people and I certainly cannot see how their anger could be associated in any way with the poisoning. There are also a number of people throughout the world who wrote some pretty awful things about the Church and me when we moved here. Of course, there are many terrorist groups here in Africa, Asia, Europe and in the Middle East who hope that somehow the Catholic Church will go away. And I know that the "Incarnation Initiative" made a great number of people angry in the United States, China, Europe and Russia because of its economic impact.

Overall, the people of Africa and South America seemed to welcome the effort. Yet, I have no idea of any individual who hates me enough to kill me. I'm truly sorry I can't be of more help".

The Chief said that the information the pope had provided was helpful if not definitive. He then asked if the personnel records of the people in his household were off limits to the investigation. The pope responded that they were, but if there was something that the investigation learned that needed to be confirmed there was some leeway for those purposes. He shared with the Chief that the entire household had been together serving his predecessor for three years and had eagerly come from Rome with him.

Finally the Chief said that his investigative team was trying to resist the effort of the FBI in the United States to enter the investigation and to keep the process to the locals and the Swiss Guard. But it the pope wanted the FBI involved he would consider it. The FBI wanted desperately to be a part of the investigation and they based their rationale on the fact that the pope was a U.S. citizen. The Chief also shared that both his team and the Swiss Guard were operating on the current assumption that the pope was the target of the poisoning and that for now, until they could find Sister Sophia, she was the principal person of interest. They had nothing else to go on and could not explain her absence.

After the Chief and his staff had left, the pope called his household together to provide them with as much information as he had and to ask if anyone had any idea of what could have happened to Sister Sophia. At the meeting in the dining room, Sister Joseph Maria said that she had been worried by Sister Sophia for more than a week. The previous Tuesday, Sister Sophia received an envelope that was not a post. It was delivered to the security desk and brought to the kitchen. She didn't open it in the kitchen. But later that evening, she heard Sister Sophia sobbing in her room.

The next day, it was clear that Sister Sophia had not slept and she was extremely nervous. Over the last two days, she had left most of the cooking to Brother Juan and her and spent most of her time at her desk with her head down and praying. Sister Joseph Maria had asked her if there was anything she could do to help her and her only response was that she must pray for her.

Sister Sophia had left the kitchen early each night, but it was obvious that she wasn't able to sleep. Then, on Friday, Sister received a package that was also left at the security gate and brought to the kitchen and Sister didn't open it. Sister Joseph Maria imagined it to be a couple of books wrapped in brown paper. Brother Juan concurred that he had observed the same things and asked Sister if anything was wrong. She assured him she would be fine but admitted that she had been very nervous the last few days. She said perhaps it was just that she was getting older and more serious.

The pope thanked the group and indicated that he would inform them of any developments that came to him. He asked the Captain of the Swiss Guard to inform Chief Mebimi of Sister Joseph Maria's comments.

Chapter 16

Discernment Time

Serious Study

While Diego was managing the progress of his bill, Jordan undertook a serious study. She registered for two theology classes at Georgetown because it was closer to her apartment than Catholic University. She paid tuition for the first quarter and began attending classes and doing the readings. She was shocked. There were a couple of women who identified themselves as nuns and three priests as students in the class none of whom seemed what she imagined to be orthodox Christians.

She was interested in exploring the faith, but the classes turned out to be principally a criticism of the historic doctrines, values and leadership of the Church. She realized that she was being taught by graduate assistants. Full professors wrote and taught mainly at the graduate level leaving the undergraduate classrooms to graduate assistants. By the third class, she had had enough and determined to read on her own. What she heard at the undergraduate level left her wondering about the poor parents who were sacrificing their life earnings to educate their offspring in an expensive well regarded institution that she found provided a very light weight offering. She often thought back to what she had been given in terms of hard data and real science at Iowa State and thanked her parents for the experience.

She worried about those who populated the classes at Georgetown where she was enrolled. They seemed not to be bothered by the insubstantial nature of the instruction. She found the two courses useless to her pursuit and insulting to her intelligence.

She read widely, first, two books on atheism to test whether she was convinced by their arguments and their world view. She had little tolerance for their negative views. It was as though the authors wanted to recruit victims to their despair. She kept coming back to the unmoved mover, an un-caused cause of existence. The concept of a first cause fit with her scientific disposition. She wanted to cover any blind areas and concluded that if there was ever a case of "thinking outside the box" it was clearly required in the matter of faith. She now knew that she believed in God but she didn't really know the next step.

She went out one night with Emily Norton, one of her former room-mates who was working for the Washington Post covering the arts and religion. Emily was happy to be moved up from obituaries where she had labored for four years. She had learned a lot in obits but want to move on to live news. Newspapers had shredded staff to meet the limited demand for hard copy news. So she was given both the art and the religion assignments because the editor didn't expect her to do much in the religion area, but she was finding the religion area more interesting than the arts.

Emily was basically a cynic, but was meeting people who thought differently than she did. It was necessary for her to work assiduously to keep open her judgments or at least mask them in order to get those in the religious area to speak openly with her. She told Jordan that she was surprised when she met a number of men and women of various religions who were incredibly selfless, who had literally dedicated their lives to others simply because they believed that that was what God wanted them to do. They populated the soup kitchens, the small missions and central city work with the poor. Baptists worked with Catholics and Methodists and even some "new age" religious types. What she saw in this religion area was new to her and completely the opposite of what she found in her journalism and sociology pursuits at Oberlin.

Emily had absorbed the material pushed at her by her professors and now she was meeting and interacting with committed real people. She was astonished that the people she was meeting were not the cynical self-absorbed masters of the gullible as was depicted by her teachers. She wondered what was at work in her professors who were so critical of such good people. The idea entered her mind that there could have been a bit of envy among those who had little to believe in.

Emily was not certain but she was of the impression that her boss wasn't a believer. It was clear that she didn't want to prejudice Emily's work. So she never discussed her thoughts and she didn't want Emily to write about atheism even though it had become a topic in the news. Emily had met with and written about Muslims, Jews, Protestants, Mormons and Catholics. She had even done a short set of articles on Wiccan practices and had a brief exposure to the Hindu faith but that article had not been printed because a controversy about the placement of a Mosque in a certain neighborhood became front and center at the time. Ironically, it was a Jewish rabbi and a Catholic priest working together to assert the right of Muslims to place a mosque wherever the city ordinances would permit. As it turned out the Muslims didn't place a mosque but they did raise an issue and they did claim bigotry against them.

The people whom she was meeting and interviewing were clearly not the most sophisticated. They were not the intellectuals and pseudo-intellectuals who populated the professor roles of the university. But they appeared to be people with pure hearts dedicated to others. She was a reporter, a natural cynic, but she was beginning to believe there was something more than self and the here and now. She had begun to wonder about religion. She was not certain whether she would return to the Baptist faith of her childhood or to something else. But she liked the idea of being connected to something outside herself. Over a second glass of cabernet prior to dinner, both Jordan and Emily laughed at how they were changing, distancing themselves from the university and their former opinions and beliefs. Under the influence of a third glass of cabernet, Emily announced her hypothesis on religion "Most people who are born into a religion live with it without knowing a great deal about the doctrines that their church holds. They embrace it loosely until their young adulthood at which point they conclude that if it is real it will eventually grab their attention. If they marry, they may pursue a religion in the interest of their kids for a while but look forward to the day when they can again abandon it. It isn't until they attend a contemporary's funeral that think about their final performance review and start to think again about God and his role in their lives".

Excursion

Emily's work took her wherever she chose to go as long as she could draw a religious or art story. Jordan and Emily agreed to go to a Baptist church for Sunday worship. Emily had not been in a Baptist church in fifteen years and she was interested in knowing what might have changed from her youth. Jordan invited Diego to join them. Emily knew who Diego was and she was looking forward to meeting him. He chose to go to mass early Sunday morning and then take a workout before joining them. The girls had settled on the Baptist church in central Washington that was pastored by a minister whom Emily knew to be quite orthodox. Diego met them at the service which didn't start until ten thirty. He had been in many Baptist churches on the south side of Chicago and had always felt comfortable. There was a lot of Baptist in his roots. His father's entire family was actively Baptist.

Rev Sampson provided a stem-winder of a homily addressing the "Sermon on the Mount" as detailed by St. Matthew. It was powerful. He ended with an inquiry as to which group the members of the congregation wanted to be in on judgment day, the sheep or the goats. He then shared what he thought they ought to do to gain membership among the sheep. The list of activities and the generosity required for being numbered among the sheep described by Matthew was demanding. As they sat there, the three each began an intellectual accounting of their lives in relation to the gospel's admonitions. But then Rev Sampson indicated that the likelihood of doing all that Matthew and Christ were calling for was not enough. Doing followed believing and worship was an expression of their belief.

They left the church saying humorously to themselves that they were all "screwed". The demands set out by Rev Sampson were stiff. Maybe they should look for a church that had lower expectations of its members and was easier on their consciences. The idea of hitting their knees five times a day as a Muslim was unattractive and the rigors of Mormonism were a little much for their current commitment to exploration. Diego chuckled when Emily commented that the Catholic Church didn't seem to demand much of its members.

They decided that on the following Sunday they would attend a Catholic mass in a downtown church that was largely attended by the elderly, minorities and immigrants of D.C. There were a few younger people with children in the pews but just a few, so they assumed that the homily would not be addressed to them. They were greeted warmly as they had been the week before in the Baptist church. There was a Hispanic family in front of them and an elderly white couple behind them. The majority of the attendees were Hispanic or Black.

A young Black priest began the mass with a welcome and indicated that he was a guest of the pastor with whom he had attended seminary. The prelate was a Benedictine monk from a small abbey in Northwest Missouri that was dedicated to the work of Christian formation of lay people and seminarians with a special focus on youth. They provided retreats and ongoing online instruction. His job was to care for the physical plant, the food service and athletic programs. He was in town for a short intense management training program and he was appreciative of having free housing at the parish and an opportunity to preach to an eclectic

congregation. He always preached to young men whom he considered to be the choir.

The first reading was from Genesis and depicted the fall of Adam and Eve. The gospel of the mass was the first chapter of St John wherein he describes the coming of Christ into the world with "He was in the world, and the world came to be through him, but the world did not know him. He came to what was his own but his own people did not accept him. But to those who did accept him he gave power to become children of God. ......".

The priest began. "We're here today as people of this gospel, this good news. God created the world and each of us in love. We celebrate the fact that we inhabit the world that Jesus made for us. John tells us that it was through Jesus that the world came to be. Normally we associate the creation of the world with God the Father, probably because Michelangelo depicted that mean looking old man as God the Father, the creator on the ceiling of the Sistine Chapel. We associate the Spirit as the author of life and wisdom and God the Son as the Redeemer. But God is God, Father, Son and Holy Spirit and they are each present in the act of creation and in the sustaining of existence. St. John in chapter fourteen of his gospel tells us that Jesus said "I am in the Father and the Father is in me" in response to Philip's request to show him the Father.

When my brothers and sisters and I were little children and being taught science and about the "big bang", my mama down in Louisiana told us what was real. She used to say that that "big bang" they talk about was the love in God's heart bursting and creating the universe. From a woman who showered a family with a ridiculously generous love, I took it as gospel. Later, I learned that her theology was as true as is St John's gospel. God caused the universe because he wanted to manifest his love in creatures. Contained in that act of love is every good that has ever existed and will ever exist. In God's being is contained the manner in which all of existence will play out into eternity. At the "big bang" all of existence was seeded.

"The fact that God knows every thought you will ever have and every act that you will perform and every word or prayer that you will say doesn't mean that all is determined. You have the power to choose to love, to neglect to love others or to hate. The fact that God knows what you will do, doesn't prevent you from choosing to do it. Anyone of you could choose to stand up and walk out of this church, go to a tavern and drink yourself into drunkenness. You have that choice. You are also free to choose to drop a $1000 check or cash in basket. It is your choice. I recommend the cash.

"God wanted all his creatures to have the opportunity to choose to love and be loved. He wanted them first to be loved by God and then by others. Because he had given them free will, he knew that not every angel or man would return his love, but no one could love if he didn't give them the choice. Thus he gave each of us free will. Some of the angels rejected God's love and challenged his dominion. They became enemies of God's love and they inhabit the world with a capacity to make harming God's children attractive in the interests of power, money or fame.

"In our theology classes, we never touched on whether God gave the angels the opportunity for redemption. So I have no idea of whether he did or didn't. But because God loved the angels as he does all of his beings, it would seem logical to me that they would be given a second chance. Neither did we touch on whether God continues to create angels, but I believe each of us has a guardian angel and my suspicion is that they are newly created to protect and guide the being newly conceived in the womb. I have from time to time wondered that if indeed, a new angel is created with a newly conceived being and that being dies in the womb from a spontaneous abortion or is terminated, killed, what becomes of the Guardian angel? But that's not for me to worry over. The Holy Spirit is in charge and has that all figured out I am sure.

"Genesis tells us God created in seven days. Genesis was written by a number of people over a long period and under the inspiration of God, the Holy Spirit. There it is again, we are assigning to God the Holy Spirit a work that is the work of God, Father, Son and Holy Spirit. It was written in a manner that featured imagination and a certain poetic style to tell the story of God and man and how things came to be. There is the possibility that the authors meant that the world developed in seven stages over many millions of years.

"The current science of carbon dating suggests that that is a strong possibility. But we need to allow for the other possibility that God could, and I emphasize, could have created in seven twenty four hour days. The scientists tell us that what happened was that the earth was covered to a large extent by water. In the drying process, it produced a living cell and eventually an animate being. Further science tells us that the animate being evolved to a point of an upright being known a Homo Erectus. It appears that at the point Homo Erectus had developed sufficient mental capacity to abstract, to choose, God imbued (breathed, placed) a soul, a spiritual capacity to love in Homo Erectus and Homo Erectus became Homo Sapiens, man and woman, Adam and Eve from whom we draw our DNA.

"Some scientists tell us that this event occurred about one hundred twenty thousand or so years ago. The authors of Genesis tell us that Adam and Eve existed in a state perpetual happiness and were destined to produce God's human creatures who would share the capacity to love him and his other creatures. But they somehow chose to reject God's love and his plan for them. Genesis depicts the event as the tasting of the apple, the fruit of the knowledge by which they knew good and evil.

"According to the poets, inspired by the Holy Spirit, those who were telling the story of creation, that angel of whom we spoke before who had rejected God's love, inhabited the space where Adam and Eve existed. He persuaded them that they would be better off if they chose to do their own will. We know that angel as Lucifer, the devil and he is indeed clever. I know he works on my will every day and probably on yours.

"But God didn't wash his hands of us and abandon us. He wasn't going to let his love for us be rejected completely. His is an unconditional love. He would exercise his love in what St. Augustine calls "Oh, happy fault" the evil that led to God demonstrating his love for us by redeeming us. God was not going to force us to love him or his beings all the time. God knew that if we had free will, we would not always love. So God's plan for the world and man was to provide a human act of perfect love to show man how to love perfectly. He would come in human flesh in the person of Jesus and demonstrate perfect love. He would live, love, laugh, be tempted, teach and criticize. He would feel fear, rejection, pain, longing, misunderstanding, abandonment. He would suffer and die in agony to show us how to live and love.

"I have told you some of what I know and a lot of what I believe. Belief and reason go together. They support one another. Reason can bring us part of the way in knowing God, but reason will never bring us to Jesus. To believe that Jesus is God, that he died for us, rose from the dead and will come to us this day in this sacrificial thanksgiving requires the gift of faith that allows us to step into the abyss of belief and be lifted by accepting that we are blessed with the belief that Jesus is God. Then we have to step farther into the unknown and embrace all that he has told us about his heavenly kingdom.

"That embrace requires us to love people we don't like, to trust people who break our trust and to suffer the rejection of those who don't understand us and refuse our faith and our love. If faith doesn't appear at that point, the only thing for willing people to do is to pray for faith and take the chance on God. That is the baptism of desire. Philosopher Pascal had a wager argument that, paraphrased, essentially said that if you believe in God and act on that belief and if you are wrong, you may have lost a few pleasures. If you gamble on there not being a God, and act on that lack of belief and there is a God, you may have lost it all. God loves us all and you may be blessed with just the desire for faith. Faith is not knowing. Faith is believing.

"As a Christian, I believe that existence is a mystery only a part of which God has chosen to share with us in this life. I don't need to know everything. I can only conclude from what I have observed that along with Albert Einstein, I believe that everything is a miracle. There are so many things I don't know that I don't know, that I can't spend time thinking about them. I try to learn every day but most of what I learn are things that will not change my faith. Nor will I allow the Church, its priests, its bishops or people to diminish my faith. My faith is in Jesus and it was given to me by God.

"I *believe* I know why God created the universe and human beings. I don't know if we are the only universe, I don't know if we are the only occupied planet, I don't know if scientists have found the smallest particle of matter and I don't know why God chose to evolve man, if he did. It may have been necessary in God's plan that in order to sustain a being with such a complex nature, it took a very long time for the being to fully develop the capacity to reason and abstract. Man needed to attain a delicate physique and an intellect and will. We will know all the answers if we are told to line up with those lambs at our judgment. St John of the Cross has told us that all that will really matter at our judgment is how much we have loved. If existence is all about God and if God is perfect love that seems reasonable to me.

"The small message that I hope you will take from this homily is that we live in God's world, we live among God's children and that we have the choice to love or not love them. If we choose to love God's children, we will commit ourselves to those actions that St Matthew describes. We will feed the hungry, comfort the infirm, visit the prisoners, clothe the naked etc etc…. Well anyway you get the idea. Stand with the lambs. St John is telling us that this is God's world even though he if not recognized by those of us who inhabit the world that Jesus, who is God, made. Look around you and look for Jesus in everyone you see. He is there. It is up to us to find him and feed him. Keep in mind that we are all God's kids. May God bless us all".

Faith Required

They stayed for the rest of the mass. Their minds were churning with their personal thoughts and responses to the homily. Each of them knew that at the consecration, believers accepted the fact that the wafer of unleavened bread and the cup of wine would be turned into the actual body and blood of Jesus. Diego firmly believed it. But none of them knew how this could occur. The girls were working the idea as a part of bumping up against faith and the people who believe. They struggled with the notion of a person in the bread and wine. Acceptance would require something that they didn't seem to have that morning. They found much of what the priest had said was rational for those who had faith.

They went to breakfast after the mass. Initially they spoke of their assessment of the décor and design of the church. They were quite taken by the Gothic influence. The structure was very old and in generally poor condition. It needed renewal. They spoke of the warmth of the reception which surprised them. The girls were surprised because other times when they had been in a Catholic Church, they had found a rather cool reception. Jordan broke the spiritual ice and said she was stunned. It was as if the homily had been prepared exclusively for her and her quest.

While she still had major questions about the Church and faith, she found she was encouraged. She would need to read, formulate her questions more clearly and talk to someone like that priest or a minister with the same sense of orthodoxy. She didn't need to be entertained by jokes, orchestras or dancers. If she was going to explore religion, she wanted it straight up.

Emily indicated she was impressed by the homily of both men but she wasn't as excited about further pursuit as Jordan was. She said that she found it interesting that both preachers had included St. Matthew's gospel on the judgment. Reporter that she was, she had an interesting take. She said that the priest had told a magnificent story. She had heard parts of it before, but she had never heard it all put together in one homily, never delivered as a whole in that manner. Like St Paul, she said that if the story isn't true and Jesus didn't rise from the dead, the whole thing was a great con.

The idea of a personal God was attractive to her, but she thought implausible. The idea of a personal God becoming man, the son of a virgin was preposterous. And the idea of the God who became man rising from the dead was outrageous. If he could convince people to believe that story, he was clearly the greatest con of all time or God. She said that those who believe are either fools or have a really strong blessing of faith which she clearly didn't share. But, she said she'd like to have that kind of faith. It would make her feel more secure in life and death. She didn't have a problem with there being a God, but Jesus was a different matter for her.

She had read enough as part of her preparation for her role at the newspaper to learn that Jesus was different from the other principals of religions. Nobody else claimed to be God. Jesus was the only one who demanded a commitment by his claim. The others either claimed they had discovered the way to God or they were God's prophets. The Buddha, Moses and Mohammed never claimed to be God. A bunch of nuts and cons over the years claimed to be God, but Jesus was the only one who made billions of people believe. That bothered her. She had rejected her Baptist upbringing big time and couldn't see herself going back to religion. It might make her feel phony and it would likely cramp her life style. She was pretty comfortable in an open sex life and most religions frowned on that matter. If she was going to go religious, she would go all the way as she did with everything she did. But unlike Jordan, she didn't feel ready for that kind of change. She indicated she had a little of St Augustine in her. She would like God to make her holy, but not just yet.

Priorities

On his way home from breakfast, Diego received a

phone call from Renaldo indicating that their mother, Carmen, had taken a turn for the worse and may not have a lot of time left. The doctors were surprised that she had outlived their projection of one year. The diagnosis included metastasis of the colon cancer to the liver and they projected a life span of one year. She had already outlived that projection by six months, but sheclearly was eager to die. She suffered with grace, but she would prefer, as she said, "to return home and to Frankie and God."

His Drug Free America bill was about to be introduced in the senate on the following Monday, but it would be managed by his co-sponsor from Pennsylvania who had lost a son to drugs. Diego wanted to be there but he didn't worry his absence would be a factor in whether it would pass or not pass. The Holy Spirit could handle it. He had his priorities and his mom was at the top of the list. He would go home.

Chapter 17

Carmen's Legacy

A Time to Suffer

She sat back in the recliner and he could sense that she was in intense pain. When he would ask if he could do anything to comfort her, she would say that she had "just a little discomfort in my back. I'll be alright in a while. I've felt worse". He knew that she was not being entirely candid. The oncologist had given a prognosis of one to two weeks indicating how difficult it was to tell with the advanced cancer. The doctor had determined to manage her pain with morphine. Diego had experienced plenty of pain himself and knew what it did to the mind, but he was worried about her reluctance to take more morphine than she was. Even without much of the morphine, she seemed to drift off to another place for a while and then return to him. He wondered what was going on in her mind during the time when she seemed not to be with him.

When the hospice people had told him to keep her as sedated as possible, he was a little reluctant because he knew she didn't like being in a haze. She told him that she wanted to be as alert as she could under the circumstance when she went to meet her Lord. She indicated early on when she began to suffer that it was God's will and that there was reason to it. She could help the poor souls. He tried to dissuade her but she would hear nothing of it. He thought back to his high school religion class where one year every day they would read about a new saint. He recalled how some of them would endure pain in the satisfaction that it was what God wanted of them. He couldn't buy it then and he didn't buy it now. His mom needed the pain relief. However her refusal fit his image of his mom. In his view, she was more saintly than many of those in the book and certainly more saintly than anyone he knew. She had devoted every second of her life to others and now she was concerned that she might burden others with her sickness and death.

He had no tolerance for pain. When he had experienced intense pain, he had never worried about his survival, but he eagerly sought relief. His playing days had provided a lot of minor injuries with a lot of pain. When he woke up in the Air Force hospital in Ramstein, shot in the shoulder, the doctors had told him he would survive his trauma. All he wanted was pain relief and to get back to business. He got relief from the pain pills but they almost did him in. It was a challenge not to use pain pills when the season began. His body was always stiff, bruised and beaten. He could easily have gotten all the prescription remedies he wanted. There was always the challenge to depend on them and avoid all pain, but he knew better. He managed without them. A couple of aspirin a couple of times a day was all he allowed himself.

Her pain was different. Her pain was dying pain. She had rallied six months ago, but this was final and both of them knew it. She was dying and she welcomed it. She had said that she would get through the pain and then go to God and Frankie. That made her happy. She told him at least a dozen times that she enjoyed the life God had given her. She had loved the family from which she came. She loved Frankie and she loved her children. She said she knew that the God who had given them that life and love would surely have an even better life for them in heaven and she was eager to get there. She trusted God totally.

He had seen her suffer before, but never physically to

the point of this day. He saw the emotional pain she endured when his father died and the pain that she felt every day in having to leave the children early every morning to work in the kitchen at St Rita's. But it was her only way of supporting them. The pension from the police department simply wasn't enough to support seven kids and to keep them in housing, food and clothes. She had gotten a break on tuitions and she knew how to skimp. In fact she was a master. Everything in the house and on their backs was either given to them or bought second hand. She never bought retail. She was skilled at keeping them in nice attire cheaply and she was proud of it.

Little did she know then that one day she would live in luxury for a few years before the terminal cancer diagnosis. Well, she had had a few comfortable years in the new house Diego had bought for her. She traveled several times to Mexico to see family and took many of them on vacations. Once, she and Rosa took ten of her nieces and nephews to Europe for two weeks. The family was ever present in Carmen's house. Diego's success was generously shared. But considering their modest start, most of Carmen's kids had done extremely well and they didn't need or want Diego's charity. His resources went outside the family. His favorite charity was to the scholarships he had created at St. Rita's and each year he would host the senior class in Washington for two days at his expense. He would accompany them to all the symbols of freedom and explain the reasons why he thought they were worth fighting for.

Sergeant Frankie Freeman

Sitting in the dark room, he was reminded of his father's death. He drifted off into a memory of nearly thirty years earlier. He was at his "daddy's" funeral, the mass, the pungent odor of the incense lingering in his nasal passages, the somber Mexican brass and the rhythmic Black chorus echoing spirituals like no other mass. St. Rita's was packed. The mayor and lots of officials and policemen had come to honor Frankie. Mr. and Mrs. Goldman of Allsave were there. The city officials and politicians in their dark suits poured out of big black cars. The police officers were in their dress blues, the state highway patrol officers in tan and many with Smokey the Bear hats. There was much brass and miles of thick and shiny black leather belts holding their equipment. He remembered the cemetery mostly for the "Tenshun!!!" and "Hodar Harms" the command of the Captain of the honor guard.

He watched the slow movement of the procession to the gravesite. Flags led each contingent of officers and they were followed by the horrible wailing of the bagpipes and then the crack of the rifles, ten of them giving a salute at the cemetery. The sound of the distant trumpet and Taps lingered in his memories. In his mind he could see the American flag that was draped on Frankie's casket and then hung in the front room of the house reminding them of Frankie's service to his country and to others.

He still remembered screaming his objection when his mother allowed the men to lower the box with his daddy's body into the deep dark hole. He was told by his brothers to be brave like his dad, but he couldn't be. He cried for a week and couldn't rid himself of the image of his daddy in a dark and crowded wooden box in the ground.

Now, as he sat next to his mom, he was beginning to understand something of what life was all about. His mom and dad were givers. Jordan had been a great comfort to him when he found out about his mom's diagnosis. She built a hedge of faith around everything he was experiencing. She made it all rational, logical and showed him that reality could be either blessed in faith or cursed with a painful doubt based on how you reacted with your spirit and attitude. She had put a hopeful cover on his thoughts. She placed his mother's condition in the context of salvation. Ironically, she herself had newly come to belief, but it seemed much stronger, more informed and wiser than his own. She was taking her existence and her new found faith more seriously than he had seen in anyone.

At thirty six, he was just beginning to grasp some notion of what things meant. He had begun to sense that life was not a pre- season game and that there seemed to be only two alternatives. Either there was a God with a plan for existence and each of us or it all ended at the grave. He had never doubted the existence of God, but he had never spent much time contemplating the implications of Christ dying to save the people in his own life like his mom and dad. He had faced death himself without giving much thought to its implications.

Jordan bluntly pointed out that there was no way out of this world without somebody suffering. In this case, it was his loving mother and the entire extended family that she had loved and nurtured. He had no doubt that she would simply bounce from her death bed into a glorious place with God in a world of peace and joy. But it was still difficult for him. She had been the rock to whom all of them were tethered, but he thought he would miss her the most. At this point, everyone else in the family, except Angel was married and had children. It was at times like this that he had realized how fast his life had moved. He knew his life wasn't normal like the other kids and he was missing a lot. He simply hadn't had time to consider marriage until Jordan came along.

As a child he had lost his father and now he was losing his mother. He was close to the family but not like he was close to his mother. The feeling of his world changing was already occurring and she was still sitting beside him in the recliner, fading. He remembered how much his world changed when his daddy was gone and now it was changing with his mother's death. From the day of his father's death forward, he had a consciousness that he was different.

He was not at all happy about being different. Some others had both mothers and fathers. He never really felt complete after his "daddy's" death. Teachers and family friends treated all the Freeman kids different after Frankie's death. It was as though they needed to remind him that he was different because he didn't have a dad. When he would go to a friend's house and the friend's dad was there, he had an odd feeling of some envy. Of course their dad wasn't as good as his dad had been. He simply could not figure out why God decided to take his dad? Dads belong with their kids. Diego's "daddy" was truly bigger, smarter and a better dad than anyone else's could be, but sometimes he wished he could have any dad.

And even with those whose fathers had left the family, guys could rely on them coming around on birthdays or maybe Christmas when it was important to have a dad. And they could be reassured that their dads were still living and unless they were in jail or drunk they could be called upon for support even if they were not always present. How many times had he thought if only he could turn back the clock, get back to just the night before his dad died and lock in that moment and stay in it forever secure with both a mom and dad.

Now he was watching his mom die. Well, she would have what she had wanted for a long time, to be with Frankie and her God. She had always told him that there were three parts to the human race and he only saw one. She said that we were all related in Jesus and that he should never forget that he was close to his dad even if he was not next to him at the table or in the car. His dad was among the "church triumphant" those who had already made it. They were with God. He liked the "triumphant" thing and he liked to think that his dad was one of those who had "triumphed". She told him he was equally related to those who were suffering in purgatory who she called the Church "suffering", those with a chance to clean up their act, getting prepared to see God and he should always pray for them and "offer up" any of his pain or disappointments to help them get out of purgatory. If he "offered up" his pain for them, God would apply his suffering for them. They couldn't do anything for themselves once they had died, but others could help them by offering their suffering which she said she was doing. He didn't really understand it too well, but he tried it when he was in Ramstein in case any of his buddies who had been killed needed the help.

He didn't really do well at suffering. And of course, she always said he should offer up any pain and pray for all the people around him. She called them the "Church militant". He thought that was kind of funny. He didn't think of his brother Renaldo, Jose or his sister Rosa or Isabel as militant. But he always liked his mother's teaching.

At two in the afternoon, he called Renaldo and told him to gather the family because he was going to call the priest. "Mom is ready to go and we don't want to hold her up" he told Renaldo. Father Kevin was only a block away. He came and administered the sacrament of the sick. Diego held one hand and Rosa held the other hand and she died peacefully before the others arrived.

Carmen had made all of her own arrangements. The readings and the music for the mass would be the same as she had chosen for Frankie's funeral. For the mass, she assigned a role to each of her twenty one grandchildren. The music would include the Mexican brass and the black gospel singers. She had picked out her cedar casket from a monastery catalog. All the family had to do was order it delivered to the funeral home. St. Rita's had stopped using the basement for wakes.

The wake occurred at Conley's Funeral Home. Because of all the friends of the seven children and the twenty one grandchildren, the funeral home was packed with people and there were lines outside waiting to pay their respects. In addition to the friends of the children and grandchildren, there were kids from the school whom she had fed over the years and their kids. In addition, there were notables and scads of politicians and ball players. Mayor Perez came and there was an auxiliary bishop and five Augustinian priests whom she had lavished care on over the years, a lot of teachers, parishioners and a lot of kids.

Diego's sadness was cast into peace by the homily Father Kevin provided. It was so beautiful and faith filled that he wanted it to go on and on. Father Kevin took passages from the gospels and showed Carmen's personification of them. The luncheon was in St. Rita's cafeteria, certainly not because the family couldn't afford a restaurant but because that was her domain, the place where she had met the children and the children's children who would be present. The last meal her family would have with her was in her kitchen and she had even decided the menu. Her friend Edwina had retired but she came back and oversaw the kitchen staff in the preparation and presentation of the meal. It had to meet Carmen's standards.

Jordan had come to Chicago the night before the funeral and had come directly to the wake to be with Diego. She surprised him by showing up in the line. He couldn't have been more pleased with her presence. Diego had told her so much about Carmen that Jordan felt she knew her well. But she felt like she knew more about Carmen by seeing the character and the values personified in her son.

Not only did she love him, but she admired Diego more than any man she had ever met. He was honest, hardworking, humble and eager to help others. It was a great relief to Diego to have her there because it took a little of the sadness out of his heart. His mother was gone but his future was standing next to him. Carmen was with God and Diego was with Jordan. He introduced her to all of his relatives as "my friend, Jordan". He didn't need to say that she was his future wife. All could see the love.

The day after the funeral, Diego had lunch with Renaldo and the aging Brother Mark who was about to retire from teaching. They discussed a lot of things. Renaldo assured Diego that everyone in the family was doing well financially and there was nothing to worry about with any of them including the grand kids. All his brothers and sisters had homes of one sort or another and at least one of the parents had jobs sufficient to keep up. Renaldo had done well and was president of a large community bank where he had been for twelve years. After lunch when Renaldo had left to go back to work, Diego shared with Brother Mark that he didn't really like congress and was thinking of retiring. Brother Mark was surprised and urged him to think long and hard about that decision. He told Diego to take a long time to make a decision and suggested that he might want to stay in congress. He told him his congressional work was important to the nation and the city. He could do a lot of good in his position.

They talked about Carmen and how happy she would be with God and Frankie. Brother Mark said that he was kind of envious of Carmen. She had successfully managed her suffering from cancer and had obviously done a lot of poor souls a lot of good. He said that now that he was retiring he would have time to prepare to die. Diego asked if Brother Mark was sick. He responded that he was still in good health but he hoped to get better prepared to die than how he felt at present.

Diego quizzed him further about what he meant. Brother Mark said that he wasn't afraid of dying. But when he contemplated his death, he thought about how radically different it would be when he died. For seventy three years he had measured his life in minutes, hours, days and years. But in death there is no time. He was convinced that eternity wasn't static because a person is in the presence of God whose very being is dynamic. But he found it difficult to imagine heaven other than that it was the full experience of love, of perfect happiness packed into a second and then stretched to an unending peace. He mentioned that he was a little outside the Magisterium's box when it came to the theology of heaven. He reasoned that if we make it to heaven and are in a place without time, the waiting for the last judgment to occur was impossible. "I'm pretty well convinced as your mom was that at our death we're given our glorified bodies. If we experience perfect happiness by seeing God after we die, we don't become more than perfectly happy at the last judgment by getting our earthly bodies back. When Jesus spoke of the resurrection I think he had that in mind. God's clever enough to handle the business of our earthly bodies deteriorating at Mt. Olivet cemetery and to give our glorified bodies to us at our death.

He told Diego about how Father Kevin had preached that man would be so occupied by knowing God that it would not matter if their relatives were with them in heaven. Carmen had walked into the sacristy right after mass and told Father Kevin that the theologian that thought that needed to have kids because there would not be a single mother in heaven who would be happy without her babies. But I just don't worry about that". All Diego could say was that Brother Mark's and his mom's observations were "interesting".

Brother Mark was taken by Jordan who had returned to Washington. Diego shared with him Jordan's pursuit of the faith and that he was going to propose when he returned to Washington. He hoped to be married within the year. Brother Mark was pleased and commented that he thought surely it was about time for Diego to marry at age 36. Brother Mark said that he had more time now that he was retiring and would be pleased to pray for both him and Jordan and their future together.

A Time to Think

Jordan continued to read. She read philosophy, theology and even some church history. As an engineering student, she hadn't been exposed to a lot of the liberal arts, history or the humanities. Her reading was enlightening and informative. She began to see the nation and the culture in a new light. She witnessed the influence that Christianity had had on the whole of Western civilization. She was particularly interested in the Church's relationship with science over the centuries. She had always been taught that there was conflict between theology and science. One thing that struck her was that there was a period when the Church totally dominated the Western mind and to a large extent the politics of Western civilization. The authority of the Church and the authority of its hierarchy held both the temporal and eternal hammer. But the Church had faded in importance in the scientific age.

Those who attempted to move to a dualism of reason and faith, theology and science were kept within the boundaries of the Church's teaching until the sixteenth and seventeenth century but science and reason took hold. Copernicus, Galileo, Newton, Bacon and Descartes broke out and the sway of the Church over the Western mind was largely lost.

Reason however sustained the natural law and science guided the world of discovery. There was a separation of reason, science and faith. That separation caused a tension for the Church and science. Jordan was aware that many scientists saw no conflict with theology and faith. But there were also many, who lacking faith, attempted to exploit the division, the fact that one couldn't reason to belief. In her studies Jordan had observed the philosophical principle that "nature never acts in vain". Every being has its purpose. Surely man was a major part of creation and consequently has purpose.

She was impressed by the position taken by Pope Pius

XII took on behalf of the Church in the 1950s, when, exercising reason and a measure of courageous faith stated that there could be no conflict between theology and science because they both were declaring truth and truth was not divisible. He indicated that the Church welcomes science provided it is guided by natural law.

One commentator on the topic of faith and science impressed Jordan with her observation that science had brought us to a point where science and technology had outgrown man's reasonableness. The author, a bioethicist, concluded that humans have to examine the use of the gifts of science in light of some generally acceptable standard that falls within the wide parameters of whether God does or does not exist. If God does not exist, then it is logical and acceptable for man to act in the place of God and use his science to any end he chooses. But she observed, too many people want to act as God in determining what is natural and acceptable.

Based on Jordan's awareness of the standards published by the Presidential Bioethics Committee in 2036, much was left to be desired. She concluded that the one good decision that continued to be maintained by the Committee was that cloning of humans was unacceptable. The admonishment meant nothing to some scientists who were devoted to cloning and had produced some unconscionable outcomes without sanction by government.

Jordan was comfortable with the Church's position on the role of science in the world and that there was a clear separation of theology and faith, but the relationship was affirming and not in conflict. The Church was comfortable rejecting any use of science that did not measure up to the natural law, but the Church did not deny the facts of science.

The week after the funeral, Diego returned to D.C. and he and Jordan went to dinner. When they had settled into a drink, he told his congressional work was a disaster and his bill was not going well. He wanted to hear about her and some good news. She said she was happily moving toward her baptism and all was going well.

A Serious Pursuit

The following Sunday, Jordan and Diego went for a ride. Washington's cherry blossoms and the glorious spring weather made for a romantic time and they decided to travel to Monticello and to walk the grounds. The day, the venue and the mood were the perfect time for a relaxed conversation. Most of the conversation was about family. When they headed home, they went for a beer and a light early dinner at a local watering hole and started to talk. Jordan shared that she had gone to the pastor of the Catholic Church where they had gone for Sunday mass and asked for some time to talk. Father David, the pastor was a Benedictine monk and had only been in parish work for a short time.

He agreed to a meeting the following day in the park next to the church after her work. He wanted to meet with her in a setting that would not constrain her by being on foreign soil. His office was very Catholic with a large crucifix and a lot of symbols of the faith. He didn't want to push her too far. He first wanted to get a fix on what prompted her interest at that time in her life. He asked a few baseline questions to learn just how serious she was and where she was in her search for faith.

She persuaded him that the search was real and central to her life at the moment. She was eager to learn whether she was indeed blessed with faith or to learn that she was stuck in ambiguity with an eagerness for faith that would not be satisfied.

He indicated that he thought she should move ahead with the pursuit of knowledge of the faith and to see where it took her. He told her to drop by his office the next day and if he was not there he would leave a couple of books that he thought might help her. One was by an atheist. He left a note with the books. The note simply asked "Do you think you believe in God"? When she met with him the next week, she said that she had no doubt about the existence of God. She just didn't know enough about him to feel comfortable devoting her life to a God she did not understand. She thought of answers to nearly everything that was mentioned in the book and that given sufficient time, she could write a response to almost every idea of the atheists sufficient to satisfy her. She was very comfortable with the idea of a personal God who created. That was not where she was. She wanted to know whether she had faith in Jesus.

He then recommended that she begin to read the New Testament and to start with Matthew. He would leave more books for her to read. She was pleased the next day when she showed up at the office and found the books he had left. Both were short reads. The first was the "The Purpose Driven Life" by Rick Warren, an evangelical minister and the other was a book entitled "Jesus of Nazareth" by Pope Benedict XVI. After finishing both books she went on line to wade through some websites that she hoped might attract her. The priest had asked if she wanted to go to liberal or conservative theologians. She described herself as conservative in matters of science, dress and lifestyle, so she assumed she was inclined to the more conservative theologians.

The priest recommended C.S. Lewis's "Mere Christianity". She had finished the first two books. When she realized that both Lewis and Warren were not Catholic, she asked the priest in humor if he didn't like Catholic authors. She had read four books, two by Protestants and one by an atheist. C.S. Lewis had given her a feeling of comfort in her search. He had had the same experiences traveling through reason to faith.

He reported that some of his stimulation to pursue Christianity was sparked by his friend and fellow author J.R. Tolkien who shared his imagination and faith. She had read Lewis's "Chronicles...." in high school but had not connected them with faith, only with adventure and imagination. She saw the "Chronicles" in a new light after she had read Lewis more widely.

Later in the week when Diego and she went to dinner, she asked him if he had done any reading about Jesus or the Catholic faith after finishing college. He said that he read the readings of the mass and read some materials from a couple of Catholic philosophers for his classes at Northwestern but he had not had time to do much other spiritual reading. They talked a while about how easy it was to function in their crowded lives without having to spend any time thinking about the big picture, the end game. It was so easy to stay in the moment of work, entertainment, shopping, cleaning, internet etc that the brain could virtually or actually be occupied for all their waking hours.

Jordan told him that she feared that the purpose of her life could be lost in the living her current life style. She felt a need for change and she was getting serious about it. She reached in her oversized bag and handed him "Jesus of Nazareth" and "The Purpose Driven Life" and told him that it was important to her that he read them. She hoped he would read the books before Easter, so they could discuss them and he agreed. She wanted to know if they were on the same page with what they thought.

She shared that there was a time when she thought that Jesus was a great philosopher with very human admonitions. She had read a book by a theology professor at Yale who was part of the "Jesus Movement" a group of modern Gnostics who didn't regard Jesus as God, just a great prophet. She was surprised at how wide the "movement" was. She told him that she wished she could have been converted as Paul of Tarsus was when he was knocked to the ground and blinded, but it was not so. She just gradually came to the belief that Jesus must have been divine. Jordan considered the most profound miracle that he had wrought was to convert billions to believe that they should love their neighbor. That wasn't to say that they did love their neighbors, but they knew it was what they should do.

Then, she told him that she was going to be baptized at Easter. Diego was not surprised. He was delighted that she had been successful in her search. He ordered champagne to go with their spaghetti. She asked Diego to be her baptismal sponsor and he readily agreed. She knew she would need a second sponsor for baptism and asked if he had any ideas. He agreed to think on it.

When they arrived at her door, he pulled her close to him, kissed her and told her that he loved her. She said 'Back at ya big guy. I think I loved you when we went to dinner on the first night and you couldn't wait to know if I was married'. He asked how she knew he wanted to know that and she said "A woman knows". He wanted to pop the question right there at the door but he hadn't formulated the words he wanted to say nor had he purchased a ring. It had to be perfect.

Chapter 18

Debate

Nothing Subtle

The Drug Free America act went to the Senate where Diego had secured two sponsors, one of whom had been a highly successful and very articulate drug addicted surgeon and the other, the mother of a young woman who had overdosed on cocaine on her twenty first birthday. He doubted the bill would pass the Senate, but he had had an opportunity to provide some education to the congress and to urge them to "think outside the box" on the issue. To his surprise, the bill passed Judiciary and went to Appropriations. The money was not the real issue. It was the possible changes that states would be permitted to make in their drug policies and the goal of the program with youth. He knew there would be opposition to spending federal dollars to help kids to understand that there was a God-given purpose to their lives. He wasn't interested in pitching God, but people a lot of people understood that if there was talk about a purpose, God would have to be in the picture. It would be hard to talk meaning without God.

The opposition started in the Appropriations Committee. A Maryland Senator, a Catholic by birth objected to the idea of funding a program that depended on kids learning that their nature, their origin and destiny was in God. She said "Clearly, the focus of this program calls for something that is unconstitutional. We are wasting our time passing something that addresses religion and forces kids to believe in God. I object and I urge you to vote this down". The ACLU had her in their pocket for years and had used her as their "useful idiot" more than once. But the bill passed Appropriations by one vote with bi-partisan support. When it went to the floor there was another heated debate.

More Than One Way

The bill fell apart on the floor of the Senate over the issue of God in the game. The ACLU was aided by a number of organizations which were suspect of any initiative that had to do with identifying life with a purpose beyond just being and doing. They clearly didn't want kids to think beyond the grave or to find a purpose in their existence. They crippled the bill with church and state gobbledygook and frightened the weak Senators with a pernicious interpretation of the constitution. Ironically, they were joined by the Republicans who opposed the states having an opportunity to articulate drug policy for their states. The federal government had failed miserably in attempting to interdict drugs but the Republicans felt that all drug policy should come from Washington. Jordan felt Diego's pain and told him that she had recently read a comment by Mother Teresa that said something to the effect that "We are not called to success; we are called to be faithful". She told him that he had done his best and that was all he could do.

He told her there was more than one route to his goal. He had checked his assets recently and he found himself better off financially than he had anticipated. Renaldo had put him together with a friend in Chicago who was running a hedge fund. Entry level participation was ten million dollars. Diego had placed thirty million into the fund and had been rewarded handsomely. Despite his generous contributions to his foundation, his total asset beyond the hedge fund money was just over one hundred million. His agent had negotiated contracts with large amounts of his income deferred. The approach was now paying off.

He could take a chunk of the asset and the interest to create another specific tax exempt foundation to test Jordan's and his program ideas. He could keep government out of the picture and go full bore with the same plan. He doubted that the Internal Revenue Service would dare to challenge the idea of the foundation on the basis of a Church- State conflict. He needed a smart tax attorney to put the foundation together. Angel, his younger sister had specialized in tax law and did the job eagerly.

Diego and Oscar had stayed in contact at least monthly over the last few years. Oscar had been drafted as a wide receiver by Oakland and was immediately traded to the Jets. He had spent most of his first year on the taxi squad and was moved up and played the last three games of the year.

He earned a steady berth for the next year and spent four years as a regular wide out. The Jets management offered a bonus to popular players to stay in New York City in the off season and to engage in public service. In his first year he became very popular. There were not a lot of NFL players of Mexican descent and he stood out both because of his play and his nationality. He stayed in town in the off season and visited a lot of hospitals and youth groups. He had a great contract and used the extra money to fund a retirement annuity program for his mother, Evelyn, so she could retire from her job at the Cook County Jail. She had been there for fifteen years and the annuity helped to cut about five years from her schedule. He also made a couple of well paying commercials that he used for the same purpose.

On a visit to a children's clinic at Columbia Presbyterian Hospital he met a pediatrician with whom he was taken. Anna Gonzalez was born and raised in Puerto Rico. She secured a scholarship to Columbia University School of Medicine where she took a residency in pediatrics. They married after the next season and immediately began a family. In his fifth year with the Jets, a new coach who had less regard for Oscar benched him for the last four games of the year. Oscar was weary of a new coach every two years and had had a couple of significant concussions. Anna asked him to consider retiring and he readily agreed. He had lost his interest in pro football.

He was offered an executive position with an insurance company in Milwaukee. Anna was burned out after five years at the clinic and was eager to start something new. When they arrived in Milwaukee, she worked only part time as a volunteer in a free clinic and their family grew to four children.

Two days after Diego's bill failed, Oscar came to Washington on business for a few days. When Diego and Oscar went to dinner, Oscar consoled Diego and shared that he was beginning to think about moving on from insurance. He wanted to go back to Chicago and Anna was willing. He had been successful, but the objectives and goals he had set for himself had been achieved quickly and he was looking for something new. Diego asked him if he wanted to run for Diego's seat in Chicago. Oscar demurred. Politics was the last area he was interested in.

Then the Holy Spirit banged Diego on the head and helped him to see how perfect Oscar would be for running the foundation. He too had had a family member destroyed by drugs. They had a laugh about the times with "Hoghead", but there was a sad end to that story when Jorge simply could not get off the drugs and overdosed in his early thirties.

After he returned to Milwaukee and after a long discussion of the idea with Anna, they called and asked Diego where he would have to live in order to run the foundation. Diego told him he could live wherever he chose. The foundation could come to Oscar in Chicago. It would be the perfect laboratory for the program. Chicago had remained the most dangerous city in the country for young men under twenty five. Drugs and killing were the hallmark of the city. Oscar started the foundation from scratch. Both he and the foundation flourished. After failing in his effort to interest the faculties of the schools of psychology or religion at DePaul and Loyola Universities, Oscar turned to the University of Chicago and developed a unique program. The School of Social Service was willing to train a cadre of young students suitable to a domestic mission to work with elementary, high school and college age people identified by law enforcement, school authorities or self identified as users.

The simple goal of the program was to stimulate a deep spirituality and sense of life's purpose in the young people who agreed to come into the program. Three years into the existence of the program, it was deemed a success and half a dozen secular foundations wanted to participate and further the model. Five years into the program the foundation had become the largest private and most successful anti-drug program in history and schools found a way to get past the ACLU and include the program in the social studies curriculum.

There were still drugs, gangs, overdoses and ruined lives, but there were also a lot of kids who thought of themselves as having a reason to live, a purpose to their existence, meaning. When the program began to see public acclaim, Cardinal Hurley came to Diego and urged him help with sustaining some of the Catholic schools in Chicago but it was too late. The schools were a matter of the past.

Chapter 19

Jesus of Nazareth, (the Book), The Purpose Driven Life

Diego's Assignment

To fulfill his promise to Jordan, he read the books. They were not long or difficult books to read. Both held his attention. He finished the books, one per week. The "Purpose" book was supposed to be read over a forty day period, but he was given permission by Jordan to read it all at once. He had ordered the books for his electronic reader and spent some time on the floor of the House with them when routine matters were being carried on or someone was droning on about some irrelevant matter. The night he finished the "Purpose Driven Life", he lay awake for a long time. He was thinking of his mother and father and wondering what they were doing, how time was spent in heaven. Then he remembered learning from Mr. Robinson in physics, that there was no time in eternity. He tried, but he simply couldn't imagine it. It was frustrating. He knelt down next to his bed. Normally, he was quick with his night prayers. He would normally hit the floor for five minutes, go pro forma and off to sleep.

His mind began to roam. All of a sudden he was struck with a consciousness of being. He thought to himself that he existed, not just his body, but "HE" Diego, existed. He was intensely aware of being and of coming "to be". The thought, I am, had a powerful impact on him. His parents were part of the near cause of his existence, but the ultimate cause of all existence was God. He considered that at one point in time, he didn't exist. Now he did. Like it or not, he would continue in existence as his parents did. He was temporal. His earthly life was linear with beginning and end. But he was also eternal. He was social with friends and assoicates, but he realized that his only absolute permanent connection with another being was to God.

He had always had something to occupy his mind, to think about. But he had never thought about being. His awareness was intense. He began to sense adrenaline coursing through his body. His heartbeat and his consciousness increased. He realized he didn't have anything to do with becoming. There was no free will involved in his becoming. Nor did he have any say about whether he would continue to be. He pondered Shakespeare's query about "to be or not to be". It was purely rhetorical. Once a person exists, they will remain in existence. That was something he had never thought about before. But it was important.

He had thought about dying and heaven, but his existence had never been as real to him as it was at that moment. Perhaps, the thought was more important than any thought he had ever had. His thoughts were coming quickly without any filter and his head was full. It occurred to him that he was really alone in the world except for one relationship that would last forever. It was just himself and Jesus who is God. He had family, friends and associates. But in the long term, eternity, it was really just him, Jesus, his God and whomever God decided to include in that relationship. He hoped it would be his mom and dad and brothers and sisters and now certainly Jordan. But he knew that the one constant and sure being would be God.

He was exhausted. The thinking had lasted a long time and had literally worn him out. He could finally go to bed and rest. It was 3:30 A.M.

When he awoke, his first thought upon his feet hitting the floor was that this is the first day of something new, a new perspective. Whether he wished it or not, his life would be divided by last night's experience. He knew things would be different somehow. Every morning started with the television news. Washington was a good place to get the latest important news of the world. The first thing that he noticed was that he had no desire to turn on the TV or radio because he had no interest in the news. While he showered and shaved, he thought about his experience the night before. But he had no idea of what it meant to his future behavior. He simply had a new consciousness.

He recognized that he was fully in God's control. He had always thought of himself as being in control of his life, except for the bullet in Nigeria and of course, the many times when his blockers missed their assignments and he was in the hands of an angry 320 pound defensive guard at full speed.

He needed to think. His mother had always told him to put his troubles in God's hands, but he tended to think that that was just a pious thought of all mothers. Besides, his new consciousness could not really be considered a trouble. Perhaps it was a blessing and one he was in need of at this time. He needed to talk to Jordan and Brother Mark, in that order.

His desire for quiet was new, a result of last night. He wanted to concentrate. He wanted to think about his life. Prior, the I-Pod, the I-Phone, the I-Pad and congressional business filled every moment of his life except for the moments with Jordan which he cherished. He would still have to use all those aids to carry out his responsibilities which he took seriously. But he would simply not let them control his life. He would take control.

He needed to talk to Jordan. He called to make a dinner date. They went to a Mexican restaurant near her condo. While they were drinking Margaritas, he told her about his experience the night before. He indicated that it was likely prompted by the content of the books. They seemed to focus his mind on the spiritual and that gave rise to his thinking. She listened intently and asked him what it meant for him in the long term. She said that she had had an experience that was somewhat similar, but it had no long term implications for her and probably was not nearly as intense as he was describing. She was interested in knowing what it meant to him.

Her experience with intense thinking was six or seven years earlier, but her experience was absent the idea of an eternal existence of her consciousness. She was a junior at Iowa State. She had had a couple of glasses of "two buck Chuck" with some friends. They had had a conversation about dying and deliberating whether there was anything on the other side of death. One of her friends was sure there was something. The other two thought it was nonsense created by those who wanted to control people's behavior. That night she had an intensified sense of being, but it wasn't anything to do with God and it passed. Jordan added that he should not let the experience fade. He should embrace whatever implications it might have for his life and to use the consciousness to grow. On his way home that night, Diego's thoughts were of how much he loved Jordan, how smart she was, how good she was and how holy she was.

Diego contemplated how he was living his life and found he was deliberating changes. As he had shared with Brother Mark, he was not being fulfilled by his work in congress. He would go back to Brother Mark again and discuss his future. Often he found his mind drifting away as he sat listening to debate in the House and in meetings. He wondered where he would be ten years from that time. And he was comforted by the hope that it would be with Jordan.

The next night, Diego called Jordan and told her he was tied up for Monday and Tuesday and asked if they could go to dinner on Wednesday. He had forgotten that she spent Wednesday nights at the pregnancy center where she volunteered. She had gone to the center to counsel once a week on Wednesdays for the last year. Her connection to the center had come through other volunteer work with Alisha Simmons, a young woman whom she was mentoring. Jordan had been working with Alisha, a seventeen year old from Washington High for the last two years. Alisha wanted to be an architect. She was a capable artist but knew there were not a lot of jobs for artists. She was poor and wanted to be rich. She had the ambition and needed guidance with respect to how to put the ambition to work. She would need a job that paid well.

Jordan had worked to find a scholarship program that could help her go to college and to avoid debt as best she could. Jordan had seen friends who graduated with so much debt that they either put their lives on hold in order pay their loans or they stiffed the taxpayers and felt guilty. She wanted to help Alisha avoid that problem. Jordan had found three programs that could get Alisha through her first year without any debt. Alisha was eager to begin her studies.

But there was a problem. Alisha had been with Richie for two years. She lived at home with her thirty four year old single mother who had had four children out of wedlock. Alisha was the oldest and tried to help her mother, but she wanted to avoid that trap. Her mother got food stamps, lived in Section 8 government housing paying thirty two dollars per month for a four bedroom apartment and had government health care. She baby sat other kids in the neighborhood from time to time. She would bring men into the house for short periods with the understanding that they would reward her kindness with dollars. But she was still fighting a losing battle. She had been trained on a government loan as a "Certified Nursing Assistant" but the number of hours she would have to spend away from the other three children prevented her from working. Besides she had a "bad" back and lifting old people was hard on her.

Alisha was dealing with the problem of Richie. He had been booted out of the house by his single father for not working and contributing to the household. Alisha's mother allowed Richie to live in Alisha's bedroom with Alisha. Somehow Alisha got pregnant. It was the second time in two years. She had lost the earlier baby and she didn't want this baby to interfere with her study and career. Richie found a new living arrangement when Alisha began to put on weight and had her first morning sickness. Richie packed his clothes while she was at school and was not seen by Alisha for almost a year.

Alisha asked Jordan if she could help her with her problem, perhaps a loan to take care of the matter. Before Richie had left her, he took Alisha to Planned Parenthood. But it was going to cost five hundred dollars to "terminate the pregnancy" and Richie had nothing. That was the reason he moved. He didn't want the bitching. Jordan reviewed the yellow page listings for "pregnancy" and found a number of diverse listings and ads. She wasn't looking for an abortionist. She wanted real help. There were twenty six large ads in English, Spanish, Vietnamese and Chinese for organizations which could solve "problem pregnancies quickly, privately and painlessly". She called a couple of them and learned that those were code words for killing unborn babies at just about any stage of development. Washington D.C. had been successful in avoiding any of the strictures that had been placed on the killing by some of the "red states". The killing in D.C. could occur right up to the moment of birth. Jordan's inquisitiveness compelled her to ask the cost of such procedures and learned it could range anywhere from five hundred to three thousand dollars depending upon the complexity of the case due to the age of the "fetus".

Jordan conferred with a woman in her office who along with her husband had adopted a baby locally. She asked how that process had played out. The woman didn't want to go to a foreign country to adopt. She contacted a local lawyer who had a history of successfully arranged adoptions. He was linked to a lawyer who did "pro bono" legal work for a "pregnancy help center" an organization whose aim was to save unborn babies from being killed and to aid the mother or facilitate adoption. The woman in Jordan's office was Black. She said everything went smoothly until they met with the mother to-be who was white. The lawyers had not told the mother to-be that the potential parents were Black. According to the woman in Jordan's office, the mother to-be was taken aback. But after further discussion, a dinner together in their home and an offer of an "open adoption" where the mother was free to associate with the child as the child matured, the mother to-be became enthusiastic about the adoption. The relationship developed and all went well for the child, the adoptive parents and the birth mother.

Jordan asked the woman in her office to join Alisha and Jordan for a luncheon and to discuss with Alisha the possibility of adoption. When Alisha evidenced some comfort with the idea, Jordan put her in contact with the "pro bono" lawyer at the pregnancy center and the adoption occurred. Alisha didn't have to deal with the race matter because both she and the adoptive parents were white, but they were not agreeable to "open adoption". Alisha balked at this to begin with but gave in, thinking that if she really wanted to follow up with her child she would find a way.

As a consequence of becoming familiar with the work of the pregnancy center, Jordan volunteered and became active in the "pro life" movement, an exercise she would never have imagined just five years previously. She shocked herself by the change in her attitude toward killing unborn babies and took issue with those who promoted it. She had great empathy for people wanted to adopt and could not understand how people could destroy an unborn baby. She became a vigorous opponent of the killing.

She invited Diego to come to the center and then they could go to dinner. He was uncomfortable, but agreed to join her. The people at the center recognized him and knew he was a Democratic congressman. They assumed he was pro choice and wondered why he was with Jordan whose views were well known to the group. Diego had seen graphics of unborn babies in high school. But for the first time in his life he saw some three dimensional pictures of fetal development. He could see clearly that as early as the eighth week the being in the womb was a baby. He wondered how people could think anything different. He was astonished that so many people considered it moral to kill unborn babies.

He remembered Brother Mark's comments from his senior year at St. Rita. He hadn't spent any time since then thinking about abortion. He was a Democrat and he knew it was a plank in the party platform but never really thought of himself as a supporter of abortion. He had never heard anything from the pulpit concerning the issue. So he assumed it was low on the Church's list of issues of morality.

Upon reflection, it occurred to him that it may be the most important issue that the nation and he had to address. He knew that this issue, like drugs did not lend itself to government. It would take a change of hearts. The Federal government and the Supreme Court were clearly not the bodies to make that happen. If anything, they had shown distain for the will of the people in matters of morals and had shown their disposition to kill the unborn. The executive and the courts seemed to be eager to support the killing.

The gross graphics of abortion were on display at the pregnancy help center. They depicted the reality and facts with respect to the damage that was done to society. Curtailing the killing would have to come from a change in hearts. The end of slavery which involved man's freedom came from a bloody civil war but the end of abortion which was the end of man's life would have to come from changed hearts, hearts that valued the sanctity of life.

People who had nothing to gain economically were fighting those whose business was killing unborn babies for a profit. He vaguely remembered that there were debates at the state level when he was in high school and college about the baby in the womb feeling pain as early as fifteen weeks and there were efforts to prohibit the killing before twenty weeks. A lot of states had done so and cases were still going to the Supreme Court to reverse the state decisions. In 2016, the President was presented with the opportunity to appoint two Supreme Court justices. There was a long drawn out battle in the U.S. Senate over the confirmation of two justices who had records as supporting the killing of unborn babies in the womb. But in the final analysis they were both confirmed and sat on the Supreme Court, coloring the court liberal. Prior to their appointment there had been six Roman Catholics on the Court, but two were nominal Catholics and pro death. Consequently, the 1973 Roe v Wade decision approving the killing remained the law of the land. Each time a case came to the court, the justices would find some specious basis for keeping the Roe v Wade decision in- tact in the same manner it had first been decided. The nation had to wait a long time to reverse the Dred Scott case and this battle had lasted even longer.

On the way to dinner, Jordan asked how the pictures had affected him. A tear came to his eye and he said that he was angry with himself for his own selfishness in not making opposition to abortion a part of his life. He didn't tell Jordan, but he determined to make up for it. He would find something he could do. Here it was again, a woman who was not yet been baptized leading him to a fundamental tenet of his faith, the sanctity of life. He had known it all his life but had never made it apart of his passion. It would be now.

During his term in the house, he was still in the majority. He had little chance to impact anything in the area of abortion except to vote with Republicans. His frustration grew and he became very conscious of what was in appropriation bills. He studied every sentence and provision. As he began his second term, the senior Illinois senator announced that he was retiring the next year. Mr. Goldman and Mayor Perez approached Diego and indicated they would support him if he chose to run for the Senate seat.

He really wanted to leave politics, but he thought a Senate seat may be new opportunity. He agreed to run. With the mayor's support and Mr. Goldman's money, he assumed he would easily obtain the nomination. His primary opponent was a woman who had not held office other than two terms in the Illinois Senate. He was leery however because he knew how that had played out before when a two time Illinois State Senator became a less than one term U.S. Senator and then became an inexperienced and confused President.

There was no mention of abortion during his senate campaign until near the end. With just two weeks left in the race, at a debate, the question of abortion was introduced by his opponent. She asked Diego how he would reconcile his Catholic faith with support for a "woman's right to terminate her pregnancy"? Diego stood before an entirely Democratic group of primary voters, the base of the party and said "Perhaps the saddest situation that any woman could face in life is to be forced by some horrible circumstance to contemplate the notion of killing the child that is growing in her womb. No woman does this willingly or without pain. She may have been abandoned or threatened by the father of the child, she may face the wrath of a parent, she may have the fear of loss of career, impoverishment or loneliness. She knows that she will regret such an act, but the fear is so great that she is overwhelmed.

We all have a vested interest in the child that is in her womb. That child is our brother or sister. My mother, who gave birth to seven children and knows about children, has always told me that the child in her womb is a child of God as each of us is. Wouldn't it be a truly a loving and human environment if that fearful mother could find in us, in our society the support, both financial and emotional for both her and her child. We Democrats have always been for the weak, the helpless, the defenseless, the innocent. How in the world did we come to make them our enemy"?

Diego surprised his opponent and the audience and all of his supporters by indicating that he thought that the decision concerning abortion should be made by state legislatures and that he would support a state constitutional amendment to ban abortion. The Illinois Democratic Party and the mayor pulled their support for him and their money the next day. Mr. Goldman stayed with him. Diego won the nomination and went to the senate.

Chapter 20

A Time for Love

Mr. and Mrs. Juan Diego Freeman

When he had to campaign for the Senate, he found it difficult to be without Jordan. Finally when he returned to Washington as a 36 year old Senator, they continued to spend a great deal of time together. He took an apartment closer to hers. The romance flourished. He picked her up every morning for early mass and breakfast. By design, their conversation excluded politics. Because he voted with the Republicans on any issue that in any way involved the sanctity of life, she labeled him in their private conversations as the only Republican senator caucusing with the Democrats. He acknowledged it in private. He assumed he wouldn't get the nod for the senate the next time around and began to think about what he would do with his life. He didn't really care as long as what he did was with Jordan.

A month after his return as a senator in January, they went to a play in New York on Friday night. He put her up at the Plaza and he stayed at the Carlisle. After breakfast on Saturday, they strolled along Fifth Avenue and by Diego's design ended up at Tiffany's. When the clerk asked them if she could be of service, Diego told her that his friend wanted to pick out a diamond ring. When they entered Tiffany's, Jordan thought that perhaps they were just browsing, seeing how the rich lived. She didn't expect a ring. When he said diamond ring, she blushed and choked a bit. He had not formally proposed. Was this the proposal? Couldn't he say the words? She paused for a moment, looked at him and said "Are you sure you want to do this"? He breathed deeply and said "I have wanted to do this for two years. Now let's do it. Pick the one you want to wear for the next seventy five years and don't worry about the price. We can afford it as long as we give up eating and clothes".

They both wanted to start their life together sooner rather than to

wait. Diego would gladly have eloped just to be married to Jordan. But he never suggested it. He wanted his bride to have a wedding that would sustain her with wonderful memories throughout their lives. There was much to do. Jordan was to be baptized at Easter at St James Church the first week of April. Diego's sister Angel whom Jordan had come to know well by virtue of Angel's frequent trips to Washington on legal matters was going to be Jordan's baptismal sponsor along with Diego. At Jordan's request, her parents and her brother would be coming for her baptism. Diego willingly went along with the old fashioned idea of asking her parents for Jordan's hand in marriage and they planned a quick trip to Omaha the next weekend. Jordan had alerted him to the fact that her father was a Bronco's fan, but her father had commented to Jordan that he thought that Diego had been a great ball player and that he was very eager to meet him.

Upon meeting him, Jordan's dad, John was immediately taken by Diego. There was a firm and friendly connection that registered both approval and warmth. It might just have been that they both loved Jordan and saw all the goodness in her. He could sense that Diego would take care of his "baby" and that was what he cared about. John had always liked the Bears any day that they weren't playing Denver and Diego was comfortable with that. There was no tension from the difference in political parties. Jordan had shared with her dad that Diego was a sort of closet conservative even though he was an elected Democrat. She knew he was ready for something more satisfying than fighting an uphill battle even in his own party. And it would take no convincing of Jordan to leave Washington after he finished his current term in five years. The five years seemed too long. But she knew of no way for him to gracefully and justly leave the senate. She knew he would do his duty.

The Crawfords had a lot of confidence in their twenty nine year old daughter, but they had never met the man she was to marry personally and that was scary to them. They liked everything they knew about Diego from the sports pages and the newspapers and television. At least they knew some things and it relaxed them a bit. But marrying their daughter was something else. They weren't at all concerned with the fact that Jordan was white and Diego was a Hispanic Black. Because he was such a handsome person, they expected some very good looking grand children and they couldn't wait for that. They certainly weren't concerned about his being able to support her. It was just the suddenness. They knew she had dated him but they didn't know it was as serious as marriage. Nonetheless, they were delighted at the prospect of Jordan marrying. Because of the suddenness of the wedding they did give a moment to wondering if she was pregnant when in fact the only sexual contact Jordan and Diego had had was kissing. They were not very modern in their courting routine.

When Jordan's parents came to the baptism in Washington at Easter, it was an entirely new experience for them. They had traditionally celebrated Easter by attending the special brunch at the country club. There had never been any religious content to Easter for the Crawfords. After Jordan had shared her plans to be baptized and the reasons why, Caroline began to wonder why religion had never been a part of John's and her lives. She hadn't given any thought to it prior to Jordan's plan. They had a dozen friends who were church goers in various denominations. A couple with whom they were close were active practicing Catholics, but religion had never surfaced as a discussion point. Each couple had their own private lives, areas where friends didn't intrude. Occasionally a comment would be passed concerning something that had some religious substance or controversy involved but it always passed quickly. Religion, politics and sex were off limits and happily so to the couples.

A couple of years prior to Jordan's announcement of her baptism, Caroline had done some ancestry exploration on the net and had learned that John's relatives had emigrated to the U.S. from Ireland. John's great uncle had recorded a history of the family's arrival in the U.S. from comments of various relatives. The family had come from County Mayo shortly after the beginning of the potato famine in the 1840s. The family was Catholic. After their arrival in New York City, the parents and the six children lived for a year in the basement of their cousin's home. The father, Brendan Crawford, her John's great great grandfather had had a small farm in Ireland. But he was without money when he came to America and stuck in New York until he could save enough to move west where there was farming. He went to work in New York as a "hod carrier" tending brick and stone layers with their mortar. He fell from a ladder and broke his back. During his convalescence in the damp basement he caught pneumonia and died. The mother, Nora, died a year later and the children remained in the basement but had to work the streets stealing and selling what they stole to secure food.

Eventually, John's great grandfather, Kevin, was picked up by the authorities and shipped to Nebraska to a farm near Lincoln where he was in effect indentured until his eighteenth birthday. The farm family was good to him but they had no contact with the city except to secure supplies. They had no social or religious affiliations. So Kevin had no contact with religion until he married a woman who had a slight connection with the Presbyterian Church. But there were no churches near where they lived. So the children had no religion though they did have a bible.

Kevin worked as a carpenter and with the permission of the builder, lived in the unfinished homes under construction. After a few years, he had saved enough to build a home which he sold and built two more. Crawford Construction of Lincoln Nebraska became the family business and John's father continued to expand it. John had no interest in building homes but he hoped to found a construction company that would build roads. He would work for the Department of Transportation for a few years to learn the trade. But he ended up staying with the Department for his entire career.

The wedding was scheduled in Omaha in June just five months from the date they had purchased the ring. Diego was the one pushing for an early wedding. He knew Jordan with her organizational skills could put it together even from Washington. The only one seriously taken aback by the date was Jordan's mom, Caroline. There was so much to do in such a short time and Jordan was needed in Washington. Caroline was thankful for all the communications devices available to her.

Jordan contacted Dan Sullivan with whom she had been friends in grade school and high school. They had debated each other in high school and had become friends. He had gone on to become a Jesuit priest and was teaching at Loyola University in Chicago. But she knew he still had connections to Omaha. She asked if he would celebrate the mass and witness the marriage. If so, could he arrange to have the wedding take place in the chapel at Creighton University? Because Jordan's parents weren't Catholic there was no parish to consider. The priest called back three days later and indicated that if they made the wedding in late June, there would be room. The early weeks were already taken for marriages. At Diego's request Father Kevin would con- celebrate the mass and Brother Mark would be on the altar as well.

John Crawford had been born in Lincoln, studied at the University of Nebraska and had played guard on the "Big Red" for his first two years until he blew out his knee and couldn't seem to rehab it to the point of any speed. He was able to retain his scholarship and finished his degree in business. He and Caroline wed and the union bore two children, Jordan and her younger brother, John junior.

John senior went to work for the Department of Transportation, a job which required the move to Omaha. Later there was another stint in Lincoln after Jordan had graduated from high school. But at retirement the Crawfords returned to Omaha where Caroline's mother was residing in an assisted living facility. John had risen to the Director of the Department after fifteen years in the ranks and consequently knew a half dozen governors and state representatives and senators. They couldn't invite everyone he knew to the wedding so they settled on close friends and a few politicians.

The two Nebraska U.S. Senators were both Republican. Diego had done some battle with them, but Diego wanted to invite them and they had graciously accepted. A lot of Chicago Bears and their wives came and a half dozen Northwestern Wildcats and their wives came. Diego's extended family including the kids numbered in excess of fifty people who joined them for the celebration. There were two altar boys and one altar girl among the kids so they too were in the wedding. It was difficult for Diego to choose a best man between Renaldo and Oscar. But Renaldo was family and he was chosen. All three of the Freeman girls were bridesmaids and the kids served as the flower girls and ring bearers. Oscar insisted on an opportunity to toast the couple at the reception. He shared some of the incidents that had colored his and Diego's lives and how they were able to be at the wedding because they each had diligent and tough Guardian Angels who had worked overtime. While they still needed protection, Anna had lessened the burden on Oscar's angel and he hoped Jordan could do the same and ease the burden on Diego's.

They honeymooned in Rome and stayed in the center of the city at the Grand Hotel Plaza. The hotel was old but magnificent. The public areas were unmatched with anything Jordan or Diego had seen. The ample marble and the huge carved lions that guarded the splendid curved marble staircase were impressive to Jordan. They stayed the first two nights in the San Pietro penthouse with extraordinary views of Rome and the Vatican.

But when Jordan learned from Diego the twenty five hundred euro cost of the room, she insisted that they move to a less expensive five hundred euro room which had its own patio. She enjoyed luxury and she knew they were on their honeymoon, but she also knew that there were people starving in the world and her newly acquired Catholic guilt kicked in. She was shocked that a hotel would name a twenty five hundred Euro a night room after a poor saint who was crucified upside down by the Romans.

The hotel couldn't have been more perfectly located. It put them within walking distance of the monuments, restaurants, the Spanish Steps and the beautiful Trevi Fountain that had supplied a main water supply for the city through the Vergine Aqueduct a project that would interest any engineer. Jordan had studied so much about the construction, the architecture and the history of the building of the cathedrals of Rome and the rest of Italy that she wanted to see them first hand. She had some difficulty believing that some of the ancient churches were built over hundreds of years.

People had patiently devoted their entire lives to a

portion of the construction of a single cathedral and the graphics that she had seen on the net and in coffee table books had left her greatly impressed, but no more impressed than when she stood in the center of the Basilica of St. Mary Major and strained her neck to see the glory of the ceiling and the magnificent sculptures and frescos. She was in heaven. It was not only a magnificent work of art; it was an engineering wonder and a spiritual moment for her.

Though Diego was not as deeply taken by the architecture, he was taken by the commitment of the faithful to the construction. It simply had to be that their lives were built on a faith that what they were doing was holy and pleasing to God. They were using the talents with which God had equipped them and shaping the materials God had placed at their disposal to form beautiful structures that lifted the minds and hearts of the believers in their worship of their God.

Added to the delight of Jordan was the first morning in Rome when they participated in a mass at St. Peters and were joined in the joyous music of what must have been a choir of professional musicians in praise of God.

She felt she had arrived home when she saw the incredible front doors of St Peter's. When she entered and looked down the long nave to the Bernini columns and the main altar she marveled that her faith journey was so wrapped in the glory of creation and the wonders of artists and architects. It was heaven to an engineer with faith. She knelt and asked Diego to join her. Together they said a prayer of thanks, thanks for their lives, their lives together, their parents and siblings, their faith and their freedom. She included a prayer of thanks to God for all the artists and construction workers who had built the marvelous structure. Her circumstance nearly took her breath away. To her right was the Pieta, the work of Michelangelo. How could an artist take the saddest scene in the history of mankind, the perfect act of love that was necessary to salvation and depict its sadness with such beauty? Only the Holy Spirit could be behind that act.

It was a Wednesday. The visit to the Sistine Chapel was a heady experience and they would stay for the papal audience that would occur at noon. But their seats were so far from the pope's location that the person giving the blessing might have been a fake for all they knew. When the soft soothing voice issued from the speakers asking God to bless all those in the audience with the peace of Christ it was clear that it was Pope Paul VII invoking God in their name. That was all they needed for the day, to be blessed by the pope with the peace of Christ whom he was representing on earth.

The Pantheon was a delight for her engineering eye and the plazas left her wanting to stay in Rome forever. The luncheons with too much pasta and wine made for enjoyable afternoon siestas. The romantic late night dinners on their patio with more wine than she was used to drinking made the honeymoon a totally enjoyable love fest. They were perfectly matched in their needs and wants. Life with Diego was going to be a warm wonderful union of two souls seeking salvation and enjoying the way. They had committed themselves to do whatever they could to help the other and those they encountered on their journey to God. How could she have ever told him to back off as she did early on? But life was much more appreciated now that she had the greater sense of what it meant and she needed that introspection. She needed the faith she had been given.

They spent three days in churches and art museums. They then headed to Florence early in the morning on the fastest and smoothest moving train they had ever experienced. Florence was more flash than Rome, fewer churches, though enough to know that Italy had once been a Christian country. It wasn't that Rome was not secular, it was. It was that Florence was art, art,

art. Jordan was not much of a shopper, but even the least shopper in creation could not be but tempted by the shops on the Ponte Vecchio, the bridge that spans the Arno. The bridge was thought to have been first constructed in Roman Times but had undergone reconstruction many times. It now housed hundreds of merchants of art, gold, leather and ceramics. Diego thought it important that Jordan have a gold memento of their honeymoon. While they ambled along Diego spotted a bracelet, an old style but with a substantial measure of gold. They asked the merchant if they could look more closely at it and to try it on Jordan's wrist. The jeweler indicated that the bracelet was no longer made and that this was a San Marcos, the largest of a style that was very popular until it became too expensive to make because it was solid 18 k. gold.

When Jordan felt the bracelet on her wrist, she remarked that she would certainly know if she lost it because it was so heavy. The jeweler pointed out that it weighed 105 grams and cost 15,000 euro. Jordan demurred and wanted to walk away. Diego insisted. They would insure it as soon as they left the jeweler and she would wear it the remainder of their honeymoon as a reminder that they were married forever. When they returned to Washington, she started to wear the bracelet often and each time she felt it or looked at it she remembered the moment they purchased it. It was important to her for more than one reason.

Six weeks after their return, when the gynecologist gave her the news that she was pregnant, the birth date was timed to that night in Rome. It was June 29, just over a week from the summer solstice, so the Roman sun gave light until almost nine P.M. They had champagne, dinner on the patio of their room and retired early. With the news of the pregnancy, they decided they would wait to learn the sex of the baby and asked the ultrasound nurse not to disclose it. If it was a boy, it would be Frankie. If it was a girl, it would be Caroline. The night they got the news of the pregnancy, Diego suggested they do what the Freeman family did whenever they got good or bad news. They knelt and recited the Joyous or Sorrowful decades of the Rosary dependent upon what the occasion reflected. Most often the Freemans said the Joyful mysteries.

Chapter 21

Evil Explores Opportunities

Back to the Ponte Vecchio

At the exact time when Jordan and Diego were thanking and praising God for her pregnancy, Abdul Ishmala and his associate Fareed Hussein were engaged in reconnaissance at the Ponte Vecchio. A jihadi operative in Rome who was known to have access to Saudi funds had invited them to Rome to explore a joint action. They had visited St Peters and other churches to determine the number of sightseeing visitors that would gather at various times during the day and they had calculated the challenge of bringing a bomb into the facilities. The Carabineri seemed to be everywhere in Rome and it would be difficult to penetrate their coverage. They were thorough in searching bags and very observant of attire. They had an excellent reputation for protection of people and structures.

The same was true of the train stations and the train itself. On their trip to Florence, the train seemed to be totally covered with security. But when they began to walk around Florence, they began to see some weaknesses and to think creatively about how the weaknesses may be penetrated. They saw particular opportunity right in the middle of the Ponte Vecchio. A powerful enough suicide vest worn by a young boy would kill and maim and do considerable damage to the structure. A second boy with a suicide bomb would be devastating if both bombs were detonated by cell phone at exactly the same time. There would be a substantial cumulative effect from the two bombs. A second possibility was the detonation of the second bomb when responders came to rescue the injured. But they would have to make sure that the second bomber was a significant distance from the first in order not to have the first bomb detonate the second by mistake with the explosion.

Abdul and his associate were promised the funding and the Roman contact had indicated that he could assemble the bomb materials and put them in a location but would have nothing to do with the bomb making. That was up to Abdul and Fareed. Abdul had had some training in bomb making but was a little leery of his skill. They either had to experiment which could be dangerous or recruit someone who had the skill. Going on the internet or borrowing books from libraries had become too obvious to the authorities and was a threat to freedom. If they got caught in just the training or the bomb making they would be losers. Abdul's ego could not handle that. The most likely candidate may be found among the parents of the children in the madrassa, but that would be a little dangerous if other parents thought they could be training their children as suicide bombers. They would go to every mosque in Islamabad and listen to the participants after the prayers. If they found a jihadi, they would subtlety inquire if they knew a bomb maker. After ten visits they linked with a jihadi, Ishmael, who himself could make bombs if provided the resources and the proper target. He was not inclined to attack the government or its agents. Infidels were his only interest.

They could bring the man to Rome. But they would first need to test Ishmael's skills in Pakistan. He would make a bomb. They had already selected and had begun to train six potential child suicide bombers. They would pick a target in Islamabad or Rawalpindi as a practice target in advance of bombing the Ponte Vecchio. But the target would have to be infidels.

The materials for the first bomb were relatively easy to assemble without detection by shopping in various stores in cities as far away as Peshawar near the eastern end of the Khyber Pass. The bomb maker did indeed make what looked like a serious weapon but the problem of where to detonate it as a test had never occurred to them in their eagerness to secure the bomb. They would have to trust that the bomb maker and take a chance that it would work on the first try. They would have to pick the brightest of the suicide bombers in the event that it didn't explode after he had yelled Allah Akbar. If it failed the bomber would have to have a story for authorities that did not include their involvement. Training such a child would be difficult but necessary.

Chapter 22

Freemans of Georgetown

Preparing for Caroline or Frankie

They knew they needed larger quarters when the baby came. They questioned whether to buy or rent. They planned to be in Washington only the five more years until Diego would finish his first term as a senator. The housing market was expensive and not very expansive. They purchased a three bedroom townhouse in Georgetown and settled in. Neither of them were very fancy in their tastes but Jordan's mother who was an excellent decorator offered to be of assistance if they were interested. Jordan's parents came to Washington for two weeks and they were treated royally while Caroline worked on the townhouse. She did wonders at a reasonable cost and they were delighted. They left the color of the nursery white until the baby was born at which time they would paint it.

Jordan's work remained demanding and Diego suggested that she might think about retirement or at least a leave of absence until the baby was at least a year old. After discussion with her obstetrician, Jordan said that she would stop work at the midpoint of the pregnancy. She ate right, worked out lightly and read voluminously about the baby and its development in the womb. She knew the progress from the conception to every moment of her pregnancy. She was happily aware and proud that she and Diego were participating in bringing a new soul into God's kingdom. She would do whatever she could to make his or her entry a healthful one.

In her third month of pregnancy, after Sunday mass, they

were riding home in the car. Jordan turned to Diego and said "Do you ever worry about how blessed we are and wonder why"? As he drove he looked briefly at her and said "What are you saying"? She asked "Did you see the poster in the back of church that announced a collection for the Catholic Relief Services, the one with the African child with the tiny arms, the pot belly and no shoes? It causes me wonder when I think about how blessed we are; we have a child who may never have a worry about food or shelter, we have our health, our faith, our families, we are free, each of us has interesting work for which we are well paid and many people in the world have nothing. It just causes me to think about why God allows it to be so. I was just wondering if the same thoughts occur to you". Diego thought for a moment and then said "Of course they do, I think about it a lot and I thank God, especially that we have each other, but I have no idea of why it is so and I don't think anyone does. If anything, it seems like more of an incentive to do for others than for something to worry about. God has his plan and his reasons that will someday be ours to know".

When they arrived home and were having breakfast, Jordan mentioned that she was asked to accompany a delegation from the House and the State Department along with a half dozen representatives of the major technical companies to Pakistan to consider a joint effort to construct a small American University devoted to technical education in Islamabad. She would be gone about a week. Diego said that if she was going, he too was going and asked who was heading the delegation. It was a congressman from New York whom Diego knew. He would call him the next day and ask to join the delegation. It was just a formality. He had a right to go if he chose and he chose. Jordan was a little taken aback because she thought he was stepping into her work arena. It was their first difference of opinion of their marriage. He indicated that even if that was so, he felt as though he didn't want her going to a part of the world that in his view was never settled. He didn't want her to go without him. Finally she agreed and asked him to wait until after she told her boss that he wanted to go.

Her boss had no problem with Diego going. She thought that having a senator in the group may lend importance to the group and may lift the interest and the fiscal investment of the Pakistani businessmen who were backing the university idea. The trip was scheduled for late October and they would travel on a private jet supplied to the State Department for the trip by the consortium. None of the representatives would be accused of taking gratuities from commercial interests if it was a State Department trip. They flew to Islamabad and then traveled by bus to the Rawalpindi where the university was to be built. The negotiations went smoothly. The U.S. would encourage as many tech companies as were interested to join the effort to build the university and the related light industries surrounding the campus for manufacturing.

They spent two days in the negotiations and stayed in a five star Westin. They returned to Islamabad and stayed in the Islamabad Marriott

for another day. The hotel was within a modest bus ride to the Benazir Bhutto International airport for an early flight the next day. Diego went to breakfast with the rest of the delegation in the main dining room of the hotel but Jordan had a bit of morning sickness and didn't want to eat a regular breakfast before the flight. She asked Diego to secure some bananas and grapes for the flight in case the private jet didn't stock them. Their bags had been handled by the porters and placed in the bus. So Diego didn't plan to return to the room. She told Diego she would meet him on the bus.

An Evil With an Innocent Face

All the businessmen on the trip wanted to talk football with Diego and at every meal he was deluged with questions about this game or that, about this quarterback or that and who was really the best coach in the NFL. He was always polite because he felt he had been blessed by the game and people really wanted an insider's views. Often, as a consequence of being polite, he was the last of the group to finish his breakfast and leave the dining room. He waited at the table while the dining room staff packed a half dozen bananas and a large bag of grapes for Jordan.

The young boy with the newspapers standing next to the bus looked as innocent and as lovable as any child Jordan had ever seen. His huge dark eyes and curly black hair drew her in. She felt sorry for him because he was too chubby and he was wearing what looked like a winter jacket in such warm weather. She smiled at him through the window as she took her seat near the front of the bus where Diego would join her. She settled in for a short trip to the airport but a very long nineteen hour flight to D.C. They would stop in London for refueling. She hoped they would spend some time off the plane to relax. On the way over they had spent two hours in a private VIP lounge at Heathrow and she looked forward to breaking up the flight. She prayed that the morning sickness was over for the day.

Surviving witnesses said that the blast lifted the bus off the ground and made a hole the size of a small car when it blew open the side where Jordan was seated. In addition to Jordan, eleven others on the bus were killed immediately and fifteen were seriously injured. But they couldn't be helped until the emergency personnel arrived with the proper equipment. There was no way to get to them without the right heavy instrument, torches to cut the steel that had melted and reshaped the entry door. It was impossible to pry open the windows wide enough to gain access and remove the injured.

Another dozen people waiting to enter the bus and seven near the front of the hotel were killed. Those at the front of the hotel were employees, Muslims who were collateral victims along with the infidels. Abdul was fifty feet from the bus and was backed up against a wall so he would not be knocked down by the explosion. But he did suffer a cut to his face from a small rock broken from the sidewalk near the bus. He had detonated the bomb as soon as the bus appeared to be full and before young Ahmed had his chance to shout "Allah Akbar". He had promised the boy the opportunity to shout the praise in order to obtain his eternal reward, but failed to honor the promise. Fareed stood with his cell phone fifty feet farther from the bus in the event that Abdul's phone didn't detonate the bomb. As they saw the bus explode, they both smiled.

Fareed joined Abdul and they slowly walked toward the bus and joined an assembling crowd to view the carnage. When they saw the damage they had done they smiled to each other and engaged in a congratulatory mutual pat on the back. Now, it was on to the Ponte Vecchio, a larger more romantic target. They acknowledged that the Ponte Vecchio would be more difficult, but also more rewarding. It was beyond their borders. But they still would not use their phones or computers to plan the project. They didn't dismiss the success or impact of their current endeavor. They had executed an action and killed thirty people, mostly infidels, without a flaw. Because they kept the operation close there was no information available to the American intelligence agencies, the Central Intelligence Agency, the National Security Administration, Homeland Security or the State Department or Federal Bureau of Investigation. Pakistani police would be dumbfounded. The billions of dollars spent by the Americans to detect terrorists had failed once again. If they had not secured the assistance of the night desk clerk at the Marriott, they might never have known of the visit of the American delegation. But they had been blessed by meeting him six weeks earlier after Friday prayers at a mosque that they had attended almost by accident.

Diego was leaving the dining room when he heard the explosion and the burst of the huge flames. He rushed to the bus and when he saw the damage he screamed her name, but no one could answer. His wife and his baby were dead. The damage was so extensive that no one could even get into the burning bus. Hotel staff came with small fire extinguishers but they were inadequate to the task. He couldn't even see her. He didn't know where to look. He went to the opposite side of the bus to see if she was there. He threw his bag of fruit at the bus and fell to his knees screaming at God. His anger was as intense as any man's had ever been.

This was the second time God had crushed his world and this time he would not take it. He would take his revenge. He would exercise his anger. He didn't know how, but it would happen. He would find whoever it was that detonated this bomb and they would pay. There was no room for mercy. He had turned his cheek for the last time in his life.

Hotel staff came to comfort him but there was nothing they could do. He stood looking at the bus with tears streaming down his face. Everyone associated with the trip was either on the bus or waiting to enter it when the blast occurred. They were all dead. He was alone. He knew he should do something but he couldn't save anyone. They were all gone. He wanted to roll up in a ball and cry, but couldn't even bring himself to do that. He just stood and looked at the burning bus and swore. When the emergency crew finally arrived, they had to wait until the fire department had cooled the bus to a point where they could get close enough to use the torches to cut the bus open. He asked to go on the bus to look for Jordan but they wouldn't let him get near it.

The emergency crews bagged the bodies before removing them from the bus. Diego wanted to view every bag before it was loaded into the ambulance so he could ride to the morgue with Jordan, but they wouldn't allow him. He would have to go to the morgue. They told him that he would be the only person at the morgue who was in a position to identify any of the bodies. But when an embassy representative showed up, she indicated that she would be able to identify at least a couple of the people from the State Department whom she knew. He was trying to remember what Jordan was wearing but she had dressed after he had gone to breakfast so he didn't even know what color clothing to look for. He did remember that she had worn a black pants suit on the flight over and thought she might wear the same outfit for the flight back.

He sat in the waiting room of the morgue for eight hours while the staff did their best to prepare the mutilated bodies for viewing. They had done their best to match body parts based on the clothing that covered the remaining parts even though they were separated. He was unable to identify many. Because Jordan was located near ground zero of the bomb, there was little left of her body. The doctor in charge of the morgue tried to dissuade Diego from looking at the parts that they had assembled that they thought belonged to Jordan. But Diego insisted. He briefly fainted when he saw what they had assembled. When he was able to speak, he indicated that he thought that the outfit was the one she probably was wearing. They tagged the body and the next time he saw what was identified as her body was a cloth covered casket as it was being loaded on a U.S. Navy troop carrier that had been flown into transport the bodies back to the U.S. He insisted on being on the plane with Jordan's body for the flight to D.C.

He had called her parents prior to boarding the plane. They had already been alerted by the State Department that she had been killed, but the person who had alerted them thought that Diego had also been killed. They were stunned when he called. They asked if he would bring her back to Omaha for the funeral and burial and he indicated that that was his intent. He would contact them as soon as he arrived home so they could schedule the funeral.

When he arrived home, he was totally immobilized for two days. He couldn't answer the phone. He couldn't eat or sleep. He sat in a chair and stared at Jordan's picture taken on their wedding day. She was stunning, so beautiful, so pure, so loving. Gone. Why couldn't he have gotten to the bus and been sitting with her? Why couldn't he be with her now? On the third day, Renaldo and Brother Mark came to his townhouse and knocked on the door until he finally opened it. They had brought some food but Diego wouldn't eat. He was somewhat incoherent. Brother Mark recognized it as the beginning of dehydration and asked if he had had any liquid. Diego didn't know. Brother Mark went to the kitchen and got two bottles of water from the refrigerator and directed Diego to drink them. Slowly he drank but he didn't communicate. Renaldo tried to persuade him to eat a couple of bananas and Diego said "No. No. No" and that was all he could say. Later he did take some soup and a few crackers. Brother Mark persuaded him to take a beer and then another and it began to relax him but he didn't want to talk. Soon he drifted off from exhaustion, not having slept for four days.

When he awoke about four hours later he asked how they had gotten into the townhouse. They shared with him that he had been slightly incoherent when they arrived. Then he remembered that he had not called Jordan's parents as he had promised. While Diego slept, Renaldo and Brother Mark concurred that he was suffering mainly from a shock but that he was likely also suffering from a lack of hope. Diego had always had an abiding faith, but hope was a different matter. It was challenged in this circumstance. He had lost his connection with life, with his reality. His new reality was that Jordan was with God even though he didn't want her to be. He couldn't accept it because he didn't want it to be. Neither of them had any idea of what to say to him other than that they were there to support him through this tragedy.

Jordan's parents were so stunned by her death that they couldn't bring themselves to plan a funeral. Their son John had to take over. He talked with Diego and together they decided to ask Father Kevin to celebrate the mass. They would all return to the Creighton Chapel less than six months after the wedding. Brother Mark's primary thought was that Diego needed to know that he had a child with God who was positively a saint and a wife who was a saint through her martyrdom. The people who were on that trip were trying to do good. They were trying to express love and that was the criterion on which they would be judged. They were with God. Jordan and his child would be advocates for him for the remainder of his life.

The Crawfords put Diego's sister Rosa in touch with the person who managed the Creighton chapel and they agreed to host the funeral. Rosa worked with Father Kevin to plan a fitting liturgy and Father Kevin prepared a homily. He remarked to Brother Mark on the flight to Omaha that it was the most difficult homily he had ever prepared and that he hoped it would somehow be of value to the Crawfords and to Diego. He was aware that the Crawfords were not Catholic but that would not prevent him from sharing what he believed to be the true meaning of Jordan's life and death. Jordan had searched and found faith and she loved.

Diego returned to Washington and the Senate, but his heart couldn't be brought to his work. His mind was but one place. Both Rosa and Renaldo pushed him to join a bereavement group at a local hospital, but it was of no value. He went to three meetings as he had promised Rosa but didn't connect with the content of the discussions. He didn't want to hear psychological explanations of why he felt sad, what he needed to do not to feel sad. He didn't belong there. He didn't feel sorry for himself, nor was he a victim. He had been married to the most wonderful person in the world and now she was gone. He knew the reality. He was alone. It was part of God's plan. God had his life all mapped out. The only thing that he could do was to survive God's plan somehow. He had to get through a few years, die and be with Jordan and his child, his son or daughter. He would have to wait to know. There would never be another person who could begin to know his pain or fill the void in his heart made by Jordan's death.

As he was sitting on the senate floor and someone was discussing defense issues, he thought about how all the agencies of the government devoted to detecting the evil of terrorism had failed to see the terrorists who killed his wife. He didn't blame the agencies or their people. Evil was difficult to uncover. Then his mind wandered to a day in their marriage preparation class where the woman of the couple that was conducting the class said something to the effect that "every marriage ends in tragedy". The woman paused. A young woman in the back row of the room said that that was a terrible thing to tell people about to be married. The woman asked her to think about how marriage ends. It could be divorce or separation, both of which were surely tragedies. The only alternative was the death of one of the spouses and that too was tragic. Diego thought how that meant nothing to him at the time. Now it was his reality, his painful reality.

That weekend he went to visit Brother Mark, his personal bereavement group. Diego sat in the quiet presence of Brother Mark and thought. He would make occasional comments, engaging in a stream of consciousness, while Brother Mark prayed the rosary. If Brother Mark thought Diego could benefit from a comment, he would make one. He simply sat and urged Diego to talk it out. Then together, they prayed, invoking the Holy Spirit, Jordan and the baby asking for guidance for Diego. He asked Brother Mark what he thought of him leaving the Senate and Brother Mark asked what he would do when he left. He didn't know. Perhaps he could come back to Chicago and work with Oscar at the <u>Frankie and Carmen Freeman Foundation</u>.

It was doing good work and he could spend his time there. Brother Mark was candid. "Oscar is doing an excellent job of leading the foundation. Leave him alone. Give yourself another full year in the Senate. If you don't find yourself doing a better job than whomever you think would replace you, then you need to stay on. If there is someone out there whom you think can do a better job, then you can step down". Diego asked him what he thought of Rosa or Renaldo assuming that one of them might be willing to run. Brother Mark said he would think about it.

On the way back to D.C. on the plane, he made a resolve. He would stay in the Senate for two years. That would be more than half of his term. He would tell the party in Chicago that he was going to retire so they could groom someone to replace him. He knew he would not get the nomination anyway because of his position on the sanctity of life. He could never understand why the Democrats were not supporters of the sanctity of life, protecting the most defenseless, the unborn and the aging with illnesses. He had decided that he didn't want to encourage either Renaldo or Rosa to even consider going to the Senate. They were both happily married and doing a great job of rearing their children. Why disrupt their lives or the lives of their children?

He served two more years. He remained a leader of a minority faction of contrary thinkers. He promoted a number of bills that addressed life issues, terrorism and drugs. Often his bills would pass the Senate on Republican votes and then die in a house committee which had been taken over by the Democrats. He voted with the Republicans as often as he did with the Democrats.

After a year, people began to ask him if they could fix him up for a date. He continued to say he was just not interested and eventually they stopped asking. He had found a way to stay in contact with Jordan. Brother Mark had urged him to do what he called "journaling", tracking his daily thoughts about life and Jordan. After about three months he saw a pattern in his writing that reflected a one way communication with Jordan. It was as if he were writing to her every night about his day, his thoughts and his eagerness to be with her and their child. This continued for more than the two years he had promised that he would remain in the Senate. He would constantly ask her to guide him to what she thought that he should do when he left the Senate.

Departing the Senate

At his departure from the Senate in late January of 2043, Diego took the privilege of a final floor speech. Of the one hundred Senators, there were slightly more than fifty on the floor. They were there because the speech occurred about fifteen minutes before the body was to be called to order for a vote. There was very little business in congress that week except for a vote on the defense budget which had been left to the week before Christmas vacation. C-SPAN was live when he came to the podium with a warm smile. He turned to his colleagues and those in the gallery and greeted them with thanks for paying attention to the business of the nation. He thanked his constituents for sending him to Washington and his colleagues for their friendship and support. He begged their forbearance because he intended to address what he called "things that matter and are important to the nation and not very often mentioned in the congress".

He began "It is with great gratitude to the author of our rights, our privileges, our material blessings of freedom and prosperity that I address you. I thank God for our blessings. I thank each one of you with whom I have enjoyed serving and I look forward to a productive future with many happy memories of shared moments of celebration of our successes. And I will be reminded of some our shared sorrows over our disappointments and our failures. We live in the greatest county in history and we live at a time in which we are lavished with scientific and technological gifts. We live at a time when we are freer than any county at any point in civilization. At one time, we enjoyed greater prosperity than any nation, but that time is now past. Perhaps that is for the best because I believe we have become more realistic and more humble. We have remained an international and military power superior to any other country and we can be proud of the manner in which we have used our leadership and power. We enjoy a moral high ground in this regard.

"Our national patrimony was the gift of values informed by Western Civilization which had been wrought in the image of Christianity. Those values fashioned our democratic republic on a foundation of freedom, a freedom to excel as individuals and as a nation. But we have begun to stray from those blessings. Three crucial Christian values shaped Western Civilization; belief in the sanctity of every God given human life, the freedom of the human will and the belief in man's redemption and expectation of an eternal life of reward or punishment based on how much man has exercised his freedom to love. The freedom of the human will allows man's capacity to choose the good. The sanctity of human life provides man the reason to act justly and to love his fellow human even to the extent that some have given their lives in defense of others. It is the recognition of the sanctity of human life that is the predicate for all positive human interaction.

The humanism of the Christian confession articulated by Aquinas justifies the sacrifice involved in acting justly and charitably to all not just fellow believers. The secular humanist ideology that fosters fairness and generosity predicated on the conviction that we are all "fellow travelers" on spaceship earth seems too shallow a basis for us to sacrifice our lives, pay extra or even inconvenience ourselves in the interest of our "fellow travelers".

This proves particularly true if that "fellow traveler" is unwilling to contribute to the common good or pull his own weight. We continually ask ourselves why we have been so blessed by God. We ask what is expected of us as a nation and as individuals. We need to ask if we have nurtured the values that were provided us by our founders and our families. Have we achieved a position of moral rectitude as a culture? Is our current culture worthy of emulation or disdain? Our freedom is designed to help us excel. Have we not often used our freedom of will to choose chaos over order and depravity over dignity? We measure the quality of our national values by examining how we treat our most defenseless, particularly our children. I choose to examine how we have valued our children over the last century.

"Who in this body hasn't heard each one of us with a self- interest in being re-elected portray ourselves as advocates of the children, *we have to do this or that for our children*"? I have heard more pious thoughts uttered in this chamber about how important our children are to us than I have heard on any other topic. We speak eloquently about their health, their education and welfare, their present and their futures and we do so as though we are seriously concerned about their wellbeing. I wish it were so. I was naïve when I came to congress. But I have been educated and I am obliged to share what I have learned about our congress, us and our children. The facts concerning the lives of our children tend to belie the hopefulness and graciousness of our words.

How did we arrive at our current level of neglect of our children? I want to share my view of how that neglect occurred, how dangerous it is to our culture and our country and how we might reclaim our children, give them their due and build their future.

"Independence is a blessing and has played a powerful role in our personal lives and the life of our nation. But we have been both blessed and cursed by independence. With the development of the scientific age in the seventeenth century, many eagerly declared their independence of the authority of the Church and many from God. That was their right. Independence from the dominance of the Church was one thing. Independence from God was another matter altogether. Both were core elements of most people's lives who were a part of Western civilization. Later, the other core institution of their lives, the family, suffered a blow from independence as the young left behind the cultural and family constraints and immigrated to the cities to participate in the industrial revolution. Jobs and technology drew them from the drudgery of the farm and the shelter of a supportive kin. As the farm became mechanized the value of children as workers was diminished. Households shrank. Family values did not always follow the youth to the city. But for the most part the family survived.

"In the United States and Europe, World War II provided a burst of independence on the home front for mothers and children. This was a further jolt to the stability of the family. Women left the home to populate the factories of war production. They learned that they could support themselves. Upon return from the war, many husbands learned that while they were desired, they were no longer indispensable. Abuse, addiction, neglect and boredom did not have to be tolerated forever by the more independent women. Divorce was a comfortable option.

"Science and technology had changed the world. The existence of the atom bomb was a reality that needed to be accepted in not only national defense, but in the way people looked at their lives. In the worst case scenario, life could end in an instant. Sulfur drugs, penicillin and preventive care fostered longer lives but added a costly dependence of the elderly on the young. And in our modern world, because of cost, we witnessed the fostering of health care rationing and the promotion of euthanasia. Some of our states have vigorously embraced euthanasia as both social and economic policy.

"The traditional family culture was twisted by the advent of television, where parents, particularly fathers were and are frequently depicted as bumbling helpless or hopeless bores. The hip people eschew family values. Television provides access to the horror of violence, anti social values and lifestyles that had never been known by most. During the sixties, the authority that could not successfully defend its existence was thrown off and the mores and morals of the past were jettisoned. Perhaps the single most significant development was what came to be known simply as "the pill" due to its widespread use. It comfortably and conveniently separated sex from procreation and made sex a recreational pastime available to all ages at all times and to all marital states. "Free love" flourished. And when the pill was forgotten or the condom failed, a cowed Supreme Court accommodated the demand of some tough, loud women for the availability of legal killing of their unintended or unwanted offspring in the womb.

"Marriage was further modified by those who chose whatever definition of family met their needs. Despite the clarity of nature's physiology and a plethora of state referenda that consistently defined marriage as between a man and a woman, legislators and judges continued to rule that marriage was between anyone that cared to define their relationship with any person or group. This was so despite the couple's inability to engage in what God had created and was commonly referred to as the "marriage act" which had the potential for children. There are now so many disparate interpersonal arrangements that are honored as legal marriage that there is chaos.

"Woven into the fabric of this tapestry is the value that we place on the sanctity of human life. The value that has been recognized, if not honored in all civilizations, has radically changed. It has deteriorated to the point where many have no idea of the meaning of sanctity when it is mentioned. The tarnished values addressing human life have been enshrined in our law, in medicine, in bio-scientific research and in the general tenor of the society during the last century. The most dangerous place to be in the United States for almost one hundred years has been in a mother's womb and it remains a very dangerous place. One third of the children to whom we give life in the womb are killed there in a legal conspiracy of mothers and doctors often paid for by the poor burdened taxpayers. These unborn are not allowed to survive the womb. And the legal threat to their survival lasts until the moment of their birth.

"We have reached a tipping point in the manner in which our children come into the world. More than fifty percent of those who are allowed to be born are born to a pernicious threat. Their God given right to a father and mother is denied them not by some violent tragedy involving the death of a parent, but by the careless and insidious neglect of the two people who enjoyed their physical union as recreation at the expense of the child that was conceived. That denial of justice weighs on the child throughout what is often a life tortured by poverty or depression. A high risk insurance company would place out of wedlock birth as the first factor in any algorithm that determined the premium for indemnification of a child against failure.

"In the case of more than seventy five percent of Black children and fifty percent of Hispanic children, the children of my culture and color, the challenge of living as a minority in a country not yet free of racism is further compounded by being born without a legal father. And this injustice is at the center of their existence throughout their lives. The large number of "fatherless" children is clearly the most dangerous threat imaginable to our county. It is that condition, fatherless children who are prone to drop out of school, become addicted, be imprisoned and commit suicide. Though such a threatening peril did not exist at the time, Abraham Lincoln was referring to such a danger when he observed prior to becoming president in his 1838 Lyceum address "if destruction be our lot, then we ourselves must be its author and finisher. As a nation of freemen, we must live through all time or die by suicide". Fatherless children are the weapon by which we are destroying our nation. Addressing the matter is not as much a matter of money as it is of supporting a cultural standard that acknowledges how unnatural the condition is and shames the perpetrators. There is however the paradox of the young woman who has been used and abandoned by the father. She must be supported in her condition and credited with placing value on the sanctity of the child's life and not killing it though she may be fearful of her own future and that of the child.

Flushing the filth from our culture, the violence that Hollywood,
television, the internet, politicians and the stars spew on the youth of our country is the best place to start the renewal of our culture and our nation.

"I acknowledge and applaud the many parents who are

extremely attentive to their children. There is a great deal of energy, attention, love and money expended on the needs and wants of children; education, health, I-Pods, I-Pads, I-Phones, clothes, video games, toys, cars, soccer, hockey, lacrosse, golf and baseball, camps etc. Children are good for the economy. But the data from all government and private research paints a nasty picture of our treatment of our children. For the two thirds who survive the womb, life is tough. The United States ranks poorly in infant mortality. More than fifty percent of all children under 18 do not live with their birth parents and nearly fifty percent live in single parent families. More than one million children become children of divorce each year. Many of the children of divorce automatically become impoverished. The statistics that record the reports of child abuse continue to climb and its spread remains rampant. (This includes the four thousand who each day are subject to the ultimate child abuse of being killed in the womb without ever having looked into their mother's eyes or felt a motherly caress). The young victims of human trafficking and sexual abuse cry out to us for justice but we are busy with more important matters.

"We are all too familiar with the tragedy of our public education system and the consequence of the outrageous number of school drop outs. If our children were our priority, we would reform and reverse the structure that places teachers unions and their members at the center of the educational universe. Parents and youth ought to be the focus of the enterprise with parents given the ability to choose the place where they send their child and their educational dollars. The proper education would heal many of the nation's wounds and would result in a robust economy. The youth unemployment rate would change. Its current state is an outrage for a free country particularly as it pertains to minorities.

"Ladies and gentlemen, let me share with you what I believe to be the sine qua non, the single most important thing you can do to recapture the spirit of America, to improve the lives of our children, of our nation, to lift our culture, to insure our future. Embracing the sanctity of all human life in law, in government, in medicine, in culture and in lives of every family is the fundamental, the only path to return to the self evident truths "that all men are created equal, that they are endowed by their Creator with certain unalienable Rights, that among these are Life, Liberty and the pursuit of Happiness. As I leave this august body, the gathering that governs this great nation, I implore you to embrace the fundamental value that gives meaning to all of our work. I beg you to place the sanctity of every human life at the foundation of your law making. May God continue to bless you, your families and the people of the nation you represent. Thank you".

The gallery which was prohibited from cheering was generous in their applause. Those present on the floor of the Senate offered a courteous response, but nothing special. Their souls remained unstirred. Life would go on in the most exclusive club in the world with or without Diego.

Chapter 23

An Investigative Dead End

Confusion Reigns

Chief Mebimi had gathered together the entire one hundred fifty person detective unit with two objectives. First they needed to consider a new approach to the search for Sister Sophia and secondly they needed to determine which motive of the three outlined by the pope was most likely. Was it inside haters, terrorists or the Chinese? They needed to work quickly. The further they get from the time of the crime, the colder the leads would become. They would work on the presumption that the poisoning was a crime that involved Sister Sophia in some manner. But what would prompt a holy woman who had been a nun for twenty five years poisoning the pope and his household? The Chief outlined what the pope had mentioned.

One, the pope was always a target of those who would do evil, but they were many. The three groups the pope acknowledged were; the radical Islamist terrorists for whom the Church and its leader were prominent infidels. The Chief, himself a Muslim, did not reject that possibility. A second possibility was those who were aggrieved by the pope disrupting the Vatican by moving his offices to Nigeria. They were widespread and very angry according to the pope. Many threats had been issued the minute the announcement was made. The threats came from all over the world, although not a large number of threats from Italy. And finally, those who were hurt financially with the success the spiritual celebration of the Incarnation initiative that had lessened the Christmas market.

The Chinese economy was damaged the greatest, but all

retailers in developed nations suffered. Retailers in the underdeveloped countries benefitted when the funds flowed to the poor in those nations. The sale of consumer goods in those countries skyrocketed in late March and the first part of April. But the business cycle with Black Friday was broken.

The Chief broke the group into five panels of ten each and asked them to discuss the likely motive and return with their reasoning. Regrouping, the most popular motive was terrorism. They rejected the merchant notion partly because they would not know where to start to look for perpetrators. They rejected the idea of angry Catholics because they found it hard to believe that Catholics who believed in hell would kill the pope. Because he seemed like a decent guy who hadn't shown any dark side and didn't really hurt anybody by moving to Africa where the people who believed were, they doubted that motive. The detectives knew a lot about terrorists, especially the Boko Haram who had spread throughout Nigeria. They had driven the Christians from the north to the south and then recruited the dispossessed youth in the south and terrorized the Christians there. Terrorists believed in their mission and would do anything to obtain the money to carry it out. The collective opinion of the detectives was that they could find an informant easily and solve the case.

The Chief had been told that the American bishops posted a reward of a million dollars funded by the Knights of Columbus for information that led to the arrest and conviction of the person who conspired to kill the pope. The South American bishops had put up a half million. Nothing came from Europeans. They would have had to borrow from the Chinese to fund a reward.

The detectives had canvassed the neighborhood where Sister Sophia's brother lived and they were successful in learning a great deal about the time before Sister left the building. In

Lagos, at the time, the police did not enjoy positive relationships in some neighborhoods and that was the case in the area where Sister Sophia's brother lived. Only two detectives were assigned to the canvass so as not to intimidate the people in the community. They found Sister's brother's house empty but the front door was unlocked, an unusual circumstance especially in that particular neighborhood where some had more possessions than others. The people in the house next door were obviously reluctant to talk to the detectives. They said that they had heard nothing and seen nothing. The neighbors on the other side said that at about five AM the day before they had been awakened by some yelling next door. They were friendly to the neighbors and had never heard any yelling before. They could not figure it out. But it stopped and they heard two cars drive off in a hurry. They didn't think anything more of it and went back to sleep. Later in the day, the woman of the house went to Sister Sophia's brother's house to ask if everything was all right and no one was at home. That was all they could offer.

When the detectives visited the house directly across the street, they found an elderly woman in a wheel chair. Initially, she was reluctant to talk to them but one of the detectives made some nice talk about how his grandmother had been in a wheelchair for years and had never let it keep her from being active and aware of her neighborhood. Before long, he was drinking a cup of fresh coffee and chatting about all things other than what the woman might have seen.

He asked if she knew Sister Sophia's brother and his wife well and she acknowledged that she did. In fact, she used to baby sit the boys some times. But when the fourth came along, she was too old and not up to the task despite the fact that they were well behaved and very bright children.

When the detective told her that they were worried about the couple and the boys, she opened up. She normally rose at four thirty AM and had her coffee while watching the sun rise through her front window. The day before, at about five AM, two cars pulled up in front of the house. There were no lights on in the house until she heard the door bang open and four men entered the house. The people who were driving the vehicles, a sedan and a suburban stayed in the cars and waited. There was yelling and all of a sudden, she saw Adam, the father being pushed to the car rapidly and put into the back seat and the man behind him followed him to the back seat. Then that car pulled away. She thought it might have been an old black Lincoln. All the men were black except the man who was directing them. He held a gun like you see in American films. It was shorter than a shot gun and bigger than a pistol. He didn't fire it.

After the cars had left, Mrs. Irheido, Sister Sophia's sister in law came out of the house and saw that the cars were gone. She took note of the fact that the telephone line had been pulled from the house. She was crying and went back into the house. The old lady said that she initially thought it may have been the police and perhaps something had happened to someone in the family and they were taking Adam to the hospital or an accident scene or something.

Then it dawned on her that no one was in uniform. She thought she should call the police, but she was afraid. Sometimes the police made things worse. It frightened her too, to think that maybe the people who came were criminals and would come back to hurt her if they knew she called. So she did nothing. She told them she hoped nothing was wrong with the family. She indicated that she knew that Adam's sister cooked for the pope and she wondered if anyone had alerted her to the events. They lied and said that they had alerted her and that Sister Sophia was fine but didn't know anything about Adam. The old lady clearly didn't know that there had been an attempt on the pope's life.

The detectives assured her she would be safe and that, even if she had called, it wouldn't have made a difference. Then they asked if she would be able to identify anyone. She said the men were too far away for her to tell if the white man was Chinese or just white. They left and told her that if she thought of anything else, she should call. They left a card.

Chief Mebimi shared all the information with the group of detectives and decided that they should start to look for an informant among the Boko Haram or Al Shabaab. The detectives found that it was not as easy as they had anticipated. They had half dozen valuable and reliable informers in the city, but none of them indicated they had any information when approached. Three of them said that they thought they could gather some information if the price was right. The detectives were authorized an unusual amount for the offer, up to five thousand but they told the informants that they could come up with only two thousand which was a thousand more than the highest they had ever provided. One of the informants came back in two days with information that a member of Boko Haram had been contacted but had turned down any involvement because they knew that the pope was from the United States and they feared bringing down all that fire power. Boko Haram was aware of Delta Force and Seal Team Six and wanted nothing to do with them. The informant assumed that the work was done by some people from other than Nigeria, possibly from Somalia or Yemen because they would do anything for money. And, they were not smart enough to fear anybody. He asked for money and they gave him just one hundred dollars and told him to get more information.

The detectives told him that they didn't think the man who was leading the group was black and they needed to know who he was. When the informant came back two days later, he said that he had been told that the men were from Algeria and were being led by a White man who had employed them. They have left Nigeria with the nun and her brother and his family, but he didn't know where they went or how they left the country. He said that his source didn't know where the white man was from or even if the man was an Asian, but that he knew he was not a black with white makeup. He heard that the men were former military personnel who were for hire to do anything anywhere in the world as long as their employer could get them in and out of the country. The detectives gave him five hundred dollars and asked if he could bring in his source. He said he doubted the source would come in but for a thousand each he would do all he could. The detectives agreed and mentioned that there were big awards out for the right information.

But after a full week of work, they were dead-ended. The following Monday the informant came back to the detectives and said that his source told him the men were not from Algeria, but were Boko Haram. The detectives gave him five hundred and said that if he did not come back with information in three days, they would go after him and that they had plenty on him that would put him back in jail.

Chapter 24

A New Life

Rio

In his last two years in the senate, Diego was assigned to the Foreign Relations Committee and as a minority member, he became a bit of a specialist on Brazil. The country was bursting with people, economic progress, corruption and poverty all at the same time. During his senate years, he made five trips to Brazil. On the first trip he met with a female Deputy Secretary of the Interior who was in charge of what was essentially the country's welfare program. All types of programs were included in her portfolio, including women's programs which encompassed birth control, child welfare, abortion, early childhood education, family life and female employment.

On one of the trips, while congress was out of session, he spent three weeks in Rio at his own expense because he considered it a vacation. The Deputy Secretary introduced him to a new lay religious order many of whom were professionals, lawyers, architects, professors, doctors and nurses. But the group also included trades people, merchants, social workers and teachers. Those who were single resided and worshipped together in a former convent that was attached to a former school. Their primary function was to address the needs of Aids patients and the addicted. They operated a clinic and worked with the poor. They also sponsored an adult school of religion. They brought lecturers from around the world to their adult education programs. They had asked Diego to speak while he was on his trip and proposed a subject, United States Hegemony in the Western Hemisphere.

At that point, Diego had no interest in hegemony or

much else. He told them he would agree to that topic but because he never charged for a speech, the speech would be about whatever he was concentrating on at the time. As it turned out he was thinking about the group and their work. Diego studied the history of the lay order and was fascinated by the life and work of the founder, Geraldo Martinez. Diego immediately identified with him when he had read about him and his life. It was to his honor that Diego spoke and to his work that Diego was attracted, so attracted that it was this group which Diego joined six months later.

De Jesus, Las Manos, the Founder

Geraldo Martinez, the founder of the group, "De Jesus Las Manos", was an unusual person. His family had been made prosperous by Carlos Slim Helu of Mexico, the cell phone magnate and at one point, the richest man in the world. He had given Geraldo's father the first Brazilian cell phone franchise for just ten percent of the profits. The business expanded to the point where Geraldo's father was a multi-billionaire. When his father passed away, Geraldo took over the business. He was thirty and he turned out to be an even better businessman than his father. He expanded and diversified the company into oil, steel and banking. He was enormously successful, married to a gorgeous former model and deeply into the political order in the entirety of South America. His grandparents had come from Portugal and he had been baptized Catholic. But he hadn't seen the inside of a church since his wedding except to attend funerals, weddings or baptisms. He had no children to whom he could pass the business.

Two months after his fifth wedding anniversary, when he was thirty five, his wife suffered a fatal heart attack while on the treadmill in their home. She had been in apparent perfect health, but in the autopsy, the pathologist found a congenital heart defect. Geraldo was traumatized and completely devastated. He couldn't think. He couldn't manage. He could barely breathe. He turned the business over to his younger brother who was trying to help him cope. Geraldo had never been a drinker. He didn't like the feeling of not being in full control. He began to drink heavily, Bloody Marys for breakfast and scotch the remainder of the day until he passed out. He didn't eat, but for an occasional snack food. He often drove his Lamborghini into Rio to go to a club. He had a driver, but wanted to be in charge. He was a danger on the road and he enjoyed it. His first accident was minor. He was charged but it didn't affect his habits. No one was hurt. He began to spend every evening in clubs and was very popular because he frequently feted the entire club to drinks and dinner while inebriated. He slept with whomever he wanted and he lavished money on those women whom he took to his home.

He hit bottom when he found himself in a public hospital in Sao Paulo. He was in tattered clothing with no identification. No one recognized him. He couldn't remember how he got there. He had been picked up in the gutter after a four day binge and he couldn't recall any of it. He was visited by a member of Alcoholics Anonymous and he quickly became a "friend of Bill Wilson" but only for a short time. He hit bottom again this time in a hospital in Rio. When he sobered, he started a new life.

He rushed into extreme activities; first, skydiving, then deep sea diving, race cars and extreme drop-in skiing in remote parts of the Alps. However, nothing could occupy his mind or provide the solace he sought after his wife's death. The danger became a bore. He was still physically alive but tired of it all. Should he end it?

Geraldo's New Experience

One morning, he rose, borrowed some used clothing from his gardener who was his size and lived on the estate with his wife and three children. He went into Rio, parked his new Maserati in a secure lot in the financial section and walked the streets, which he had never done before. For eight hours he passed through neighborhoods he didn't know existed. On the edge of the central city, he entered an impoverished area populated by drug addicts, alcoholics and handicapped. He had never seen a poor person up close and certainly had never talked with one. He sat on a curb and took off his shoes and started to rub his aching feet. A man of about his age with filthy attire, wretched beard and hair and missing his four front teeth sat next to him. He was emaciated. He asked if he could have one of his shoes. The man would give Geraldo his left shoe which had a large hole in the sole and no heel if Geraldo's would give him the work shoe that belonged to the gardener. Geraldo laughed at the proposal but on impulse he agreed to the swap. The man became his "new best friend" thanking him profusely for his generosity. The man said that if he stayed with him for another couple of hours, he would take him to dinner at a soup kitchen.

Geraldo thought for a while about whether to do so. Then he thought it was a new experience, something he needed. They sat for a while and then walked about a mile to the free kitchen. It was in a large hall that was probably the old ballroom of the abandoned hotel next door. The man, who referred to himself in the third person as "Anthony" told him that it was church people who served the meal. Those who served didn't push religion or ask for anything and it was always a good meal with dessert. Geraldo was introduced to three of the Anthony's associates who were not much interested in Anthony's friend, Geraldo. Once they had gobbled down the meal, they were gone.

Anthony shared that he had been an alcoholic since he was about fifteen, had had a lot of women but never married and he didn't know if he had kids. He had used every possible drug in his day, but could no longer afford them. He was too weak to steal and had spent too much time in jail. He wanted only to sit in the sun. He just tried to live out each day and return to his little shack where he slept. He ate twice a day, once at noon at a soup kitchen a few blocks away and then dinner here at the hall. He shared that there was a place about two kilometers away where he could shower and get new underwear and socks, but it was a long walk. That was why he needed Geraldo's shoe.

After dinner, Geraldo left him and said that he hoped he would meet him again someday. Anthony told him he loved him and Geraldo went home. By the time he reached his car wearing the shoe Anthony had given him, he knew he would not be able to walk the next day. He couldn't sleep, partly because his feet hurt, partly, because of Anthony. He rose the next day early as he always did since he had become sober. Shortly after arising, he called his new appointed AA sponsor, Father Dan Ryan whom he had met at the AA meeting two weeks earlier. Father Dan was a Franciscan priest who had gone through a ten year bout with alcohol. Geraldo needed to talk to someone who he thought had a good fix on the "higher power" of AA. Father Dan was a real Franciscan, who lived the life in slums of Rio. He wore sandals and a grungy brown habit so that those in the neighborhood would recognize him and come to him for help. He had become an institution in the slum where he worked.

There were many slums in Rio and there were other Father Dans working in them. For the first two weeks of their association, Geraldo and Father Dan would talk at a coffee shop after the AA meetings. Geraldo had not had occasion to call Father Dan at any other time. He was working hard on his

sobriety. But this morning was different. He needed guidance about his future. He asked if they could meet at the coffee shop on Wednesday rather than wait until Friday for their regular meeting. When he met with Father Dan this time it was at a lunch stand in the ghetto. He
said that he needed more time alone to discuss something that didn't have anything to do with alcohol. Father Dan said he couldn't be available until about seven in the evening. They could meet in the building where Geraldo had had the dinner with Anthony. Geraldo didn't know when he ate there two days ago that it was run by Father Dan's group.

When they met, Geraldo told Father Dan that he wanted to change his life. He was thirty nine and had no interest in business, politics or entertaining himself. He needed something to do that would give meaning to his life. Father Dan asked him why it was important to have something meaningful to do. Geraldo didn't have an immediate answer. He thought perhaps it was that Juanita, his late wife, would be proud of him if he did something that mattered. Father Dan went to a bookshelf and pulled out a copy of "The Purpose Driven Life" in Portuguese. He told Geraldo to read the book and then they would talk. He read it straight through over a few days and come back to discuss it. Geraldo said he didn't want to be a priest or a monk. He wasn't into God or church. He just wanted to do something useful that would please Juanita.

Geraldo stayed up that night and read the book through. He called and told Father Dan that he had read it and asked if they could meet the next day. When he met with Father Dan at the dining hall, he said he could give away a lot of money and then join him in the slums. Father Dan laughed and said that if he did that, he might turn back to the booze. The slums were depressing and one of the things that alcoholics love is depression. It can justify anything including the drink. Father

Dan told him that he needed to do something that would use his talents. He was creative. He needed to build something that would reflect the talent for leadership he had shown in business. But he needed to have a core principle to which he could attract others with the same needs and talents. He could start another company, a learning institution or a political party.

Geraldo spent the next few days reading biographies of people who had created organizations. He couldn't generate an idea. When he returned to Father Dan, he was frustrated and asked if he had any ideas for what he should do. Father Dan told him to look closely into his eyes and to see if there was anything there that prompted an idea. Geraldo said he couldn't see anything in Father Dan's eyes. Father Dan gave a facetious sorrowful look and said he must be a pretty poor reflection of the founder of his outfit, St Francis.

Then he told Geraldo that Geraldo had all the same capabilities of St. Francis of Assisi, the man who had founded a world wide band of friars nearly five hundred years earlier. Francis had talent. Francis was from a wealthy family. Geraldo had more experience, more money and likely more talent. But then Father asked him if he had the core principle that drove St Francis, faith. Geraldo would have to think about that. He believed in the "higher power" in his life and as a child he really admired Jesus. But he had not given any thought to him for a long time. He still didn't know where Father Dan was taking him. He wanted to do something but he wasn't sure he wanted to change his life completely. He knew he didn't want to be a priest. He may want to marry someday. He had had a happy marriage.

He began to think of people who he knew who were different than he was, people he admired and who seemed to have a sense of purpose. There were a few in his organization, some accountants, some engineers, sales persons and managers. One of the things they seemed to have in common was their seriousness about life. He called one of the electrical engineers whose work he had admired over the years and asked if they could go to lunch. He asked him about his life. He was married, had four kids and was deeply into his faith and to service. He had worked on the construction and repair of the dining room where Father Dan was headquartered and where he and Anthony had eaten. They had plans for three more dining rooms in different parts of the city. Geraldo asked if there were others in the company involved and he told him about four others, three of whom were still single and devoting a great deal of their off time to the mission.

They were a part of a very small group of Catholic laymen and lay women. Geraldo asked where the money came from for their work. He said they each contributed what they could. He asked if they needed money and the engineer told him that they never begged for money, it just came to them when they needed it, sometimes through Father Dan who had a sign over the dining room door in Latin "Deus Providebit" (God will provide) and it always seemed to work out. Where the money came from only God and sometimes Father Dan knew.

Geraldo was beginning to plan for an organization that could aid the poor, but he didn't have a good sense of why he wanted to do it. He spent the sleepless nights thinking about Juanita, where she was and what she was doing. His thoughts demanded that he think of the afterlife and God which he hated doing. He wanted to be fully alive and not think about death, but Juanita was with God, so if he wanted to think about her, he had to think about God.

A Breakthrough

Finally, one day in what turned out to be Holy Week, he

sat in the Catholic Church of Santa Cruz where he had been married. When he was a child his mother had always taken him and his brother to mass during Holy Week. But he never liked it. All the statues were covered with purple cloth and he thought that was dumb. He always wanted to see the statues. But today the covers on the statues were positive. He was pleased that he was not distracted by a bunch of colorful images of plaster saints. Even the cross was covered. He remembered that as a child he hated seeing Christ on the cross bleeding and battered. His mother had a cross with a statue of Jesus after he had risen and had on flowing robes. Geraldo liked that much better.

He thought he would just drop in and try to regain a picture of Juanita with a beautiful smile and dressed in her magnificent wedding dress, but he couldn't produce that picture in his mind no matter how hard he tried. All he could picture was the funeral, the casket and the homily. The priest knew Juanita well. She was a practicing Catholic with serious faith. The homily focused on Juanita, her faith and her goodness. He was momentarily lifted by what the priest was saying about Juanita and wanted the priest to continue to talk about Juanita. He had not totally captured the wonder of Juanita. It was the next best thing to having her with him. But the priest stopped and the horrible reality set in.

Now he was back in the church alone. Geraldo hurt badly. He cried and cried. Then he sat up and asked himself what was going on in his life. He stayed in the church for nearly four hours, thinking, cursing, praying and crying. When he left, he was exhausted. What would Juanita want him to do? She always wanted him to be more generous with the church and the poor. He thought he was generous enough. But now he was a billionaire and didn't even like money. It had become a burden to manage it all. It gave him no solace. It didn't excite him. He lived in a mansion on a hill but had no interest in it. It was just a place to be. He didn't want to travel alone and he hadn't met anyone who could in anyway measure up to Juanita. She was too beautiful, loving and unique.

He would give his fortune to a charity. He would call it Juanita's Bread and he would establish eating halls all over Brazil for anyone who wanted to come including the poor. Then he would go to them and oversee the managers. He would have something to manage again. When he went to Father Dan with the idea, Father Dan said simply that it was a nice idea. "Maybe everyone in Brazil would eat there and if they could get free food, they wouldn't have to work. It would wonderful for their dignity to eat at someone else's table every day. You would be their hero". The soup kitchen that Father Dan's group ran was supposed to be an emergency relief facility, not a place where everyone should eat every day. Geraldo got the point quickly and he didn't like Father Dan's response, but he knew he was right. So he said "O.K. wise guy, what's your idea"? Father Dan said he thought he'd never ask. He told Geraldo he wanted him to be his assistant. Geraldo said "What did you just say? You told me six weeks ago that working with you would turn me to drink".

Father Dan said "That was then, this is now. You've learned a lot since then. Humility can do things for people". Geraldo walked out of the small smelly office and went home. He wanted to run things, be the boss, not work for a broken down priest in a soup kitchen. He brooded for a week. He was frustrated. Geraldo went back to Father Dan and agreed to be his aid until he thought of what to do. By virtue of his new role, he met other lay people who wanted to be of service. He even went to confession to Father Dan and started serving his mass in a room adjacent to the smelly office. One day, he asked if he could improve the offices and Father Dan said that the people who come there may be uncomfortable in fancy offices. One day as he was sitting on a bench outside a shoe store and watching the world of poverty pass him, he saw Anthony. Anthony was dying of Aids. Anthony had been diagnosed a couple of months before, but it was too late to do anything with the drugs available to the impoverished. Geraldo had a moment of clarity. He would try to enlist a group of people to work exclusively with the Aids and HIV infected patients in the community. They would scour the community for potential patients and provide testing and end of life care for those who were dying. Geraldo would make his mansion available as a care center for those in their last days. Father Dan urged him to call the mission "De Jesus Las Manos", a concept with which patients would identify. Geraldo dedicated the care center that he built in the slum to Juanita's memory and it was a model facility with the latest technology and very attractive surroundings. The mansion was too remote from the city for patients to live, so it was sold and the funds went to purchase a facility in the city where the patients of the AIDS project could reside. The new facility was dedicated to Juanita on her birthday and its first patient was Anthony who died three weeks later while Father Dan was administering the Sacrament of the Sick.

Father Dan helped Geraldo form a lay order specific to the AIDS ministry. It didn't have any canonical connection. The connection would have required too much paperwork and would be limiting. In the first five years, more than one hundred people joined in the effort. Most were young but a few were seniors. Those who were single lived in the facility with a chapel where the mass was celebrated daily and recitation of portions of the holy office prayed. The former nunnery was remodeled with an auditorium in the former school that was used as a school of religion.

Among the early speakers in the school of religion, was Leonardo Boff of liberation theology fame. Geraldo knew nothing of Boff or of liberation theology. But he was welcomed by Geraldo. Geraldo had thought that the order might find enlightenment from a theologian. After the talk, he and Father Boff shared a meal. They both concluded that the quality of the meal was the only matter upon which they agreed. Geraldo was still a capitalist who had created thousands of jobs throughout the world. He sensed that Boff would like all those jobs and any profit from their work to be in the hands of the government.

Geraldo contracted AIDS three years into his ministry and died one year later after being felled by pneumonia. The cause of his sanctity was initiated five years later, one year after Diego had joined the order. In May of the year before the canonization started, a contagious disease doctor working with the clinic confirmed without a doubt that a man in the final stages of Aids had had a spontaneous recovery after he, along with two of the brothers, had prayed to Geraldo for a cure. Because it was before the sainthood process had been initiated, the Devil's Advocate would not give attribution of that as one of the necessary miracles. It was because of the recovery that the group had asked to start the process.

When Diego joined the lay order after leaving the senate, he was referred to as Brother Diego within the lay community. The order had never sought canonical status, had no approval from Rome and was unofficial. So they didn't refer to themselves religiously outside the community. They took a simple vow to start each day with a prayer to ask God to help them recognize each person with whom they came in contact as a child of God whose life was sacred and to foster their sense of love for them. Diego went almost immediately to work for Father Dan who was beginning to age and needed help.

But after a year, the executive committee of the order asked him to study for the priesthood. Father Dan had been an unofficial chaplain but the executive committee knew he would not last forever and wanted a permanent chaplain of their own. Diego had not intended to be a priest. He enjoyed his role as a brother. Father Dan was his confessor. He encouraged Diego and supported the group's request. He thought Diego would make an excellent priest. After meeting Jordan and understanding her relationship with God, Diego began to see how grace came to people. If asked by someone who was well intended to do something, he began to think of the request as a grace that should be responded to.

The order wanted to send Diego to Rome to study theology thinking that he would get the best theologians as instructors. Diego thought the request was a grace and was willing. Father Dan petitioned the American College in Rome to allow him to live there free of charge while attending the Pontifical Lateran University which had an interesting history. Pope Clement XIV suppressed the Jesuits and booted them from the university. They were rehabilitated by Pope Leo XII in 1824 and he gave the university back. Saint Pope John the XXIII titled the seminary the Pontifical Lateran University. Father Dan also petitioned the Vatican on the order's behalf to advance Diego's study to allow him to finish his philosophy and theology studies in five years.

Diego knew that returning to Rome would evoke memories of his honeymoon there and could generate sadness. But he had determined as best he could to always concentrate on the joys that he had shared with Jordan. He didn't want to grieve. He knew she was his advocate. He looked forward to his study and knew he would learn from the effort. After all, he was going to have time to read, to study and to listen to people who made it their lives to learn what he now considered important, God's nature, why he made us and what he expects of us. He could learn why God did what He did for us.

He was forty one years old, but he was worn out in both mind and body. Were it not for his conditioning, he would be in ill health. He had been going at life with abandon for too long and now he was re-directing all of his energies. He had known throughout his life that he was different and the path he was now pursuing was surely evidence of that difference.

During his studies, he was taken under the wing of Bishop Thomas J. O'Boyle of the Pittsburgh diocese who was the Rector of the American College in Rome. Diego was allowed to live there free because he was an American citizen and because O'Boyle wanted him there. O'Boyle was just five years older than Diego, a huge pro college and pro football fan and had watched Diego rip the Pittsburgh Steelers defensive line to shreds for five years. Bishop O'Boyle had played basketball at Boston College but had always wanted to be on the gridiron. His mother would not allow him to play football saying that any sport that required an ambulance on the field was not for her son. During the five years that Diego spent in Rome, Bishop O'Boyle regularly whipped Diego in one on one on the hardcourt just to keep him humble.

He introduced Diego to Pope Paul VII and a lot of the other Vatican dignitaries, one of whom was the Secretary of State, Cardinal Alango of Kenya.

At the conclusion of his studies, Diego returned to Brazil where he was ordained by the cardinal of the Rio diocese and went back to his community as the full time chaplain tending to the spiritual needs of both the patients and the volunteers. He came to know death intimately and felt like a little bit of him went with each of the patients to whom he had become close as they were dying. It was again a case of feeling that he was in the right place.

The decision to ask him to study was wise. Father Dan was aging and ready to cut back on his responsibilities. Diego took over the chaplaincy and served as the advisor to the committee that decided on projects that continued to be funded by Geraldo's money. Geraldo had left the trust fund to be spent for operations and twenty five million per year for new projects.

There continued to be strong support in the community to promote canonization for Geraldo for his "white (bloodless) martyrdom". Diego favored the idea and worked with the committee to support the process while in Rome.

Diego was asked to assist a committee chosen by the cardinal of Rio to coordinate a political approach to the repeal of Brazil's decision to support euthanasia. The supporters of the initiative that legalized euthanasia emphasized that there simply was not enough money to provide health care to all the elderly in Brazil. The initiative was principally supported by the youthful population of Brazil. There was progress in the repeal, but before the legislative vote occurred, Cardinal Alango called from Rome.

Three years after his return to Rio, Cardinal Alango summoned him to come to Rome as quickly as he could free himself. Diego had no idea of what the agenda was for his being summoned. When he arrived in Rome, the cardinal was blunt. He needed Diego and a part of it was that Diego had both African and Hispanic blood but didn't represent either group from a nationalistic perspective. Because he was still an American citizen he would be considered neutral in any dispute Rome might experience in dealing with the two largest populations in the Catholic Church. Africa and South America were sometimes at odds. Diego was shocked. He was ordained for the community and he felt he owed them his service. The cardinal had a dilemma. He couldn't order Diego, but he could get someone to persuade him.

Cardinal Alango had already talked to the pope. He decided to play the pope card. When the cardinal asked him to accompany him to the pope's offices, he thought it was for a blessing. But when they met with the pope, Diego was encouraged to serve with the Secretary of State. The pope assured Diego that a priest would be assigned as chaplain to his community. Diego became the Under-Secretary of State for

International Diplomatic Affairs, new post and moved back and forth between Africa and South America. After just two years in the Secretary of State's office, he was ordained a bishop. He found that he was skilled at diplomacy and seemed comfortable in his role. He liked working with both the Hispanic and African hierarchy and he enjoyed the learning about the cultures and the issues.

Chapter 25

Waking to a Call

The Room of Tears

Six years into Diego's role in the diplomatic corps of the Vatican, Pope John XXIV, a vigorous Dutch sixty six year old with no known illnesses, died suddenly of a brain hemorrhage. Diego had known him well and admired his courage and holiness. He had been rushed to Gemelli Polyclinic for emergency surgery, but it was unsuccessful. He had served for only four years. The camerlengo, the official who takes over in the event of the pope's incapacity was Cardinal Baroni who had once served as the Secretary of State and was currently the Prefect for Sacred Doctrine. He entered the pope's hospital room, tapped his forehead three times with the silver hammer and called his baptismal name each time. Why the Church switched from the candle held beneath the nose to see if it flickered, no one could determine. But the silver hammer was now the instrument for the formal determination of the pope's death. Of course in the modern age, it was just a symbol. When John XXIV did not answer to his name, the camerlengo declared the pope deceased and removed the papal ring. He had it chopped in two and destroyed it to symbolize that the authority of the papacy was changing.

Over the centuries a number of seemingly bizarre customs developed around the death and burial of the pope. Most had little to do with the faith. Pius XI who died in the twentieth century was buried with three bags of coins, one silver, one gold and the other copper. Each bag contained seventeen coins to symbolize the seventeen years of his reign. The camerlengo was conscious of all the odd customs and determined to have none of it under his auspices. He arranged for the funeral mass and the homilist. The assigned roles in the events surrounding the funeral and the various ceremonies associated with the death of a pope were very important in establishing a papal pecking order. An important role could give a cardinal an audition allowing him to be reckoned among the papabile, a possible candidate for the papacy. Such was the power of the camerlengo who was generally the past pope's right hand man. He arranged and was responsible for overseeing the conclave to elect a new pope. He called the cardinals to Rome for election even though most of them were there for the funeral and decided to stay over unless there was some critical activity in their diocese to which they needed to attend.

The period between the funeral and the conclave allowed the cardinals to discuss their wants and hopes for a new pope and to compare notes on who would best meet the needs of the Church. There was a traditional waiting period before the conclave during which there were meetings arranged to inform the cardinals about the status of the Church throughout the world, her problems and progress.

Because of the sudden death of the pope, there was an unusual measure of anxiety in the Church and even among the cardinals. The cardinals were simply not prepared for the death of a young pope. As always there were major challenges facing the Church and a great deal of conflict among both the faithful and the clergy. There was a clear divide between those who were tradition bound and those who wanted the Church to be more progressive and modern. The number of Catholics in the world had continued to grow because the Church was expanding in the countries where people were still having children. But the percent of Catholics in most countries was diminishing while the Muslims, Mormons and fundamentalist evangelical churches were increasing in percentages.

A number of cardinals thought that a factor that was contributing to the growth of the Muslim and Mormon faiths was the rigid disciplines required of its members. It had been nearly a hundred years since Vatican II when the relaxation of the disciplines in the Church made being Catholic so easy that birth Catholics often didn't seem to think Catholicism an important matter. They could take it or leave it and many did.

The cardinals gathered and determined to meet for three days before the conclave. In an effort to re- establish contacts and to be brought up to date on the challenges that would face the new pope, they sequestered themselves in a committee of the whole. The camerlengo presided and called on various members of the curia to provide deep reports. Each member struggled to prepare a status report in the brief time available to them between the death and meetings. The camerlengo prepared the agenda with the aid of representatives whom he selected from Europe, Asia, North and South America, and Africa.

The camerlengo was comfortable in the autocratic role that the structure of the Church and the conclave provided him and he made no pretense of democracy in setting the agenda. He did attempt to demonstrate a measure of collegiality, a small measure. The agenda provided for reports on finances, diplomatic relations, status of the clergy and the faithful, conflicts and challenges, near and remote. Some of the cardinals were relatively new to the "red hat". Some had never met others and some had not met face to face with others since the election of Pope John XXIV four years earlier after the death of Paul VII. They were not always called to Rome at the same time. While they were saddened by the untimely death of the pope, they were all comfortable with the role of elector and they were eager to get on with the matter of choosing a successor. While they were conscious of the age of a pope and hoped for long reigns, their most recent experience of the death of young pope made them conscious of the role of the Holy Spirit in the matter of who leads the Church.

The carmerlengo opened the first of the meetings in the general sessions before the conclave with a presentation that was meant to put all the cardinals in the same frame of mind regarding their duty. He wanted them to focus on the election of the Church leader, who was familiar with the Church's struggles and triumphs over the centuries, its current role in the world and in history and more significantly, its future. He reminded the cardinals that though the Church was presently threatened by forces both internal and external, she would survive. She had been threatened often. The Roman persecution baptized the Church in blood. She survived early schisms. She dealt successfully, if not wisely, with the Islamic threats over the centuries. She not only survived, she led during the Dark Ages, coped with the Reformation, addressed the Renaissance demands and challenged the Enlightenment. She dealt with Darwinism, met Modernism and Post-Modernism head on and continued to progress in serving the world and providing the moral leadership. And she will continue to do so.

He didn't pull any punches. "The damage done by the sexual horror visited on our children and our Church is still weighing heavily on us and our Church after nearly fifty years. The Church's mission and her moral authority even in areas totally unrelated to that matter have been all but destroyed. You undoubtedly know that the financial position of the Church has continued to suffer. There is not likely a man in this room today that does not bear some guilt concerning that vile insult to the personal dignity of so many innocent young people. We all sinned by negligence if not by action. Each of these victims has every right to doubt us, to reject our preaching and to subject us to their anger. If you were ordained at the time and most of you were, you knew someone who was or whom you suspected was complicit in those sins. Some of you may have headed administrations that are guilty of subjecting young people to vicious sexual violence. We all need to pray for forgiveness from both the victims and our God. We need to do a fitting and severe penance for those sins, promising never to allow another gross moral failure. It is not good enough to say we are human. We need to lead and we need to behave in a manner that allows us to lead.

"I have never understood why bishops simply did not utilize and allow the criminal and civil law of the lands to deal with the failure of its priest citizens. Though we are priests, we are first and still citizens and subject to the law. Whomever we elect in the coming conclave must be fully alert to the possibilities of all of our moral failures and wise enough and strong enough to address them aggressively. He needs to be a man of great intestinal fortitude.

"Most of us live in societies where the family has faltered. Absent the nurturing, the instruction, the discipline and the love and affection of the family, our youth have entered their adolescence and their adult lives weakened morally and spiritually. Most are unprepared to resist the secular culture that absorbs them into an pervasive hedonistic and materialistic narcissism. The spiritual, behavioral and moral standards that shaped Western Civilization and underwrote Eastern culture have long ago deteriorated. Some societies have fallen to nearly uncivilized levels where the sanctity of an individual's life is no longer respected or warranted as a human right. Many societies long ago abandoned the sanctity of the lives of the unborn and the criminal. Now as our populations age and the cost of their care rises, those same people who abandoned the sanctity of the lives of the unborn are now comfortably abandoning the sanctity of the lives of the aging. They are refusing to pay the taxes to support their medical and care needs. We need to regain our moral authority and challenge this slide. When it comes to the sanctity of life, we are required by duty to God, to his children and to the natural law that he has instilled in the heart of man to assert the sanctity of life no matter what the world may think of our past sins.

"You need to enter this conclave knowing that this is the conclave that elects a pope who can lead the Church in reclaiming our role. His duty is to be *the servant of the servants of God* . You are those servants. Pray to God to know and have the strength and wisdom to accomplish your mission."

The Conclave

When the doors to the Sistine Chapel were closed, locked and a Papal Chamberlain, a monsignor from Ghana was posted, there were one hundred twenty elector Cardinals all under the age of eighty. Nineteen cardinals were excluded because they were over eighty years old. There were standing rules and roles that governed the conclave. The pope to be elected was the two hundred and seventieth pope. But not all popes had come to the chair of Peter as a result of a conclave. In the modern conclave, the roles switched from day to day. The camerlengo was in charge, but new presidents, verifiers and counters were chosen for each day. Two additional people were assigned to act as the ones to share information with a cardinal who might take ill in the conclave and those who were unable to vote because of their age. There was to be no contact with the outside world and cardinals were to keep fully sequestered from the world and its happenings.

Despite their generally secular orientation, there was intense interest among the media concerning the workings, the progress and the outcome of the conclave. A scoop would merit a Pulitzer Prize and most media representatives and their organizations would expend any cost or energy or engage in any subterfuge to obtain one. Odds makers too had a high interest in the outcome and the events surrounding the elections and were willing to take wagers on every aspect of the event.

Two days into the conclave, the first vote was taken and the black smoke was released indicating that there was not yet a pope elected. A two thirds vote was hard to come by in a Church that was so diverse in its composition and complexion. Beyond any nationalisms were the splits that reflected the traditionalists and the progressives who were just about balanced in their representation. And there were outliers at the extremes of each group that found it difficult to support anyone who didn't share at least some of their views. The camerlengo began to worry a bit after twenty votes which were widely spread among some six vastly different candidates. One was a pure intellectual and would not be at all fit to the task. Another had had a sexual scandal in his diocese and another, a financial scandal. Another was what the camerlengo considered a rigid traditionalist who was working to take the Church back to the pre Vatican II era while a radical progressive had a dozen votes.

The cardinals met in caucuses in rooms in the living quarters at night. After a week and a half and having called together a total of five different small groups, the camerlengo still couldn't determine any obvious pattern in the voting or think of any way under the standing rules to legally and morally press the group to a decision. He was uneasy but decided to let the conclave progress for at least another week without any personal comment. The cardinals knew their mission and they were mature intelligent adults who were making a bona fide effort to choose a pope. But they were also becoming impatient.

In the fifth day of the second week, the camerlengo gathered with the sixth small group he had selected and asked them if they saw the same voting pattern that he noticed. Of the three leading candidates, one was black, one Hispanic and one was white. The black was traditionalist, the Hispanic was moderately progressive and the white was widely known as the most progressive cardinal in the college. Others noted the same pattern but did not see any movement in the votes. They were coming up with a three way divide, a dangerous circumstance for the conclave. Cardinal Alango of Kenya urged the camerlengo to intervene by simply pointing out the voting pattern and to ask anyone who wanted to speak to take ten minutes to share their thoughts. The camerlengo took note but did not respond.

Three more votes were taken and the camerlengo again assembled a different small group. He was not attempting to influence anyone. He was trying to learn why the vote was so and if they thought it would continue in the same manner or resolve itself. Those receiving votes were from Italy, Germany, Poland, Brazil, Kenya and the Netherlands. No one was near a majority in the twenty eighth vote. In the last two votes, only Hispanic and Black cardinals were serious contenders, but none could acquire the necessary two thirds.

Cardinal Alango, the Secretary of State was just another voting cardinal but he did speak with a greater measure of persuasion by virtue of his office. Cardinal Alango told the camerlengo that it was clear that the conclave was hopelessly deadlocked and they needed to think of some way to introduce a new candidate. The voting pattern made it clear that the Hispanic cardinals would not support an African and the Africans would not support a Hispanic.

In the small leadership group, Cardinal Alango asked to put the name of his Under Secretary in the State Department, Bishop Freeman, a Black Hispanic from the U.S. into candidacy. The others were intrigued by the idea, but bothered by the prospect of electing a bishop and not a cardinal. It was legal under Canon Law but would it set a precedent? A very long discussion resulted in the approval to nominate Bishop Freeman as a candidate. He was popular with both the Africans and the Hispanics, but they wondered if the cardinals would be willing to elect him as their leader. The fact that Diego had both African and Hispanic blood did not go unnoticed by the members of the conclave. But he would be the first American pope. The weakness of the American Church bothered some of the cardinals.

On the next vote, Bishop Freeman who at the time was in the Central African Republic involved in an effort to resolve a conflict between two factions spread over a half dozen dioceses. One group was eager to have both married priests and women as bishops and the other group opposed to the idea. When he was elected pope and advised of the selection, he appeared on television in Africa and took the name of Francisco Augustine. He wanted to be positive, but the events happened so quickly that it left him in shock. The idea of being the pope had never occurred to him. He had planned to someday return to Brazil and the lay community where he had found great happiness, where he felt close to those who believed and were joined by the love of Jesus. He accepted that God had spoken through the conclave. He prayed for the necessary grace. It took him two days to arrive in Rome, so he had no need for "the Room of Tears" to cry while they fitted him with a papal cassock. The last tear he would ever shed was at Jordan's funeral. He had never again cried.

During the two travel days from Africa there was time to think through what he might say to the Church and to the world in his first appearance as pope. He prayed to the Holy Spirit to guide his tongue. He was eager to foster the faith among both the baptized and those who longed for faith in a world where hope was fading. He wanted to speak to the people of the world whom he had met in his travels, the people about whom he had deep concern and the people for whom he had developed much love. As he prepared his remarks, he was mindful of his mother's beautiful gift of faith that prompted her service, the wisdom provided him by Brother Mark and the grace and joy that his beloved Jordan found in her faith.

He wanted to engage the full universe of communication with his first words and he wanted to include even those whom he assumed had no interest in the faith or the Church. He hoped to acknowledge that faith was a blessing, s gift that for God's own reasons was not bestowed. He needed to be realistic in a wildly secular world. He would acknowledge those who doubted and was eager to give them a basis for hope. He stood on the steps of the St. Peter's Basilica in the warm Roman August sun and said: "God has seen fit to provide his Church and his world with a pope who is humbled by his lack of preparedness but thrilled at the opportunity to be of service to the faith that Jesus shared with us. We are a people of Jesus' gospel of life and love born to serve our brothers.

"That enormous explosion, the incredible boom that physicists tell us occurred some fourteen or so billion years ago, what scientists call the "big bang" was the burst of God's love become manifest in existence, the beginning of our universe, the beginning of matter, space and time. Our world is from God made for love. It is our origin, our nature and out destiny to love. The words of love and service given us by Jesus have echoed through two millennia and come to us each day in the gospel.

"The physicists can tell us a great deal about the nature of our beginnings, the how of the explosion. In fact they have mimicked it in laboratories. But the protons they have used to do so came not from scientists, but from God. Science tells us that it is certain that the universe had a beginning. Because it is linear, the world we know will end. We learn more each day about the how of the event. But no one can tell us with absolute objective truth "why" the world exists. It is God's mystery.

"In 1927, two years prior to publication of the Hubble constant theory of inflation of the universe, Father Georges Lemaitre, a Belgian priest and physicist described the origin and expansion of the universe. Father Lemaitre labeled the atom the "primeval atom", the "cosmic egg". In that act of creation God seeded his plan for all that has and will occur. The mission God has given to each of us for our lives is in that plan. In 1933, physicist Albert Einstein, the scientist yet unequaled in his theory of the nature of the universe described Father Lemaitre's full theory of the beginning of existence as "the most beautiful and satisfactory explanation of creation I've ever heard". It was logical that a priest who was both a man of science and faith could describe creation so beautifully. The event to which he referred has now become universally known as the "big bang".

The physicists tell us that the "big bang" is still echoing all around us in "cosmic microwave background radiation". Father Lemaitre described our current state by noting that "the fireworks are over and just the smoke is left". Some theoretical physicists speculate that our universe may have come from a multi-verse that may have pre-existed our universe. But if that is so, the multi-verse had to be the result of some equally inexplicable event. In short, some sort of being is responsible for existence and that being is by nature a transcendent being. The fact that there is no objective measure for the why of existence establishes a barrier that prevents many from any exploration of the nature of reality. It prevents them from exploring faith and leaves them in a world of ambiguity. There is no barrier to seeking God. The Catholic Church and Christianity welcome every discovery of science that leads man closer to the source of his being, to God, the transcendent being who is responsible for the universe. Einstein struggled with the notion of a personal God. But he willingly acknowledged the miracles that God has wrought. He mused that "There are only two ways to live your life. One is as though there is no such thing as a miracle. The other is as though everything is a miracle". "We live in a miraculous world. All of existence is a mystery.

Pope Francisco's words were reported by a cynical media as an attempt to reflect a Catholic "Scientology" but they were met with acceptance among the faithful. In the materialistic secular world they inhabited, the reminder that life is a miracle and a mystery was valuable to appreciating the role of faith in their lives.

After two years in the papacy and much painful learning and deliberation, he announced that he would move the Vatican to Nigeria for five years to better showcase the strength of the faith and to address the problems of poverty and persecution in Africa. His additional motive was to place the church in clear contrast to the overpowering strength and the damage done to Christians by the Muslims in Nigeria. In the same announcement, he indicated that his second five years in the papacy would be spent with the Vatican headquartered in Brazil.

He had greatly enjoyed the Vatican, Rome and Italy. He found the Italians fascinating; their passion, their tolerance, their beauty, their art, music and their commitment to family, though deteriorating was still edifying. He didn't really want to leave Rome. But he felt he needed to be where the Church was and not in a location remote from God's people. He felt a need to let the world know that the Church was not the Church only of Rome but of the world. For too long people had identified Rome with the old order managed by the Italians and those whom they chose to assist them. He had seen the Church from the United States, from South America and from Africa, from the days of his youth and now as a mature man of faith. He was now the leader of the very Church from which he had almost become alienated. He had no idea of what was to come during his papacy but he sensed, as Jesus had, that he and the Church he led had enemies who would not cease. But he had to do what he thought was God's will for him.

Chapter 26

It's Always about the Money

Follow the Filthy Lucre

Unfortunately for Chief Mebimi, once the FBI learned of the attempt on the pope's life, the news spread quickly to the internet and the international community. The media became very demanding to know the status of his case. The Chief was pleased with the success of the detectives' work with the informant, but he was also impatient. He needed more information and needed it quickly. This was clearly the biggest case in the history of Africa and it was his to solve or to live with a reputation of a loser for the rest of his life. He was still a young man with fifteen more years to retirement. He was nervous and anxious.

He needed to open new fronts in the investigation but he didn't want confusion with too much irrelevant information. It appeared that Sister Sophia and her brother's family were kidnapped and that Sister Sophia may have been involved in poisoning the pope. But he had no idea of who did the kidnapping, where they came from or where they were. He assigned another group of detectives who were specialists in financial crimes to pursue a completely different approach. They needed to follow the money. Was there a large amount of money that changed hands in Nigeria or elsewhere and could they learn who received funds. The detectives were to put out feelers with money attached.

Three days passed and the additional set of detectives got a lead from someone in the foreign financial section of Nigeria's largest bank. He was not seeking reward money. He said that he was violating his fiduciary responsibility and he would not disclose his name. He said he was a Catholic and was not going to stand by while someone tried to kill the pope. He told them that one million American dollars had been wired from Italy to a private citizen in Abuja, a man who was known to be a financier of Boko Haram. He knew nothing further and he didn't want to testify in the event Boko Haram was involved.

The Lagos detectives went to Abuja and sought the help of the local police. They didn't want to bring in their federal police until they had a better lead. The local Abuja police knew the financier and had tried to prosecute him before but to no avail. He had the best lawyers in Nigeria to protect him. The Abuja detectives alerted their Chief who approved of a friendly visit with the financier. One of the Lagos detectives joined them. They didn't want to have too many officers present. They went to the financier's offices and asked to meet with him. He called his lawyer in and they all sat down. He said that he had received a large transfer of funds from a Roman bank but it was for financial consultant services that his firm had rendered over a year's time. He had deferred payment until the current tax year to avoid paying too much last year. The detectives had nowhere to go with further questions. But they began to conclude that they had been misled by their informant who indicated the kidnappers were Algerian.

They needed to go to Rome and to the Roman bank from which the funds had been wired. When they went to the bank, they asked to speak to a vice president who signed off on the transfer. She said that she didn't have time to speak with them but wrote a note while talking to them indicating that she would meet them after her work in the back of the church of St Mary Major, which was less than a half mile away, where they could talk.

She met them in the vestibule of the church and indicated that she had been with the bank for more than twenty five years. She handled most of the transactions where large amounts of money were transferred outside the country. She said she knew the name of the person who wired the money, but that no one at the bank knew his business. The money had come from a series of cash deposits over a period of six months, none of which was large enough to warrant any suspicion of illegality. She said he would deposit ten to fifteen thousand a day in cash. They assumed he had a successful restaurant or some other cash business. She shared the name of the man but didn't know if it was an alias or real. She said the man had not come to the bank since making the wire transfer. She didn't have a picture of the man, but the bank's surveillance system would have a number of tapes that would show his face. They would have to have permission from the bank president to see the tapes.

When the detectives sought permission from the president, they subtlety but aggressively let it be known that it was the most important case he could imagine. He got the message and allowed them to look at the tape. The detectives now needed to involve the Italian federal police to further the identity.

Unusual Suspect

The federal police were not at all interested in the case until the detectives shared that it involved the poisoning of the pope. One of the feds offered that he was disappointed that the poisoning had not been successful in the case of the pope. When they reviewed the tape, they couldn't find anyone known to them. The man on the tape appeared to be in his late sixties, balding, short and heavy. As they were viewing the tape, an older federal inspector, walked by and glanced at the tape. He took a few more steps, turned around and asked them to reverse the tape. He looked at it twice and then said that he thought they had a picture of Tito Moretti the son of Mario Moretti the leader of the Red Brigade group that had kidnapped and killed Premier Aldo Moro back in the seventies or was it the sixties. He thought he was in prison, but may have been released after the Red Brigade dissolved itself in the late eighties.

But what would he be doing with a million dollars of cash and why would he send it to Boko Haram? Could Moretti be involved in the kidnapping and poisoning? Perhaps? A visit with Mr. Moretti was in order but where would they find him. He was originally from Turin. Was he now in Rome? They tracked his Rome address which was a small apartment in the central city near the Spanish Steppes. But when they went there, the landlady said he had moved the week before and had not paid his rent. She asked if she could have a chat with him if they found him. They then checked with the police in Turin who said they knew where he lived and could easily bring him in if they needed him. When the Lagos detective team arrived in Turin, the Turin detectives brought him in and interviewed him, he claimed to know nothing about the deposits or the wire transfer. When they said that they had at least twenty tapes showing his face, he asked if there was something criminal about making deposits in the bank.

They told him that it was legal, but if he didn't tell them where he got the money, they would have to learn that the hard way. He could be brought back to Rome to face charges for not paying his rent and he would have to face an angry landlady. He knew that if he went to Rome under the wrong circumstance, he could disappear. He was old and not too many people would notice. He held out and asked for a lawyer. They released him from the interview. The detectives were at a standstill. They had nothing on which to base a warrant, but they needed information.

The Lagos detectives joined the Turin detectives in a four day surveillance and on the fourth day it bore fruit. Moretti left his home and went to the Concord Hotel and to room #306. He stayed one hour and then left and went to the Circolo Arci La Cricca where he met with another man for a short time. The Lagos and the Turin detectives split into two teams, one from each city. One set of the detectives followed Moretti to the restaurant and after the other man left, approached him and started to ask questions.

Confession is Good for the Soul

The other team went to the room and found Monsignor Anthony Marino, a fifty year old Italian priest who lived at the Vatican in Rome. He told them he was on vacation from his work in the Vatican Bank. They immediately realized they had a good lead. Moretti had deposited a million dollars and they had a person who had access to cash, a great deal of cash from funds paid in donations, admissions and money spent at the Vatican Museums.

The Turin detective took the lead. He said to his acting partner and to the monsignor that it was his "lucky day" because he needed to go to confession and they were in the presence of a priest who could hear his confession. He asked the monsignor if he would be willing to hear his confession and the monsignor shrugged and said that if it was that important to him, he would do so. The Turin detective winked at the detective from Lagos and asked if he would mind waiting outside the room. He did so.

When he was alone with the monsignor, he pulled out a snub nosed .38 and said "Monsignor, I used to be a Catholic, but no more. It's a lot of hocus pocus bullshit. You murder someone

one day and you are guilty. Go to the priest and confess and now God loves you. Well the truth is, about a month ago, I killed a man, but you don't need to give me absolution because I gave it to myself. The son of bitch had raped my niece and he won't rape anyone else. I did God's work. Now, I have a problem with you. I need information and I need it in a hurry. So we are going to talk. If I don't get what I think is true, you and I will take a ride.

"Once, I had a reluctant person of interest that I wanted information from and he wouldn't talk to me. So we went for a ride. At the time, my wife had just divorced me and I was probably depressed. Anyway, I didn't give a shit whether I lived or died. So we went for a ride north of here in the mountains with the steep grades and the two lane roads. We were traveling about seventy five and every other hill we went up on the wrong side of the road. We didn't collide with anyone on the first two hills, but after the second, he started to breath heavily and suddenly got talkative. I learned what I needed. We're not going to do that today. I'm now happily married. But because it is very easy for people to disappear, especially vacationers, you may go for your last ride. There is a silencer for this weapon that I keep in my pocket. If you can't help me, we will put the silencer on and I will remove every other bullet from the revolver that feeds the bullets to the gun. I'll advance the chamber and ask a question. For you, it will be like going up every other hill on the wrong side of the road at seventy five kliks an hour.

"Now, Monsignor, I suppose you understand what I am talking about. You gave a lot of cash to Mr. Moretti for a reason and I want to know why. I have a suspicion why you did it, but I don't have enough evidence to prove it in court. You need to help me if you want to see the sun rise tomorrow. Keep that in mind when you tell me what's going on". The Monsignor initially said that he knew nothing of the matter. Mr. Moretti was a distant cousin and had simply come by for a chat. The detective told the Monsignor that Mr. Moretti was being interviewed by the other detectives and if that wasn't his story, the Monsignor had a serious problem. He put the silencer on his weapon and put the weapon in the side pocket of his sport coat. He directed the Monsignor to the door and out to their car parked in front of the hotel where his Lagos partner was. He told his partner that the Monsignor wanted to talk and they would do so in a more remote location.

He then stepped out of the car and called the other team and asked if they had learned anything from Mr. Moretti. Moretti had clammed up until one of the detectives started smoking. Moretti's nerves were finished and he desperately needed a smoke. The detective offered him one. Moretti went to take it and the detective said "A cigarette and light for every answer I think is true. A false answer and Fellini here will put a 9mm in his Glock 23 C which blows big holes in peopleand when we go out of here you will need to keep an eye out for him. He is a good shot from a distance and is very sneaky. He can appear at any time out of nowhere.

Just as he was about to talk to them, Moretti got a telephone call and then clammed up again. They said that they could not easily force him to go with them, but if he left the café, they would grab him when he left. They left the café and parked down the street watching the door. When Moretti emerged and started to walk toward a four door blue Fiat across the street from the entrance, they pulled up next to the car and blocked it from leaving the parking place. Then, both detectives got in the small car and pulled their weapons.

The person in the driver's seat was a heavy set woman of about fifty. She began to scream. One of the detectives took out his handkerchief, wrapped his hand and put it over her mouth while the other detective transferred Moretti to the other car.

They took the keys to the woman's car and left the woman in the car. They met up with the other detectives at an abandoned warehouse of a produce company that had gone out of business many years ago.

On the way to the warehouse, the Turin detective told Mr. Moretti that they were going to meet with the monsignor who had already given them all the information they needed about the money. Mr.Moretti began to curse saying that he never should have trusted the "bastard". The monsignor's uncle was a "crooked p…." stealing money from the poor and then lying to everyone about it. When they drove up to the warehouse, he saw the monsignor talking to the other detectives. He asked the detectives what he would need to do to avoid prosecution. They said that they could put in a good word for him and the prosecutor would probably go light on him if they could use his information. He said he would provide information, but what he really wanted was a few minutes alone with the monsignor to make him wish he had never met him.

The Turin detective went to the detective talking to the monsignor and said that Mr. Moretti was about to talk and they wanted to keep him talking. He returned to the car and listened as Moretti told his story.

Chapter 27

Will Evil Prevail?

The Search Continues

When Chief Mebimi reported the developments in the case to the pope and later to the reporters, he couldn't unequivocally report that they had found the person responsible for the poisoning. They had learned that a cardinal in Rome had paid a million American dollars to Boko Haram for something but that was all they could prove. Sister Sophia and her brother's family were still missing and they had no positive leads. Informants came in but no one had hard information about the family or Sister. The pope was greatly saddened by the knowledge that there were those within his Church who were interested in killing him. His mother had instilled in him a consciousness of the fact that there may be people around him throughout his life who were his angels and that through them God's grace flowed to him. But she also made him aware that there may be evil people who could come to him and make him believe they were there to help him. It was up to him to be able to discern which was which. She told him "Pray to your Guardian Angel and to the Holy Spirit for that help".

The Chief assured the pope that they would find Sister and her brother. A week later, an informant came to his lead detective with information. He told the detectives that he could tell them who the white man was who led the raid on Sister

Sophia's brother's house. He didn't know his name but he was connected with the Chicago Mafia and had been hired by a cardinal in the Vatican. He said that he had gotten the information from an informant inside the Boko Haram who was working with the Saudis against the Chinese. The informant couldn't tell him where Sister Sophia and her brother were but he could get that information for one thousand dollars each for himself and the other informant. The detectives told him to bring the information and if it proved accurate, he would get the money.

He trusted the detectives because they had paid him after the fact before. They paid him five hundred American in good faith. The informant came back the next day and he shared that they had been taken north to Kano. He knew it was Boko Haram and that they were taken to where Boko Haram was headquartered. The informant had received the information from a prostitute who was his informant and had entertained one of the Boko Haram members who had participated in the raid on Sister Sophia's brother's home and had taken the brother and Sister Sophia north to Kano.

Boko Haram had kidnapped Sister's brother Adam, and held him in an apartment in Lagos for three days. During the week, they held him and sent a note to Sister Sophia with a picture showing her brother tied up in their custody. They told her that they would kill him, his wife and four boys and the rest of her family if she didn't poison the pope. From her childhood, she had known how vicious Boko Haram was and she didn't doubt their threat. Then, on Wednesday they delivered the rat poison in a gift wrapped package to the security desk with a note telling her that the pope must die before Friday.

They said that she, her brother and his family would all be safe if she did so. Otherwise, they would all be dead within the week. The note told her they would bring the brother to the " Vatican" with them, pick her up and take them to a private plane and fly the family to Turin, Italy where they could live. The note indicated that a cardinal who was representing the Curia from the Rome Vatican had paid them and ordered the killing in order to restore the Church to Rome. Then the Church would not be bothered by terrorists. The cardinal had made arrangements for them to immigrate and for their housing and employment.

Chief Mebimi shared with the pope the information about what had happened and how the poisoning occurred and told him he was certain that they would find Sister Sophia within the week.

A week later when the Chief came to the pope's office, he was crying. He told the pope that they had found Adam's wife who had escaped Lagos after her husband had been taken. She and four children were found living safely with her sister in Chad. But the police in Kano had found the bodies of Sister Sophia and her brother in a dump on the outskirts of Kano.

Tears came to the eyes of Pope Francisco Augustine. He blessed the Chief and his detective and asked if they would join him in prayer for the victims and the perpetrators of the crime. They readily agreed to do so.

The Chief went home to his wife and family and prayed. The pope went to his chapel, prayed for Sister Sophia, her brother and his family. He prayed for the perpetrators. Then he prayed for the world. He asked the Holy Spirit for guidance and wondered who else among those around him wanted to kill him. He hoped he would never know.

Moretti had told a story that made known the reality. The monsignor who had employed him was the nephew of Cardinal Marino, who had been the chief officer of the Vatican Bank for nearly ten years until he was demoted, essentially fired from the role for embezzlement when Francisco became pope. The cardinal had come from a very wealthy northern Italian banking family in the Lake Como area. He had progressed rapidly in the

Church and was absorbed into the Vatican at age forty. He became a bishop at age forty five and remained assigned to the Vatican Bank. He spent ten years as the understudy to the head of the bank, during which time he developed a practice of investing in stocks in his own name with Vatican Bank funds. He grew his portfolio to more than one hundred million Euros and enjoyed luxurious accommodations in a famous and historical villa in the hills of Rome outside the Vatican.

It was well known that he had ambitions to become the pope, but he knew that he needed to be in either the Office of the Secretary of State or the Prefect of Sacred Doctrine. He made every possible move to shift to those offices but was always re-buffed. He was cast as the "Vatican Beancounter" and couldn't shake the role. In the 2042 international monetary and financial crisis, he lost more than half of his portfolio and went into a depression. He was attached to his wealth and saw it as a consolation, a substitute for knowing he would never become pope. He widened his embezzlement to grow back his portfolio. He would pay the bank back when he had reached his hundred million.

When Pope Francisco Augustine was elected pope, he called for an audit of the bank. The cardinal scrambled, borrowing as much as possible off the books but couldn't cover the losses. It was apparent he had no recourse but to wait until he was discovered by the audit. Upon confrontation by the Commandant of the Swiss Guard, he resigned as the head of the bank and blamed Francisco Augustine. He claimed the whole matter was unfair. He only needed more time to grow back his account. Francisco fired the cardinal before he had that opportunity. While he was still in Rome, Pope Francisco engaged in lengthy consultation with a group of international bankers who were personally dispassionate regarding the Vatican holdings and whose banks were disinterested in Vatican finance.

On the advice of the bankers, he chose to close the Vatican bank. The assets were deposited in a six banks spread throughout the world, three each in developing and developed countries. He appointed a Vatican commission separate from the Curia and the Secretary of State to oversee the assets. The commission involved bankers overseen by the lay chair, a middle aged Chinese woman who had departed the communist regime in Beijing and had extensive banking experience in the Hong Cong banking business. The deposits were made in a ten year rolling mode and were based on interest rates derived from competitive bidding by the banks. The Church would no longer directly hold interests in corporate institutions and the commission was made responsible for selecting banks that held only assets morally acceptable to the Church.

The cardinal embezzler remained a cardinal and lived luxuriously. But he was angry and eager to take revenge against the pope. His reputation was destroyed and he became a recluse dealing only with a nephew who was the monsignor still in the Vatican bank. Mr. Moretti quoted the nephew who employed him. The monsignor told him that he "had the blessing of the Church". He said the cardinal was not going to sit idly by while "that half breed Spanish-negro held the keys to the kingdom and traipsed off to Africa. When Francisco Augustine was gone (dead), the "keys" would return to the Vatican and his uncle the cardinal would be vindicated for having taken the necessary action to bring them back. Mr. Moretti said the monsignor had agreed to pay him fifty thousand Euros for his work and would put it on deposit in his bank in Turin. He would pay another one million American for transfer to the Boko Haram. But when Moretti went to collect his money that day in the hotel room, the monsignor had less than half the funds and promised the rest of what was owed him in three months. Mr. Moretti was not at all happy and said he would be eager to testify if it would involve putting the monsignor and the cardinal in prison.

Cardinal Marino finally resigned from his cardinalate. There was insufficient evidence to prosecute him for anything more than financial crimes despite his nephew's testimony against him. The Italian authorities couldn't tie him to the attempted assassination. He was convicted of the financial crimes and subjected to a luxurious house arrest. He died of a heart attack within six months of conviction. His nephew, Monsignor Marino, after testifying against his uncle was found guilty of conspiracy to commit murder. He was imprisoned for ten years. Mr. Moretti testified against the monsignor and was placed on probation for financial crimes.

The authorities were unsure of who the man was who led the raid on Adam's home and the kidnapping. But they had been told he came from Chicago in the United States and had safely returned to America. The Chief requested the FBI to follow-up but they had no idea of how to find the perpetrator. After delays, nothing new had been reported to the Chief. He assumed the matter was finished.

A Growing Storm of Response

From the 1960s, a great number of Europeans had stopped having children and the Christian populations had diminished to the point of no return. Europe would never again be predominantly Christian. By 2050, much of Europe had become Muslim and the European culture had been radically changed.

In the United States, Islam had grown significantly, but there was little terrorism. The Islamic terrorist acts in the United States were small and performed by foreign terrorists. Because of Hispanic immigration and the growth of the Muslim population the birthrate and the population of the U.S. had remained somewhat stable. The culture of the U.S. had shifted predominantly to secular humanism. Relativism was the standard for all behavior. The dominance of feminism and the force of political correctness had overwhelmed the male population and the family was thoroughly maternalist.

It was not just the United States that was changing. The whole civilization was in flux. The U.S. became predominantly non White and was so multicultural that the founders would have no recognition of the nation they founded. Law changes had created a culture that reflected a confused society. The Lesbian, Gay, Bisexual and Transgender movement had achieved major influence in the schools and media and had persuaded the youthful population that gayness and same sex marriage were normal behavior.

The consequence for the falling birthrate was negative. For lack of consumers, the economy faltered. Jobs were few and with exception, they tended to require less education than was formerly the case. University education had become so expensive and so unproductive that there was a growing sentiment endorsed by progressives for government to take over the private colleges and universities, control administrative and faculty salaries and to force a dumbed down national curriculum.

Christianity was threatened by terrorists not only in Europe but throughout the world. The United Nations was both unable and unwilling to intervene. As a force, the U.N. was essentially powerless. Christians in threatened nations were weary and frustrated and ready to defend themselves and their religion against radical Islam.

The leadership of an anti-radical Islam group assembled in Rio in early 2055. The leaders of the effort were three dynamic right wing Catholic activists who had had their fill of jihadists. When Pope Francisco Augustine came to office in 2058 and left Rome, they also had their fill of him. The principal who recruited the others to the group was an angry charismatic Irish born former Jesuit lawyer who had spent his career on the faculty of

Georgetown University Law. His right wing views had become the basis for his being fired from the law school and eventually being ushered out of the Jesuits. He first tapped an enormously wealthy industrialist from Brazil whose first fortune had come from oil. The third principal was the grand-daughter of a German grocery dynasty. Her weariness with the Church had become palpable.

These were wealthy people who were significantly networked to the powerful who pulled the levers of action within the Washington beltway, Asia, Africa, Europe and South America. They were able to muster support from the conservatives in power in each of these government centers. They knew the proper buttons to prompt a wartime stance among their supporters and they were not reluctant to press them. They may not be immediately able to generate a "boots on the ground" approach to the jihadists but they knew that they could initiate conflict and cause the political and military leaders to respond in some manner. They also knew that people, particularly the Christians, feared Islam and the radical Islamic terrorists. They could count on their support.

Together they had selected and employed a retired U.S. Army four star general to assemble an army of mercenaries with divisions throughout the entire world. Money and arms were no issue. The issue was how to hold back the mercenaries among whom were former Seals and members of Delta Force and their international colleagues from what they considered their mission. They were pregnant with the urge to destroy the enemies of Christianity. It was more than just a job for them.

Anticipating an eventual showdown between Islam and Christianity, a number of otherwise peaceful groups of Catholic and evangelical Protestant organizations had secretly contributed to the defense fund. The Knights of Columbus in the United States, The Knights of Malta, The Southern Baptist Convention, Opus Dei, Christus Rex, Legionnaires of Christ, Mormons and many other conservative groups had been raising and pooling their money in preparation for the response to radical Islam. The group included representatives from India, Australia, Russia, Poland, Germany, France, Italy and many African, North, South and Central American countries. The mission was secretly supported by the Russian and Greek Orthodox Churches as well as a number of evangelical bodies. China did not join in.

Their purpose was to raise sufficient money to employ small mobile armies of mercenaries from as many countries as possible to quickly respond to each radical Islamist attack. The response was always to be with greater violence than had been exercised by the terrorists to insure immediate suppression of the attacks. If the clarity of who was responsible for the terrorist act was in doubt, the victims would be Muslims in the same areas in which the original violence occurred. The energy and anger was mushrooming and there was a beginning resolve to initiate a new crusade.

The general selected to lead the military mission of the group was fanatical concerning the threat of Islam. He had always felt frustrated as an American Army General. He believed that the presidents, defense secretaries and military chiefs of staff lacked courage and failed to address the terrorist threats with sufficient armed response. Beyond that frustration, his daughter had been killed in a terrorist attack when she was doing social work in Yemen. He was relentless in his effort to lead the group to an armed response.

Pope Francisco Augustine had vigorously condemned the group and its activity. It appeared to him an effort at an offensive war. He stopped short of threatening excommunication, but was clear about how unacceptable the group's purpose and plans were. His condemnation was clear and forceful. The group was not responsive to the pope. They would make their own rules. This new pope meant little to them because he had vacated the Vatican and had left his moral authority behind. The Church no longer belonged to him. He lacked influence over them. However, when the attempt on the pope's life became known to the group, the leadership assembled in the United States and began to plan a response with vengeance as quickly as possible once they identified a possible perpetrator. The group which labeled itself "The Fifteenth Crusade" initially assumed that the papal assassination attempt was an Islamic terrorist act. By the time when the facts became known, that it was sponsored by an American Catholic group connected to the Mafia, it was too late to hold back "The Fifteenth Crusade".

Francisco Augustine knew this was not his last challenge. But he was not at all discouraged. His faith and his love gave rise to an undaunted hope that there would be peace in his lifetime. He would continue to do what he knew was best for Christ's Church in pursuit of peace in the world no matter any personal cost. But he was completely unprepared for what he was about to face.

Three weeks had passed since the end of the investigation into the poisoning and things had gone back to a more normal pace. The Lagos Police had passed the case on to the Nigerian Federal Police because all the information they had collected pointed to the principal conspirator being an American who they concluded had fled Nigeria. And the federal police had engaged the FBI. As a local law enforcement body, the Lagos Police had found it impossible to break through the barriers shielding the terrorists inside the Boko Haram . Nothing had been reported to Francisco Augustine in more than three weeks.

Francisco Augustine and Bishop Sanchez were moving briskly on the interior walkway that connected the hospital chapel to the small building that housed the Lagos Vatican's administrative offices. They had concelebrated a six A.M. mass in the chapel for the nuns who worked in the hospital. The nuns lived and worshipped in the same building with the chapel. The sun was beginning to rise and it promised to be a very warm humid day in Lagos. The pope and Bishop Sanchez were headed to their breakfast in the small dining area attached to the offices and then start their work day. Francisco Augustine was preparing for a trip to China where he would be welcomed by a new Chinese President who was attempting to slowly foster a unique culture that honored the past and eschewed the negatives of Western culture. At the same time, she was gradually expanding human rights and reaching out to the world to normalize what had become a serious tension between China and the rest of the world. This was after a series of encounters with Japan when China would from time to time take possession of disputed islands and wars of words would be waged. From time to time, shelling of one of the islands and some deaths would occur but no war would ensue. The Chinese made shows of force but were reluctant to engage in combat. They knew they had the bomb and millions of troops and relied on threats. They suffered from terrorist elements as all countries did.

Her election came about despite the fact that females in China were seriously outnumbered because males were preferred under the single child policy that had been in effect for nearly a hundred years. Off and on it was tinkered with when an administration was worried about the limited number of females. But the voters had reached a point of disgust with the male politicians.

They had concluded that there was too much testosterone being exhibited by the males. The male population outnumbered the female population due to the general acceptance of the sex selection. But the Chinese female population was well organized and chose their first female president. Christian religions and especially Catholicism had benefitted by the work of the last President but there was still a long way to true religious freedom. Ironically the Church was growing quickly in China. St. Francis Xavier after whom Francisco had labeled himself would have been highly pleased. Francisco found it ironic that religious freedom was advancing in China and deteriorating in both Europe and the United States where outright discrimination against Christianity was becoming more common and acceptable. Very little Christianity remained in the Muslim nations. Saudi Arabia, Iraq, Iran, Syria, Egypt and most northern African nations had effectively removed Christianity from their nations.

The hundred and fifty foot long walkway between the chapel and the administrative office featured a dozen floor to ceiling windows on both sides, each about two and a half foot wide. Though the walkway was air conditioned, it was always extremely warm. Today was no exception. Both the pope and Bishop Sanchez wore cotton cassocks in Lagos. They were still very warm. They couldn't wait to get to their residence and to shed their cassocks.

The sniper's first bullet came from the right rear and hit Bishop Sanchez just below the left shoulder and exited below the collar bone. The bishop careened sideways to the left and fell. The bleeding from both his back and shoulder was severe. He went almost immediately into shock. Francisco Augustine was hit in the left buttock with the bullet exiting without hitting his hip bone. While the wound was painful, he was gravely concerned for the bishop's condition. He knew he had to get him to an emergency room immediately or he would bleed out. He picked him up in a fireman's carry. He had to navigate the fifty feet remaining on the walkway staying to the left side hoping that the sniper would have a more difficult angle. He was already shooting from their rear. He hoped too that there was only one sniper.

If he could make it to the end of the walkway, there were about a dozen stairs on the left that would take him down to the street level. He would then have at least fifty yards to cross to the front of the hospital. He was grateful that the emergency room was so near the front. He prayed that there were no snipers on that side of the hospital and no one on the ground between the exit and the front of the hospital.

He didn't realize how heavy Bishop Sanchez was until he started down the stairs. The Bishop had to outweigh him by at least thirty pounds and he was dead weight. Francisco Augustine was pleased that he had taken his own personal conditioning seriously all his life. It may contribute to saving Bishop Sanchez today. As he labored to balance the priest on his back, he remembered that he had had a meeting with the Commandant of the Swiss Guard when the "Vatican" was first moved to Lagos. The Commandant had wanted to "harden up" the whole facility and the walkway windows were a part of the hardening. But the cost of the Kevlar that the Commandant wanted to install would have been prohibitive. Francisco had indicated that he didn't think it was worth the cost for just the five years that he planned to be in Lagos. So the effort to harden the windows was abandoned. He felt guilt that his decision might result in the death of the bishop whose life was currently in the balance.

Apparently Boko Haram wouldn't give up on their effort to kill him. The initial failure with the poison had not deterred them. He was painfully aware that those around him were being killed and he was frustrated by not being able to stop the killing. He had to face the fact that there was more evil in a pope's world than he had imagined. But he knew it wasn't uncommon for evil to target the Church. He remembered the story about the woman who always had something good to say about everyone. When asked what she thought of the devil, she remarked "Isn't he a hard worker". He knew how true that was. Boko Haram was only one of those targeting the Church. It would always be so.

God Help Me

As Francisco lay in the hospital bed, his mind kept turning to the night before he was told that he had been elected pope. He was in Africa and he had prayed and fasted, asking God to give the cardinals wisdom in choosing the person best prepared to serve his Church in the challenging time. The shock of being elected pope was severe. He had no idea of what he might do if he were pope because the thought had never entered his mind. He was a bishop and not even a pastoral bishop of a diocese. He did have a titular diocese but it was not his pastoral role. He was just a Vatican administrator. He knew he was not the best candidate to serve as pope but he had to deal with reality. He was pope. Now he had to face the reality that he was leading a Church that was the object of much hatred and violence in many parts of the world. Not all the challenges to the Church were obvious or violent.

The subtle but deadly persuasion of secularism had done its damage for a long time. God's kingdom on earth was not faring well. He knew all too well the warnings and admonitions that Jesus had given to his followers when he was with them. Personally, he didn't think of himself as a particularly virtuous man. But he was conscious that symbols or people of virtue would always be the objects of derision, scorn or violence from both those who believed differently and those who didn't believe. Those who embraced virtue would be subjected to rejection and violence. Jesus' first successor, a virtuous man was crucified upside down, a pretty violent end. Jesus had directed his disciples to turn the other cheek. Throughout history turning the other cheek had always been the most difficult of all Jesus' directives for most Christians to follow. They responded to violence violently. They acted humanly.

Now he was faced with trying to hold back another well

funded crusade that he knew would be cataclysmic for both sides. But was it right for him to tell those whose lives and families were being destroyed by terrorists to stand down? Throughout the world, the Far East, Africa, Asia and America, radical Islamic terrorists were laboring to find weak spots in defenses to which they could direct their bombs. Infidels were being killed by extremists simply because they were unwilling to believe that Muhammad was the final prophet who had a special relationship with God and had written the final word on man's belief and behavior.

Bishop Sanchez lay in the next bed. The bullet that had opened his back and chest was the result of the actions of those who thought they were doing God's work by trying to kill the pope. They were believers. Idi, the informant had told the Lagos detectives that General Abula told his men "We are being paid to execute the chief symbol of the infidels. We are being paid by stupid infidels to kill their own leader. Not only are they infidels, they are Americans, the most evil of all the infidels. I would gladly do it myself for no money but we will profit and become famous at the same time. This is a mission from which we will draw much joy and honor. It will be pleasing to Allah. But to reap the reward we must finish the job. We must kill the pope".

Francisco asked himself if Jesus really wanted him to tell his flock to subject themselves to the unrelenting violence and death. This was not the first time he had faced the question of war. He had had an ongoing discussion in one of his philosophy classes at Northwestern, in the military and with Brother Mark about pacifists and just war when he was in the Marines. Brother Mark was not a pacifist and had always fallen back on St. Thomas Aquinas' "just war theory". Thomas Aquinas had taken his direction from St. Augustine and had but three conditions for a just war; a good and just purpose, waged by proper authorities, normally a state and with a goal of peace. Numerous expansions on the theory had been made since Aquinas. The School of Salamanca added the need for possible success and war being a last resort. He wondered if that was the point at which Christians now found themselves.

Those were the conditions that Francisco felt necessary for a just war while a Marine but he was no longer a Marine. He was leading the Roman Catholic Church, the mystical body of Christ, the people whose very identity was to love. He knew that it was by love that people would be judged at the end of life. Was standing down and not responding to violence an act of love or an invitation to suicide for the members of his Church? Or by not responding would the world learn that Christians were truly committed to loving no matter the cost even if it was their life. Would the world be a better place if he was killed by an assassin's bullet? Would the world be better if thousands of Christians met a violent death at the hands of the terrorists? Did the atrocities committed by Hitler, Stalin, Pol Pot or Mao make the world better? Should a Christian have stopped them before their crimes?

He reflected on how seventh and eighth century Islam had decimated entire Christian cities, massacred hundreds of thousands, looted and destroyed the holy city of Jerusalem. He was mindful too of how in the fifteenth century Islam had slain its way to dominance in the mid east and the Balkans and had brought down the Byzantine Empire. Now, most Islamic nations supported terrorist groups that were bent on the final removal of all Christians from their lands and firmly establishing Sharia law. Their attacks on the free world were frequent and deadly but most free nations found themselves without the means to address the undeclared wars. He wondered what God wanted of him in this age in which he was a factor. He was painfully aware of how a flood of Islamic radicals had used the very civil tolerance afforded by secular Europe to Islamicize a half dozen nations that were formerly Christian. Would God's kingdom be advanced by a pacifist response to terrorist killings? Or is it allowable for Christians to put an end to radical Islamic terrorism? Should it be stopped through violence? Were the crusades altogether wrong in their mission, trying to reclaim Christian shrines or was it the barbarism of the crusaders that made them wrong?

Francisco knew that Nazism and communism should have been stopped before the millions who had a right to life were killed. He knew slavery should have been stopped before it gained a foothold in the American economy. He knew the same was true of the millions of tiny beings killed while living in their mothers' wombs. That too should be stopped. He held the statistics of these moral disasters firmly in his consciousness when deliberating his responsibilities.

He saw the world though a lens colored by the evil that bore on the suffering innocents. It took a half million American deaths to stop slavery, the deaths of six million victims and more than four hundred thousand allied combatants to stop Hitler. Millions died at the hand of Stalin and tens of thousands more had to die in the fight with the Chinese communists in a Vietnam Civil War. But the statistic that made the others pale in comparison was the nearly hundred million helpless beings who were meant to be future American citizens who had been killed in the womb during his lifetime.

Should he give a green light to those who were willing to protect the defenseless by engaging in seriously disruptive civil disobedience? Should he give the nod to The Fifteenth Crusade to wage violence for violence? He was mindful that Jesus, who opposed violence, had rebuked Peter for trying to defend him with his sword.

He had literally reached the point in his life where he was eager to go to God. He knew that a part of his eagerness to leave this world was his weariness. But he was also looking forward to what he regarded as the most exciting day in his life when he would see God and join Jordan, his child and his parents.

Would anything be gained for the Church from his death at the hands of terrorists? Would his death promote the love that God wanted people to share? He was painfully conscious of the irony he saw in the attempts on his life. Those attempts were apparently prompted and paid for by American Catholics who were angry with him for doing what he believed was what Jesus wanted him to do. He was ever mindful that both those who supported him and those who would kill him were children of God.

His faith told him to put all his questions in God's hands. But he needed to have God tell him what to say to his people. He needed the Holy Spirit to take charge of his words. After all the hateful response that his initiatives had set off, he wondered if the Church of Jesus could take one more fearful step in the direction that Jesus admonished? Could Catholics and other Christians turn the other cheek? Should they?

The bullet had gone through the left cheek of his buttocks. The irony of being asked to turn the other cheek was not lost on him. The stitched repair of his buttocks allowed him to rest but not sleep. He felt pain. But his thoughts would not allow any rest or any indulgence in self pity. He needed to concentrate. He knew the day was near when he would be required to act.

He knew too that the Holy Spirit was still in charge of what occurred in the world and that in the end he would be guided by the Holy Spirit. The Spirit would let him know if he should encourage his people to respond to the radical Islamic terrorist threat with violence or to practice a passive resistance.

He needed to pray. "God, you made your world of love. You made each of us in your image to know and to love you and your children. When man rejected your love and chose to do his own will, you came as man to show us what perfect love does.

You willingly died on the cross out of your love for us. You repaired the bond of love that unites us and provides us with the hope of eternal joy with you. You come each day in your glorified body as our sacrificial gift at the offering of thanksgiving. You come in our Eucharist to nurture us. You come in the Spirit to enlighten, inspire and energize us. I believe in you. I hope in you and I love you. I am your servant. Please enlighten me. Help me to know what you want me to say to your children".

AUTHOR'S NOTE

It could be said that the seed for "The Fifteenth Crusade" was planted in the late 1970s when a friend shared her copy of Thomas S Klise's only novel "The Last Western" a story of a mixed race athlete "Willie" who rises suddenly and surprisingly to the papacy in which he exhibits extreme concern for the poor. Klise, who died not too long after the publishing of his book, received his early theological education a few years prior to mine by the same Adrian Dominican elementary school sisters at St. Augustin's school in Des Moines. Much of Klise's allegorical message was imaginative and entertaining, often drawing on the bizarre and extreme to illustrate his point. I considered the yarn, spun often at the edges of the imagination, a valuable vehicle for sharing a more direct social, political and theological commentary.

I have chose to channel Klise. Two elements of "The Fifteenth Crusade" mimic Klise's effort; a mixed race male athlete and "Willie's" radical papacy registering concern for the poor. That's where the similarity ends.

Six years ago at age seventy three I realized I should get busy on a few of the items on the "bucket list" and I began to write off and on. Three years ago, while wearing a brace for four months to repair a broken vertebrae, I was forced into sufficient seat time to get serious about the book. Because we are now pleasantly blessed with a living Pope Francis who personifies some of the same qualities of Pope Francisco Augustine, I now realize I should have exercised greater dispatch in completing the novel, lest the subject matter and the timing of the publication be considered a bit redundant. But Diego became Pope Francisco in 2008 prior to our real Pope Francisco occupies a battered "Chair of Peter" in a future and different age in a wildly secular world.

John Wright

12659473R00204

Made in the USA
San Bernardino, CA
24 June 2014